Populist Parties in Europe

Populist Parties in Europe
Agents of Discontent?

Stijn van Kessel

*Department of Politics, History and International Relations,
Loughborough University, UK, and
Institut für Deutsches und Internationales Parteienrecht und
Parteienforschung (PRuF), Heinrich-Heine-Universität Düsseldorf, Germany*

First published 2015 by
PALGRAVE MACMILLAN

Palgrave Macmillan in the UK is an imprint of Macmillan Publishers Limited,
registered in England, company number 785998, of Houndmills, Basingstoke,
Hampshire, RG21 6XS

Palgrave Macmillan in the US is a division of St Martin's Press LLC,
175 Fifth Avenue, New York, NY 10010.

Palgrave Macmillan is the global academic imprint of the above companies
and has companies and representatives throughout the world.

Palgrave® and Macmillan® are registered trademarks in the United States,
the United Kingdom, Europe and other countries

ISBN 978-1-349-49012-7   ISBN 978-1-137-41411-3 (eBook)
DOI 10.1057/9781137414113

This book is printed on paper suitable for recycling and made from fully
managed and sustained forest sources. Logging, pulping and manufacturing
processes are expected to conform to the environmental regulations of the
country of origin.

A catalogue record for this book is available from the British Library.

A catalog record for this book is available from the Library of Congress.

Contents

List of Illustrations   vi

Acknowledgements   vii

List of Abbreviations   ix

1 Introduction: Studying Populism in European Party Systems   1

2 Populist Parties across Europe   33

3 Paths to Populist Electoral Success and Failure: fsQCA Analysis   74

4 Populist Parties in the Netherlands   99

5 Populist Parties in Poland   121

6 Populist Parties in the United Kingdom   144

7 Conclusion: Populist Parties and Their Electoral Performance   169

Appendices   184
Appendix A *List of Consulted Country Experts*   184
Appendix B *Country Expert Questionnaire*   186
Appendix C *QCA Data*   187
Appendix D *List of Interviewees*   194
Appendix E *Expert Survey (Case Studies)*   196

Notes   198

Bibliography   204

Index   229

List of Illustrations

Figures

1.1   Explanatory model concerning the electoral performance
      of populist parties   28
3.1   Plot of cases' membership in POPSUC against their
      membership in CREDIB   86

Tables

2.1   Populist parties in Europe that gained parliamentary
      representation after national elections between 2000
      and 2013   71
3.1   Conditions in the fsQCA   77
3.2   Calibrated data for the fsQCA (period: 2000–2013)   84
3.3   Truth Table   88
3.4   Paths implying POPSUC (period: 2000–2013)   91
3.5   Paths implying ~POPSUC (period: 2000–2013)   94
3.6   Paths implying POPSUC (last election)   95
4.1   Dutch parliamentary election results 1998–2012, in % of
      the vote   104
4.2   Motivations of PVV voters (spontaneous response to
      open-ended question), in % of PVV-voting respondents   111
5.1   Polish parliamentary election results 1997–2011, in % of
      the vote   124
6.1   UK general election results 1997–2010, in % of
      the vote and seats   154
A.1   Election results of populist parties between 2000 and 2013   187
A.2   Raw data for the PR, ECOHARD, EURSCEP and CORRUP
      conditions   190
A.3   Calculation of UNRESP values   191
A.4   Calculation of NATIV values   192
A.5   Data for the fsQCA concerning the latest election results   193

Acknowledgements

I would like to thank the many people who have provided valuable substantive feedback and/or moral support. The research done during my time as a doctoral student at the University of Sussex forms the basis of this book. First of all, I thank my former supervisors Aleks Szczerbiak and Paul Taggart. Thanks to their intensive guidance at the very early stages of the process, I was able to promptly and confidently get the project underway, and the meetings that followed always provided me with a clear sense of direction. I look back with pleasure at the enjoyable discussions, and I am particularly grateful for their encouragement and enduring readiness to provide advice. I would also like to thank the other members of the department for contributing to the friendly and collegial atmosphere. Special thanks go to those of the preceding 'generation' of DPhil students who were present at the time of my arrival, and throughout most of my years at Sussex, for making me feel at home so quickly: John FitzGibbon, Martine Huberty and Dan Keith. I also thank Elisabeth Carter and Paul Webb, who provided me with useful comments and feedback during my *viva voce*, and the *VSBfonds* and *Prins Bernhard Cultuurfonds* for their support at the time of my doctoral studies.

In my post-Sussex period I ended up in various departments, where colleagues have also contributed to the finalisation of this research project. I would like to thank in particular Niels Spierings and Andrej Zaslove at the Radboud University for valuable feedback and support. At the VU University in Amsterdam, my former MSc supervisor Ben Crum provided feedback and advice during the embryonic stages of the project. I subsequently started my lectureship at Loughborough University, and I am very grateful for Loughborough's readiness to grant me a two-year research leave at the Party Research Institute (PRuF) at the Heinrich-Heine-University Düsseldorf. This gave me the opportunity to concentrate fully on this book. My fellowship in Düsseldorf has been made possible by the *Alexander von Humboldt Stiftung*, which I thank for its generous support. I would also like to thank Thomas Poguntke for his advice and readiness to act as my academic host during my postdoctoral fellowship.

Moving beyond my immediate working environment, I am grateful to the many scholars listed in Appendix A who have kindly shared their knowledge of party systems covered in this book. Among those I harassed most frequently are Daniele Albertazzi, Sergiu Gherghina, Duncan McDonnell and Jens Rydgren. The (anonymous) scholars who participated in the three conducted expert surveys have also been of great help, and I am further indebted to the interviewees listed in Appendix D who took the time to speak with me and to share their insights. I would also like to thank Simona Guerra and Bartek Napieralski for their feedback on an earlier draft of the Polish case study chapter, and Sabina Avdagic, Emelie Lilliefeldt, Carsten Q. Schneider, Barbara Vis and Claudius Wagemann for their comments on preliminary or more advanced draft QCA analyses. Naturally, any shortcomings and errors in this book are entirely my own responsibility.

I would further like to thank the members of the team at Palgrave Macmillan who have been involved in this book project Amber Stone-Galilee, Sara Crowley-Vigneau, Andrew Baird, and Jemima Warren. Several other academic colleagues and friends have also provided feedback and support throughout the past years, and should also be mentioned for their more general kindness: Simona Guerra, Saskia Hollander, André Krouwel and Andrea Pirro. I could, furthermore, always rely on my loyal friends Jochem Brons, Chris Heijs and Wouter Prause for their unfaltering assistance in moving my possessions between the countries I lived in. Last, but certainly not least, I would like to thank my brother and sister, Nard and Jaco van Kessel, and their other halves, Rinske Piek and Ruben Klaphake, for their love, support and encouragement. I am also indebted to my parents, Jos and Klarie van Kessel, for having provided me with the biological stuff that enabled me to finish this book, and with a safe and loving environment for me to grow up in. I am particularly thankful to my mother, who taught me the values and discipline which helped me in completing my work. It saddens me deeply not to be able to share my experiences with my parents or to show them the results of my work.

List of Abbreviations

AWS	Akcja Wyborcza Solidarność (Solidarity Electoral Action, Poland)
BNP	British National Party
CBOS	Centrum Badania Opinii Społecznej (Public Opinion Research Centre, Poland)
CD	Centrumdemocraten (Centre Democrats, the Netherlands)
CDA	Christen Democratisch Appel (Christian Democratic Appeal, the Netherlands)
CP	Centrumpartij (Centre Party, the Netherlands)
EP	European Parliament
EU	European Union
fsQCA	fuzzy set Qualitative Comparative Analysis
LN	Leefbaar Nederland (Liveable Netherlands)
LPF	Lijst Pim Fortuyn (List Pim Fortuyn, the Netherlands)
LPR	Liga Polskich Rodzin (League of Polish Families)
MEP	Member of the European Parliament
MP	Member of Parliament
NF	National Front (UK)
PiS	Prawo i Sprawiedliwość (Law and Justice, Poland)
PO	Platforma Obywatelska (Civic Platform, Poland)
PR	Proportional Representation
PRR	Populist Radical Right
PSL	Polskie Stronnictwo Ludowe (Polish Peasant Party)
PvdA	Partij van de Arbeid (Labour Party, the Netherlands)
PVV	Partij voor de Vrijheid (Freedom Party, the Netherlands)
QCA	Qualitative Comparative Analysis
SLD	Sojusz Lewicy Demokratycznej (Democratic Left Alliance, Poland)
SMP	Single Member Plurality
SO	Samoobrona Rzeczpospolitej Polskiej (Self Defence, Poland)
SP	Socialistische Partij (Socialist Party, the Netherlands)
TON	Trots op Nederland (Proud of the Netherlands)
UKIP	UK Independence Party
VVD	Volkspartij voor Vrijheid en Democratie (Liberal Party, the Netherlands)

1
Introduction: Studying Populism in European Party Systems

> I am deeply concerned about the divisions that we see emerging: political extremes and populism tearing apart the political support and the social fabric that we need to deal with the crisis; disunion emerging between the centre and the periphery of Europe; a renewed demarcation line being drawn between the North and the South of Europe; prejudices re-emerging and again dividing our citizens.
>
> José Manuel Barroso[1]

It may be clear that populism, a term used in the gloomy prognosis of former European Commission President Barroso, is often associated with developments which are deemed adverse, or even dangerous. Particularly since the dawn of the financial and economic crisis in 2008, various European political actors have expressed their concern about the rise of populism, more often than not associating the concept with political extremism and xenophobia. Yet what precisely constitutes this 'populism', and which political actors embody it, is often left unsaid. This book aims to clarify the manifestation of populism in European politics between 2000 and 2013. The focus is on political parties, which are still the key actors in contemporary European politics in terms of democratic representation. I first aim to apply the concept of populism to party systems across the continent and to identify parties that stand out from the others in terms of their consistent expression of a populist discourse. Second, I seek to explain the electoral performance of those 'populist parties' in national elections. Does the success of these parties in Europe denote a reactionary and destructive mood, as certain commentators and representatives of the political elites would like us to believe, or is this interpretation incomplete, or even flawed?

It is something of a cliché to start a text on populism with the observation that agreement on a definition is lacking and that the term is used for many different types of actors through time and space. Although this may still be true, there has been a surge in academic contributions on populism in recent years, and many scholars – at least those who apply the concept with care – tend to talk about the same phenomenon when they use the term. Populism is generally associated with a Manichean vision of society (pitting the good 'people' against the corrupted 'elites'), a conception of 'the people' as a homogeneous entity, and a defence of popular sovereignty (see e.g. Taggart 2000; Mudde 2004; Abts and Rummens 2007; Albertazzi and McDonnell 2008a). While many scholars broadly agree on what populism *is*, it is still debated in what *form* populism manifests itself. Disagreement exists about whether populism can best be seen as a strategy, a style or a political ideology. This, in turn, makes it unclear whether the term 'populism' denotes an ideological attribute of a bounded set of political actors, or whether it constitutes an (opportunistic) rhetorical tool which can be applied by any politician. By relating the concept of populism to party systems in Europe and aiming to identify 'full' cases of populism, I seek to shed more light on this question.

Although the academic debate on populism may be well developed, in the vernacular sphere the term is applied in a less precise way (Bale et al. 2011). In the European context, populism is habitually associated with xenophobic politics and parties of the extreme or radical right (and therefore considered to be dangerous). This is not surprising, since populism in Western Europe has often been expressed by parties characterised by a nationalist and culturally conservative ideology, and hostility towards immigration and multiculturalism. The European academic literature has therefore also mainly considered populism as an element of 'the right' (see e.g. Betz 1994; Kitschelt and McGann 1995; Betz and Immerfall 1998; Mudde 2007). Populism, however, is not necessarily related to xenophobic politics or to any of the other properties of the radical right. Outside the European context, populism is actually often associated with politicians, parties and movements of a very different kind (see Ionescu and Gellner 1969; Canovan 1981; Taggart 2000; Mudde and Rovira Kaltwasser 2013). Although the focus of this study is on Europe only, this book also considers cases of populism beyond the radical right, as I am interested in the phenomenon of populism (expressed by political parties) in itself.

Another feature of the literature on populism in Europe is that, at least until fairly recently, it predominantly dealt with long-established democracies in Western Europe (e.g. Albertazzi and McDonnell 2008a). Although contributions have also emerged on populism in post-communist countries (e.g. Havlík et al. 2012), pan-European research projects have remained scarce. Since Central and Eastern European countries have been marked by the legacy of communism, it was difficult to provide a meaningful comparison between the party systems of long-established and post-communist European democracies. A quarter of a century has now passed since the post-communist countries' transition to democracy, and many of these countries have joined the European Union. While it would be wrong to disregard the still prevailing differences, it now makes sense to compare parties and party systems across the whole of Europe. Cas Mudde (2007) and Luke March (2011) set an example in their studies on populist radical right and radical left parties, respectively. This book has a pan-European scope as well, and provides a systematic analysis of populism and the electoral performance of populist parties in party systems across the continent.

By taking this general approach, including populist parties with different ideological traits and analysing them in a wide variety of countries, it can be expected that the study will include cases that have little in common apart from their populism. This is in line with the notion that populist parties are 'chameleonic' in the sense that they adopt an ideological 'colour' and focus on issues relevant to their specific context (Taggart 2000). As far as their electoral performance is concerned, this study assesses whether, in spite of ideological differences, the success or failure of populist parties is dependent on the same logic. While many comparative studies on the electoral performance of populist or other radical 'challenger' parties have focused on institutional variables, the economic and political context, and positions of mainstream competitors, the role of the challenger parties themselves has often been overlooked (see Mudde 2007; 2010). This study explicitly concentrates on the electoral credibility of populist parties themselves. In addition to the presence of a conducive environment, the agency of populist parties is deemed crucial in explaining their electoral performance.

As will be discussed in more detail towards the end of this chapter, the electoral performance of populist parties in national elections will be assessed through a mixed-methods approach. My first analysis assesses populist party success and failure in 31 European countries (EU-28 plus Iceland, Norway and Switzerland) by means of Qualitative Comparative Analysis (QCA) techniques. QCA can demonstrate how different (combinations of) explanatory conditions underlie the same outcome across various contexts. This is of crucial importance in view of the diversity of populist parties and countries studied in this book. After this analysis, the book continues with three qualitative case studies, which provide an in-depth analysis of populist parties and their competitors in the Netherlands, Poland and the United Kingdom. The first two countries have experienced the rise as well as the fall of populist parties since the start of the 21st century, while populist challengers have been unsuccessful in UK general elections up until 2010.

On the basis of the analyses in this book, several key messages can be formulated. First, it is important to avoid using the concept of populism too indiscriminately to describe or classify political parties. Some parties may voice populist rhetoric only sporadically and for a limited amount of time, and grouping these parties together with more genuine cases of populism leads to conceptual confusion and misclassification. Several post-communist countries, in particular, pose a challenge. Due to the more general presence of anti-establishment sentiments in many of these countries after their transition to democracy, it has been difficult to distinguish between populist and non-populist parties. As far as electoral performance is concerned, the rise of a populist party in a given country ought not to be seen as a mere reactionary backlash, but, rather, as the result of a perception that established political parties are unresponsive with regard to certain salient political themes. Populist parties, at the same time, only do well if they present themselves as credible alternatives to the political establishment. This means that researchers should pay more attention to the agency of populist parties in their effort to explain their success and failure. Populist parties are fairly ordinary players in the domain of party competition, and they should not be dismissed as dangerous pariahs out of hand, as their rise tells us something about the state of representative democracy (e.g. Canovan 1999; Mény and Surel 2002; Taggart 2002; Panizza 2005; Rovira Kaltwasser 2014).

The remainder of this chapter discusses the conceptual, theoretical and methodological starting points of this book. First, I provide a brief overview of the academic use of the concept 'populism', followed by a discussion on how populist parties can be defined and identified. I will then turn to my explanatory framework concerning the electoral performance of populist parties in Europe. The remaining section discusses the study's research design and the outline of the book.

(Problems of) populism

The concept of populism is not new, but its application in scholarly contributions has witnessed a surge in the past few decades, especially where the European context is concerned. This surge followed the appearance of political parties in Western Europe which were often described as extreme or radical right-wing, and also 'populist' (e.g. Ignazi 1992; Betz 1994; Kitschelt and McGann 1995; Taggart 1996).[2] It is important to recognise that studies on populism in other parts of the world, such as the United States (e.g. Kazin 1998; Ware 2002) and Latin America (e.g. Weyland 2001; Roberts 2006; Mudde and Rovira Kaltwasser 2013), include political actors of a different kind. As this book focuses on populist parties in Europe, the main aim of this concise literature overview is to outline the main issues faced when applying the concept in the European context. I will first introduce frequently identified elements of populism and several definitions, and then touch on discussions about the manifestation of populism and its relationship to democracy. In the subsequent section I will discuss in more detail the elements central to the definition of 'populist parties' I apply in this book.

Populism and its manifestation

One of the earliest accounts in which populism is described quite systematically is not devoted to the concept as such. Edward Shils (1956) discussed populism in his book on American security policies and associated anti-communist senator McCarthy with the term. According to Shils (1956: 101), populism is 'tinged by the belief that the people are not just the equal of their rulers; they are actually better than their rulers and better than the classes – the urban middle classes – associated with the ruling powers'. Populists are highly sceptical of bureaucracy and impatient with institutional procedures, which supposedly hinder the direct expression of the popular will. Politicians would have to be 'at best errand boys with little right to judgement on their own behalf if that judgement seems to contradict popular sentiment' (Shils 1956: 103).

The ground-breaking edited volume of Ghiţa Ionescu and Ernest Gellner (1969) showed that the use of the concept was by no means restricted to the American context.[3] The editors observed that populism was used to refer to actors from a wide range of countries and ideologies. In search for common elements of populism, the individual contributions touched on a range of cases, including the 19th-century movements in the US and Russia, and 20th-century populism in Latin America, Africa and Eastern Europe. The various authors identified a broad range of populist attributes. Peter Wiles (1969: 166), for instance, argued that populism is based on the premise that 'virtue resides in the simple people, who are the overwhelming majority, and in their collective traditions'. Wiles subsequently composed a long list of populist characteristics, including the notions that populist movements tend to be leader-centred, loosely organised, anti-intellectual, opposed to the establishment, and nostalgic in their dislike of the present and aim to 'mould the further future in accordance with its vision of the past' (Wiles 1969: 170). Similarly, Angus Steward (1969: 193) emphasised populism's dislike of the state in its present form, and parliamentary politics in particular, and also spoke of the 'charismatic' leadership of populist movements. Peter Worsley (1969: 244–246), in turn, argued that populists stress the supremacy of 'the will of the people' and the desirability of popular participation in the political process. In the end, however, the Ionescu and Gellner volume showed a reluctance to provide a clear-cut definition of the concept.

In her study on populism, Margaret Canovan (1981) was also pessimistic about a single, globally applicable approach to populism. After having described a broad range of historical and more contemporary populist movements and politicians across the world, Canovan (1981: 133) argued that it is not possible 'to unite all these movements into a single political phenomenon with a single ideology, program or socioenomic base', and instead distinguished seven general categories of populism. In later work, Canovan further claimed that a single (explanatory) theory on populism would be 'either too wide-ranging to be clear or too restrictive to be persuasive' (Canovan 1982: 544). It was, according to the author, best to build a descriptive typology 'which clarifies the ways in which the term is used while being spacious enough to do justice to the diversity of the movements and ideas concerned' (Canovan 1982: 550).

Several authors have, more recently, been less reluctant to provide a clear definition, or a universally applicable description, of populism. In his construction of an ideal type, Paul Taggart (2000: 2) identified six key themes: populism is hostile towards representative politics, identifies with an idealised 'heartland', lacks core values, is a reaction to a sense of crisis, is self-limiting and episodic, and has a 'chameleonic' character. Cas Mudde (2004: 543), in turn, defined populism as 'an ideology that considers society to be ultimately separated into two homogeneous and antagonistic groups, "the pure people" versus "the corrupt elite", and which argues that politics should be an expression of the *volonté générale* (general will) of the people'. Daniele Albertazzi and Duncan McDonnell (2008b: 3) added a third group (the 'others') in their definition of populism as 'an ideology which pits a virtuous and homogeneous people against a set of elites and dangerous "others" who are together depicted as depriving (or attempting to deprive) the sovereign people of their rights, values, prosperity, identity and voice'.

As is evident from the last two definitions, populism has in recent years often been perceived as an ideology or, more specifically, a 'thin' or 'thin-centred' ideology (Mudde 2004; Abts and Rummens 2007; Stanley 2008; Rovira Kaltwasser 2014). Following Michael Freeden (1998: 750), a thin-centred ideology is an ideology 'that arbitrarily severs itself from wider ideational contexts, by the deliberate removal and replacement of concepts'. Along these lines, populism as such lacks a 'programmatic centre' and ideas about how to deal with societal issues, but it can 'cohabit' with more comprehensive ideologies (Stanley 2008: 100; Rovira Kaltwasser 2014). This is similar to Taggart's (2000) assertion that populism is chameleonic in adopting the ideological colour which resonates with the values of the 'heartland' in which the people reside. This is not to say that there is no substance to the populist ideology; following Stanley (2008: 100), 'the absence of a common history, programme and social base, whilst attesting to populism's "thin" nature, does not warrant the conclusion that there is no coherence to the collection of concepts that comprise populist ideology'.

It would appear that treating populism as a (thin) ideology implies that there are political actors with populism as a defining ideological attribute. Indeed, in the European context observers often speak of 'populist parties' or party families for which populism is a core component. Mudde (2007), for instance, has treated populism as a core element of the populist radical right, and also identified two other types of populist parties: neo-liberal populists and social populists (see also Zaslove 2008; March 2011). Even though it would not be accurate to speak of a populist 'party family' (see Mair and Mudde 1998), for populist parties are not united in the policy positions they take, populism can still be seen as an important core attribute of certain types of parties.

Yet populism is certainly not always treated as a core ideological element of a certain type of movement, party or politician. An alternative approach is to define populism as an (opportunistic) strategy, employed to generate or retain support. Hans-Georg Betz (2002: 198), for instance, asserted that populism could be viewed as a rhetoric 'designed to tap feelings of *ressentiment* and exploit them politically'. In his study of populism in Latin America, Kurt Weyland (2001: 14) argued that 'populism is best defined as a political strategy through which a personalistic leader seeks or exercises government power based on direct, unmediated, uninstitutionalized support from large numbers of mostly unorganized followers'.

Yet another approach is to perceive populism as a 'style'. Jagers and Walgrave (2007: 322), for instance, distinguished between 'thick' and 'thin' populism, and argued that the latter form is simply 'a communication style of political actors that refers to the people'. Populism is, in this sense, not necessarily associated with a certain type of movement or party, but can also be applied by actors such as interest group representatives and journalists. More recently, Moffitt and Tormey (2013) have also argued that it is best to define populism as a style, and to focus on its 'performative' and 'aesthetic' features. Populism, according to the authors, should be seen in the context of the decline of traditional ideological cleavages and the increased 'stylisation' of the political, which goes together with a simplification of political discourse, the formulation of 'neat us-against-them antagonisms' and 'sound-bite solutions' (Moffitt and Tormey 2013: 387). It may be argued, then, that there is scope for a more general populist 'mood' in contemporary politics. Indeed, Mudde (2004) spoke of a populist *Zeitgeist*, and argued that the emergence of the radical populist parties in Western Europe has encouraged mainstream parties to use populist methods themselves (see also Mair 2002; Pappas 2014a).

From an empirical perspective, the fact that there are different interpretations concerning the manifestation of populism is not necessarily problematic, as long as there is a consensus about the concept's attributes. It seems reasonable to argue that populism can occur in various forms (e.g. style, strategy *and* ideology) and that its expression is not confined to a delineated set of political actors. As a matter of fact, recent contributions have measured the *degree* of populism in the discourse of political parties and politicians, through content analyses of party manifestos, speeches or party political broadcasts (Jagers and Walgrave 2007; Deegan-Krause and Haughton 2009; Hawkins 2009; Pauwels 2014; Rooduijn et al. 2014). In doing so, the question of whether populism is an ideology, a strategy, a communication style or something else might not be very important.

Accepting that the distinction between populism and non-populism is a matter of degree rather than kind does make life harder for those who seek to apply populism as a 'classifier' (Sikk 2009): that is, to use the concept in order to discriminate between certain types of politicians or party families, which involves determining which actors are populist and which are not. It is far from straightforward to determine how much populism a party should express in order to classify it as a 'genuine' populist party. What is more, some scholars even question the usefulness of an 'in-or-out' type of classification in the first place (see Deegan-Krause and Haughton 2009; Sikk 2009; Rooduijn et al. 2014). Rejecting the value of this 'dichotomous' approach completely, however, seems overly drastic. The scope for 'border disputes' also exists where other types of parties are concerned, and for some political actors populism is evidently more than a disposable rhetorical device. The study of these political actors is important, as the rise of populism tells us something about the state of representative democracy.

Populism's relationship with democracy

As discussed at the start of this chapter, it is common to see populism as a threat, or at least as an adverse phenomenon. Populism is regularly applied as a synonym for demagoguery, simplistic solutions or opportunism (e.g. Di Tella 1997; Taggart 2000: 5; Mudde 2004), and, especially in the vernacular sphere, the term is often used pejoratively to refer to vote-winning policy proposals, attempts to pander to public opinion, or xenophobic attitudes (Bale et al. 2011). Yet also in scholarly literature the term is frequently seen as a negative phenomenon. Hans-Georg Betz (1994: 4), for instance, sees populism as a means of political opportunism that is unscrupulous and exploitative of the anxieties of the electorate. Others have seen a threat in populism's espousal of unmediated popular sovereignty, which is considered to come at the cost of liberal-democratic 'checks and balances' and the protection of minorities. Abts and Rummens (2007), for instance, argued that populism is inherently incompatible with democracy; populism's conception of the people as a homogeneous body is fictional and 'generates a logic which disregards the idea of otherness at the heart of democracy and aims at the suppression of diversity within society' (Abts and Rummens 2007: 414).

A more optimistic reading is that populism is an important indicator for the health of representative or liberal democracy. Some scholars have argued that populism emerges when the political elite loses track of public opinion, or when the 'constitutional' or 'liberal', as opposed to the 'democratic' or 'popular', pillar of democracy becomes too dominant. Taggart (2002: 63), for instance, argued that populism acts as a 'bellwether' for the health of representative politics. Mény and Surel (2002: 17) have described populism as 'a warning signal about the defects, limits and weaknesses of representative systems', and argued that 'in spite of its often unpleasant tones, it may constitute an effective reminder that democracy is not a given, but is instead a constant enterprise of adjustment to the changing needs and values of society'. Canovan (1999: 11) wrote about the tension between the 'pragmatic' and 'redemptive' faces of democracy and argued that:

> When too great a gap opens up between haloed democracy and the grubby business of politics, populists tend to move on to the vacant

territory, promising in place of the dirty world of party manoeuvring the shining ideal of democracy renewed. Even from the point of view of pragmatic politics, the vital practices of contestation and account-ability grow weak without the energy provided by democracy's inspi-rational, mobilizing, redemptive side.

Still, populism is seldom seen as an unequivocally good thing. Not many scholars appear to subscribe to Ernesto Laclau's argument that populism and politics are essentially interchangeable terms and that 'the end of populism coincides with the end of politics' (Laclau 2005: 48). Francisco Panizza (2005: 30) instead described populism as a 'mirror in which democracy can contemplate itself', but argued that 'populism is neither the highest form of democracy nor its enemy'. In the same volume, Benjamin Arditi (2005) argued that populism can appear in three possible modes: as a mode of representation, as a symptom or as an underside. The first mode is compatible with liberal-democratic politics, the second presents a disturbance of democracy, and the latter entails an actual inter-ruption of democracy. Gianfranco Pasquino (2008: 28), in turn, argued that the appearance of populism is often a sign of a poorly functioning democratic regime, but that populism, for instance due to its unrealisable promises, has a negative impact on the democratic framework itself.

In a more recent edited volume of Cas Mudde and Cristóbal Rovira Kaltwasser (2012), an attempt has been made to move beyond theoret-ical assumptions about the relationship between populism and democ-racy, and to test empirically the consequences of populism in several countries in Europe and the Americas. Based on the various case studies, the editors conclude that populism can be a corrective as well as a threat to democracy. Populist politicians can, for instance, place issues on the agenda which have been ignored by the political establishment and give voice to excluded sections of society. Especially in unconsolidated democracies, on the other hand, populism can also undermine liberal-democratic institutions in view of its monist conception of society and disdain for 'checks and balances'.

The theoretical arguments made by several of the aforementioned authors thus seem to have empirical consequences. For my study, it is particularly relevant that populist parties appear to mobilise in situa-tions where the political establishment is seen as unrepresentative, or unresponsive to the demands of a certain segment of the electorate. The chapter will later turn to the analytical framework of this study in more detail. The following section first discusses how populist parties can be defined and identified in the European context.

Defining and identifying populist parties

Defining populist parties

In this book I seek to use the concept of populism to classify political parties in Europe and, through this, to investigate whether it makes sense to distinguish between populist and non-populist parties. I start out from the idea that populism can be a durable defining attribute of certain political parties, and thus potentially more than an (opportunistic) strategy or style. Populist parties embody resistance against the political establishment in defence of popular sovereignty, and it would be impossible to characterise such parties without taking their populist anti-establishment discourse into account. The way populism is applied here is in line with the accounts considering populism to be a 'thin' ideology; populist parties do not all adopt the same substantive policy positions. In terms of defining populist parties, this study seeks inspiration from the previously mentioned contributions that treated populism primarily as a set of ideas. Even though differences can be noticed, there is a substantial overlap between recent definitions of populism. Four crucial, distinct but interrelated, populist properties are captured well by Ben Stanley (2008: 102):

- The existence of two homogeneous units of analysis: 'the people' and 'the elite'.
- The antagonistic relationship between the people and the elite.
- The idea of popular sovereignty.
- The positive valorisation of 'the people' and denigration of 'the elite'.

Although populism is regularly assumed to portray both 'the people' and 'the elite' as homogeneous entities – emphasising the *normative* distinction between the two groups (Mudde 2004: 544) – authors have most often focused on populism's monolithic conception of 'the people' (e.g. Taggart 2000; Abts and Rummens 2007; Albertazzi and McDonnell 2008b).[4] Populists speak of 'the people' as if it were a clearly circumscribed and homogeneous group, and tend to ignore the differences between its members. It is not self-evident who belongs to 'the people', and populists themselves are often not very specific about their target audience. To be so would actually limit the populist appeal. In the words of Arditi (2005: 82):

> the populist 'us' remains conveniently vague. It is a deliberate vagueness, for it enables it to blur the contours of 'the people' sufficiently

to encompass anyone with a grievance structured around a perceived exclusion from a public domain of interaction and decision hegemonised by economic, political or cultural elites.

Populist parties, in other words, profit from an elusive characterisation of their target constituency, as it enables them to appeal to a broad, disgruntled audience. This is not to say that the appeal to the ordinary people is entirely undefined. In the words of Taggart, populists identify with an idealised and imagined 'heartland', which is the place where 'the people' reside (Taggart 2000: 95). The features of the heartland are usually based on a romanticised portrayal of the past and constitute the elements of the community which are considered worth defending. Consequently, populist actors across time and space each construct their own specific version of the heartland.

Even though the heartland concept helps in making sense of who 'the people' are meant to be, populist parties are still clearer about who does *not* belong to their portrayed heartland. The conception of 'the people' is, then, typically constructed in a negative manner (Taggart 2000; Mudde 2004; Albertazzi and McDonnell 2008b). In the words of Taggart (2000: 3), populism 'excludes elements it sees as alien, corrupt or debased, and works on a distinction between the things which are wholesome and those which are not'. It can be argued that populism is intrinsically exclusionistic, in view of its monolithic portrayal of 'the people' and its, therefore perhaps inherent, rejection of pluralism (Mudde 2004: 543; Abts and Rummens 2007). Immigrants and ethnic or cultural minorities are easy targets to brand as outsiders in particular. Not all populists are necessarily xenophobic, however, and the heartland can also be defined in non-ethnic terms. Mudde and Rovira Kaltwasser (2013: 167), for example, argued that European populism primarily has an 'exclusionary' character (excluding the 'aliens'), but that populism in Latin America is more oriented towards the socio-economic dimension, and primarily focuses on 'including the poor'. Left-wing populists in Europe also tend to place more emphasis on socio-economic themes in their distinction between the elite and 'the people' (see March 2011). Thus, in the words of Rovira Kaltwasser (2014: 479), populists may conceive of 'the people' as the '*ethnos*' as well as the 'plebs' (or a combination of the two).

Despite their emphasis on popular sovereignty, populist parties do not necessarily intend to get their following directly involved in politics, even if many support referenda and other forms of direct democracy. Following Robert Barr (2009), populism can be associated with a 'plebiscitarianist' form of linkage between citizens and the political elite; populism emphasises the need for accountability of leaders, but rather less the need for political participation by citizens. Populism is thus not necessarily incompatible with representative politics, since populist politicians can claim to offer responsive leadership, and to act as the voice of the people (see Mudde 2004; cf. Taggart 2000).

The category of 'elites', in turn, can be defined broadly, and may comprise the corporate rich, bankers, but also the media or intelligentsia whose (liberal) ideas, values and interests are at odds with those of the 'silent majority' (Canovan 1999: 3). Both populist core concepts, 'the people' and 'the elite', are thus 'empty vessels', which can be filled in different ways, depending on the context and ideological features of the populist party (see Mudde and Rovira Kaltwasser 2013: 151). If we speak about populism in the form of political parties, the national political establishment inherently belongs to the 'elite' category. In electoral competition, the 'established parties' are the main antagonists of populist parties, and portrayed by the latter as the henchmen of 'special interests' (Mudde 2004: 561). Residing in their ivory towers, the members of the political establishment are alleged to have lost track of the everyday problems of the ordinary people. In their denunciation of the whole political establishment, populist parties' criticism goes further than condemning a specific government for being unresponsive or corrupt.

These issues considered, political parties are here classified as populist parties if they:

1. portray 'the people' as virtuous and essentially homogeneous;
2. advocate popular sovereignty, as opposed to elitist rule;
3. define themselves against the political establishment, which is alleged to act against the interest of 'the people'.

A few further points of clarification should be made. First of all, this definition should be treated as a minimal definition, which includes necessary and jointly sufficient properties, and excludes the attributes that are considered to be 'accompanying properties' (Sartori 1984: 55–56).[5] 'Populist party' is thus treated as a 'classical concept', meaning that all three properties outlined above need to be present in order to include a case into the populist party universe. Alternative strategies of concept formation would be the 'family resemblance' approach and the construction of 'radial categories' (see Collier and Mahon 1993). The latter strategy entails the creation of a central subcategory which can be considered as a 'full' instance, because it incorporates all possible components of a concept. The concept, however, may still be used for cases that lack some of these components.[6] The family resemblance structure is even more flexible, in that it contains no necessary defining properties (Goertz 2006: 7, 45). The absence of one of the concept's properties can be compensated by the presence of another.

These latter approaches, however, are not suitable for the concept of a populist party. None of the components in the above definition can be left out, or substituted, without depriving the concept of its specific meaning and causing 'concept stretching' (see Sartori 1970; 1991). That is, too wide a variety of political parties would become associated with populism (Weyland 2001; Sikk 2009). Excluding the first two components of the above definition, for instance, leads to the potential inclusion of any kind of (new) anti-establishment party. Hence, to prevent concept stretching, this study does not follow the example of contributions which distinguish between categories such as 'thin' and 'thick' or 'soft' and 'hard' populism (Lang 2005; Jagers and Walgrave 2007).

Another issue to raise is that populism is often associated with characteristics which I consider to be 'accompanying properties', and thus not directly relevant in determining whether or not a party is populist. Some of these properties relate to the alleged style of populists, and include the use of simplistic and coarse language and the 'colourful' image of populist leaders (Moffitt and Tormey 2013). Two other frequently identified attributes relate more to the organisational attributes of populist politics: personalistic (or 'charismatic') leadership and the lack of a developed party organisation (e.g. Di Tella 1997; Weyland 2001; Barr 2009). There may indeed be a tendency for populist parties to be under-institutionalised and reliant on personalistic leadership, in view of their quasi-religious message of salvation and their dislike of traditional party organisations (Taggart 2000: 101–102). Yet I do not consider these organisational features to be defining properties of populist parties, since I concur with Mudde's (2004: 545) argument that charismatic leadership and direct communication between leader and followers '*facilitate* rather than define populism'. The use of simplistic and politically incorrect language, in turn, should primarily be seen as a *consequence* of the populist thin ideology; in particular populism's antagonistic position *vis-à-vis* the political establishment and its appeal to the 'common' people. In theory, a party can be populist without showing typical organisational or stylistic features, and populism should essentially be seen as a set of *ideas* (see also Rooduijn 2014a). The way populist parties organise and express themselves is here considered an empirical rather than a definitional matter. Still, as will be discussed later in this chapter, since many populist parties are weakly institutionalised and built around their leader in practice, organisational features are likely to play an important role as far as the electoral performance of populist parties is concerned. A final point to make is that the presented definition is primarily devised to identify populist parties in Europe. The way in which populism manifests itself varies considerably across continents. Populism is, for instance, seen as a more general feature of US politics (Kazin 1998; Ware 2002), and in Latin America populism is, even more than in Europe, commonly associated with individuals rather than parties (see e.g. Roberts 2006; Mudde and Rovira Kaltwasser 2012). Even though 'populism' can be defined so that it is universally applicable, speaking of 'populist parties' is primarily useful in the European context, where parties are still key actors in political systems.

Identifying populist parties

With the above definition, the identification of a bounded 'universe' of populist parties in Europe is still not an uncomplicated task. The lack of a clear populist archetype, or another basis for identifying cases of populism, poses a first challenge. Populism, after all, does not 'adhere to a single foundational doctrine, political philosopher or intellectual tradition' (Zaslove 2009: 309). Moreover, actors and movements associated with populism rarely use this label to identify themselves (e.g. Worsley 1969: 218). Even though there are exceptions to the rule,[7] populism's pejorative connotation is one reason why political actors are not keen on adopting the term for the purpose of self-identification.

Another issue is that there is a fine line between populist and essentially non-populist party families. In some ways, for instance, populists are similar to fascists, communists and minority nationalists in resenting the existing political order and making appeals to an idealised community. There are some crucial differences too, however. Fascists envision a totalitarian, hierarchically organised and organic state in which the people serve as mere parts of a larger whole (see e.g. Hayes 1973; Payne 1980; Griffin 1993). Populism, on the other hand, glorifies the ordinary people within the community, and not the nation-state as such (Albertazzi and McDonnell 2008b: 3). Fascism, like other forms of right-wing extremism, is also anti-democratic, while populism sees the will of the people as the ultimate source of legitimacy.

Communist parties, in turn, arguably share the populist claim to defend the 'ordinary' and oppressed people. The populist portrayal of the heartland, however, tends to be based on a shared identity which goes beyond class relationships (March and Mudde 2005: 35; March 2009: 127).

Even left-wing populists may differ substantially from communists, as the former do not subscribe to the idea of many Marxist theorists that the proletariat should be liberated from a 'false consciousness' and made aware of its true interests (see Eyerman 1981). Populists instead claim that the ordinary people are well aware of their interests, and actually idealise the 'common sense' of the people (Mudde 2004: 547; March 2011: 120).

Minority nationalists or regionalist parties, finally, have a clear notion of a communal identity and often share the populist resentment of the central state establishment. Unlike typical populist parties, however, they oppose a political establishment which is portrayed as 'foreign' and as an enemy 'from outside'. Certain parties, such as the Italian Northern League and the Flemish Interest in Belgium, can nevertheless be considered as 'regionalist populist' parties (McDonnell 2006). Yet it is important to stress that minority nationalists are not automatically populist, since they may not subscribe to the notion of popular sovereignty. This also applies to nationalists in general, who are not always anti-elitist and, thus, not always populist (Mudde 2007: 24).

In practice, however, these ideological boundaries may not be that clear-cut. What is more, the literature review previously outlined that populism can also take the form of a more ephemeral rhetorical device, which can, in principle, be applied by all political actors. As discussed, Mudde (2004) spoke of a populist *Zeitgeist*, which also influenced the discourse of established parties, and March (2011: 19) argued that since 1989 all radical left-wing parties have become more populist (and nationalist) in their aim to reach out beyond a traditional working-class electorate. However, one should not be overly doubtful about the 'discriminating power' of populism as a concept (Sartori 1970). On the basis of a content analysis of party manifestos, Rooduijn et al. (2014) actually showed that certain Western European parties clearly stood out in terms of their populism, while mainstream parties did not become more populist over time.

In post-communist Europe, however, the situation is less clear-cut. Politics in many Central and Eastern European countries was characterised by a lack of continuity in party organisations and ideologies. Economic crises and corruption scandals, furthermore, provided an ostensibly favourable environment for populism. Public dissatisfaction was particularly high among the so-called 'transition losers' who did not reap the benefits of the free-market economy (Bustikova and Kitschelt 2009; March 2011: 139–141). Thus, according to Mudde (2007: 41), several parties in post-communist countries have gone through a populist radical right phase in their aim to tap into a general anti-political mood (see also Minkenberg 2002; 2013; Rupnik 2007; Pirro 2014a). It has even been suggested that populism constituted a more general feature of post-communist politics, with populist rhetoric being voiced by radical and non-radical opposition parties alike (see Lang 2005; Učeň 2007). This book nevertheless provides a study of populist parties across the whole of Europe, as excluding post-communist countries in comparative research becomes increasingly artificial. In the quarter of a century that passed after the fall of the Berlin Wall there have been substantial developments in Central and Eastern European politics. Post-communist EU members, notably, have been forced to abide by the economic as well as the political norms of Western European countries (Mudde 2002a: 229). In addition, by the end of the 20st century it was possible to observe the entrance of a range of new parties in many Central and Eastern European countries, which voiced criticism of the mainstream political camps that had alternated in government after the fall of communism (Pop-Eleches 2010; Hanley and Sikk 2014). Thus, also in this part of Europe it became possible to distinguish between a (post-communist) political establishment and new parties challenging it. At the same time, in view of processes such as growing electoral volatility and partisan dealignment, Western European party systems have arguably begun to resemble more closely the changeable systems in Central and Eastern Europe (see e.g. Dalton et al. 2000; Mair 2006; Van Biezen et al. 2012).

These arguments should not be pushed too far; especially in the post-communist part of Europe many countries remain marked by widespread disenchantment with politics, unstructured party competition, and extremely weak ties between voters and parties (Rupnik 2007; Casal Bértoa 2013; Van Biezen and Wallace 2013). This may also affect the way in which populism manifests itself in this part of the continent, in the sense that populism might still be a more generic phenomenon in post-communist than in Western European politics. In the next chapter, which identifies the populist parties across Europe, I discuss in more detail to what extent one can meaningfully use the concept of populism as a 'classifier' in both parts of Europe. I will now first turn to the analytical framework related to the other core aim of this book: explaining the electoral performance of populist parties.

Explaining the electoral performance of populist parties

For my analytical framework concerning populist party performance I seek inspiration from the wider literature on radical right, new or 'niche' parties. It can be expected that there will be considerable overlap between the conditions underlying the success or failure of populist parties and those related to the electoral performance of other non-mainstream parties. Below, I will nevertheless seek to clarify why several such conditions are expected to be relevant for the performance of populist parties in particular. For reasons of space, the review of findings from previous studies is concise, and I will refrain from going into depth with regard to these studies' methodological approaches and geographical scope. This is not to deny that these factors are important in accounting for the sometimes contradictory results in the literature.

Previous studies have regularly referred to broad societal developments as a cause of the breakthrough of new types of parties. Ronald Inglehart (e.g. 1977; 1997), for instance, described the growing salience of post-materialist causes and the related rise of social liberal and green parties. Scholars such as Piero Ignazi (1992; see also 1996) and Hans-Georg Betz (1994), on the other hand, focused on the socio-economic and socio-cultural conditions favouring the rise of radical or extreme right parties (see also Taggart 1996; Swank and Betz 2003). It has been argued that processes such as the globalisation of markets, the decline of traditional (class) identities, and the related individualisation of society have generated cultural and economic anxieties among specific sections of the electorate, and fed into dissatisfaction with the established political systems. More recently, Kriesi et al. (2006; 2008) identified a new structural cleavage in Western European countries, pitting 'winners' and 'losers' of globalisation against each other.

The abovementioned studies have been valuable in clarifying the general breeding ground for parties outside the traditional mainstream – predominantly in Western Europe. Yet the identified trends do not explain cross-national differences in the success of populist parties, since they have affected countries in similar ways. Indeed, it can be expected that populist parties have electoral potential across the whole of contemporary Europe, in view of the current 'availability' of voters. This relates to the previously mentioned process of partisan dealignment in Western Europe (see e.g. Dalton et al. 2000; Mair 2006; Krouwel 2012) and the fact that ties between voters and parties have remained weak across post-communist Europe (e.g. Rose 1995; Casal Bértoa 2013). To explain the varying electoral fortunes of populist parties between European countries, I therefore seek to select more country-specific explanatory conditions for my analytical framework.

One can, first of all, think of various institutional factors which have frequently been considered in past studies. Some of these have been discarded: Abedi (2004) and Carter (2005), for instance, found little evidence that requirements for ballot access, the availability of state subventions, or access to broadcast media had an impact on the vote for, respectively, anti-political establishment (APE) and extreme right parties (see also Harmel and Robertson 1985; Norris 2005; Bolin 2007).[8] Several authors have also considered whether a federal state structure is conducive to new party success. A federal or decentralised structure may provide opportunities for new parties to enter legislatures at the subnational level and to build regional strongholds. However, most studies found little evidence for an impact of federalism or territorial decentralisation on the success of new or extreme right parties (Harmel and Robertson 1985; Willey 1998; Arzheimer and Carter 2006; cf. Hakhverdian and Koop 2007).

The influence of another institutional variable, the electoral system, has also frequently been considered. The properties of an electoral system are relevant for new and small parties in particular, and populist parties often fall into these categories. A pure proportional representation (PR) system allows parties with a relatively small vote share to enter parliament, while other systems are designed to the advantage of larger parties. Specific features of electoral systems, such as the district magnitude (the number of candidates to be elected per district) and the electoral threshold, affect the proportionality of a system (see Carter 2005). A higher district magnitude normally leads to a seat distribution that reflects more closely the distribution of votes, which tends to benefit smaller parties (see Rae 1971). A higher electoral threshold, on the other hand, obstructs the entrance into parliament of parties with only a limited vote share. Besides the mechanical effects of electoral systems, psychological effects are also likely to be relevant (Duverger 1959). When the electoral system is disproportional, citizens may be reluctant to 'waste' their votes on parties that are perceived to stand relatively little chance of entering parliament. Electoral system characteristics, then, influence not only the allocation of seats after the election, but also the initial vote distribution. At the same time, political entrepreneurs may be less inclined to found a new party, if the hurdle posed by the electoral system is deemed too high.

Studies that considered the effect of the electoral system on the support for extreme right parties have yielded mixed results. Some scholars concluded that, under certain conditions, factors such as district magnitude and electoral thresholds matter for the performance of extreme right parties (Jackman and Volpert 1996; Golder 2003). Others found less or no evidence for the expectation that more proportional electoral systems are conducive to the extreme right vote (Carter 2005; Norris

2005; Van der Brug et al. 2005; Arzheimer and Carter 2006). This study, however, does not only consider populist parties of the radical right.

Since several studies have shown that a more proportional electoral system favours the electoral performance, or the party system entrance, of new parties in general, the **electoral system** will be considered as an explanatory condition in this research (Harmel and Robertson 1985; Willey 1998; Tavits 2006; Bolin 2007; cf. Abedi 2004). Although the electoral system alone is unlikely to determine the electoral performance of populist parties, there is sufficient reason to assume that it can be an important factor in combination with other explanatory conditions.

The electoral success or failure of populist parties cannot be understood without also considering the agency of political parties. Various scholars have assessed the ideological placement and tactics of mainstream parties in order to account for non-mainstream party performance. Studies have, for instance, found that convergence between mainstream parties, or the formation of a grand coalition, benefited (radical/extreme right) challenger parties (e.g. Kitschelt and McGann 1995; Abedi 2004; Carter 2005). Other scholars, however, did not find clear evidence for the ideological convergence thesis (Arzheimer and Carter 2006; Norris 2005; Veugelers and Magnan 2005). Yet others have questioned whether measuring party distances on a single left–right dimension is a valid way to study developments in party positions and strategies (Bornschier 2010: 6). Various different issue dimensions may be relevant in accounting for party competition dynamics (see Spies and Franzmann 2011). One way around this problem is to consider the policy dimension which is most relevant to the appeal of the parties under consideration (Meguid 2008: 49; Bornschier 2010). In view of the ideological diversity of populist parties across Europe, however, a general explanatory framework for their electoral performance needs to go beyond an assessment of the ideological space related to specific issue dimensions.

What is more, in addition to more substantive policy-related motivations, a vote for a populist party is here assumed to be an expression of dissatisfaction with the political establishment (see Eatwell 2003; Bélanger and Aarts 2006; Oesch 2008; Schumacher and Rooduijn 2013). This dissatisfaction may not necessarily relate to party positions; it can also be the result of disappointment with established parties' accomplishments or neglect of specific issues (Rydgren 2005). I therefore expect that populist parties' electoral performance will, above all, be related to the perceived **responsiveness of established parties**. It can be expected that populist parties will thrive when established political parties are perceived to be unresponsive to the demands of 'the people'.

This can relate to a notion that established parties fail to address certain salient issues, have become indistinct ideologically, or have formed an impenetrable elitist cartel (see Katz and Mair 1995). If these views are sufficiently widespread, established parties are vulnerable to the rise of populist challengers (see also Hauss and Rayside 1978; Lucardie 2000; Hug 2001; Pirro 2014b).

Established parties may, on the other hand, hamper the success of populist parties by successfully retaining or seizing the ownership of the issues central to the populist party's appeal (see Budge and Farlie 1983; Petrocik 1996). Tim Bale (2003), for instance, spoke of a 'black widow effect' when centre-right parties in office are able to capture the electoral support of their radical right junior coalition partner by copying its policies. Bonnie Meguid (2008) similarly argued that an 'accommodative' strategy of a mainstream party can reduce the electoral support for a niche party, but that the success of this strategy also depends on the strategies of the other mainstream parties (see also Bornschier 2010; 2012).

Notwithstanding the importance of the established parties' agency in explaining the performance of populist challengers, I suspect it is a mistake to treat the latter as mere 'by-products of competition between mainstream parties' (Meguid 2008: 22). In this study, therefore, an additional explanatory condition is the **supply of credible populist parties**. Even if the breeding ground for populism is fertile, populist electoral success would be lacking without the supply of a credible populist party. The importance of 'supply-side' factors, such as party organisation and leadership, in explaining new, radical or populist party performance has been acknowledged (e.g. Hauss and Rayside 1978; Betz 2002; Carter 2005; Rydgren 2005; Mudde 2007; Albertazzi and McDonnell 2008b; March 2011). In single case studies these factors are also regularly taken into consideration, yet in comparative studies (of a quantitative nature) they have often been overlooked. This is hardly justifiable, following Cas Mudde's (2010) argument about populist radical right parties, since these parties' leadership, organisation and campaigning are vital in explaining their success or failure in breaking through and surviving.

The contribution of Elisabeth Carter (2005) is one of the few systematic comparative studies taking into consideration such supply-side factors. Carter found that party organisation and leadership are of key importance in explaining the varying levels of support for extreme right parties in Europe; strongly organised and well-led extreme right parties have been more successful (see also Lubbers et al. 2002; Givens 2005; Pauwels 2014). Carter also found that the ideology of extreme right parties relates to their support; parties that are anti-democratic and adhere to classical racism are generally less successful (see also Schedler 1996; Rydgren 2005; Bos and Van der Brug 2010). There is no reason to assume that factors related to ideology, leadership and organisation are any less important for populist parties, and, based on previous insights, the credibility of populist parties will be assessed by taking into account two main indicators: electoral appeal and organisational cohesion.

For a populist party, electoral appeal is assumed to relate to the following factors in particular: its leadership's visibility and persuasiveness, and its ability to dissociate itself from both the political establishment as well as political extremism. In order to break through electorally, a populist party needs to be sufficiently visible and persuasive to seize the owner-ship of salient social issues. Potential voters must be convinced that the party is able to 'handle' the problems it identifies better than its oppo-nents (Petrocik 1996). In relation to this, it is important that the populist party attracts sufficient media attention and that the party figurehead(s) make a strong impression during the election campaign (see Mazzoleni et al. 2003; Mazzoleni 2008). This is not to say that populist party voters are prone to simply vote for the most 'attractive' leader (see Bellucci et al. 2013), but skilled leadership is required to raise attention to, and support for, the party's substantive arguments.

At the same time, a populist party's electoral attractiveness is likely to remain limited when its policy positions are overly militant, or when the party is associated with political extremism (Rydgren 2005). It is impor-tant to note that whether or not a party is considered too extreme partly depends on the political context and the dominant political attitudes (see Eatwell 2003; Mudde 2007: 259; Minkenberg 2013).[9] Particularly after their breakthrough, the appeal of populist parties is likely to wane if they fail to stick convincingly to their anti-establishment discourse. This is a challenge especially for those populist parties that enter govern-ment, as they become part of the governing elite they used to oppose (Taggart 2000; Mény and Surel 2002). Once populist parties take part in office they are not necessarily doomed electorally (see Albertazzi and McDonnell 2005; 2010; Akkerman and de Lange 2012; Zaslove 2012), but it becomes at least more of a challenge for them to still present themselves as 'outsiders' in a convincing way. Government participa-tion, in other words, can be seen as the 'ultimate test' for populist parties (Betz 2002; Heinisch 2003).

The second main indicator of credibility, organisational cohesion, is also vital to the electoral persistence of populist parties (Mudde 2007). After their breakthrough, populist parties are likely to lose their credibility as competent political actors if they fail to preserve internal discipline and cohesion. Since populist parties are often leader-centred organisations in practice, they are especially likely to fall apart when the leader departs or loses grip over the party (Betz 2002; Heinisch 2003). Other organisational factors, such as the degree of internal democracy or effective internal leadership (see Mudde 2007; De Lange and Art 2011), are not considered in this study as long as they remain purely internal affairs. Intra-party procedures are not normally visible to the electorate at large and are, therefore, unlikely to affect the party's image to the outside world. This is not to deny that these factors may have an *indirect* effect on the credibility of populist parties; sound internal leadership can, for instance, improve organisational cohesion and prevent publicly visible rows and defections (see also Bolleyer 2013).

By considering the credibility of populist parties as one of the key explanatory conditions, my study departs from the notion that that such parties only rely on uninformed protest votes. Even if populist parties thrive on resentment and disenchantment, there is more to their electoral performance than the presence of anti-establishment sentiments alone. Studies have, in fact, indicated that ideological convictions and policy preferences play a crucial role with regard to the right-wing populist vote (e.g. Van der Brug et al. 2000; 2005; Ivarsflaten 2008; Arzheimer 2009). This is expected to be no different for populist parties in general. These parties need to convince voters that they can handle salient issues in a better way than the established parties, and that they are therefore a credible alternative to the traditional political elites.

In addition to the three more fundamental conditions identified (the electoral system; the responsiveness of established parties; and the supply of credible populist parties), I expect that populist parties will stand a better chance if certain issues are electorally salient. As discussed, populist parties may adopt various ideological colours, depending on the social and political context they operate in. That does not mean, however, that the populist thin ideology is entirely unrelated to the policies they focus on and the positions they take. For instance, the fact that populist parties envision the 'the people' as a homogeneous entity, and define themselves against the establishment, has consequences for their substantive policy platform. As I will discuss below, populist parties in Europe are likely to focus on the following issues or themes in particular: 1) culture and ethnicity; 2) economic hardship; 3) European integration; and 4) corruption. It is important to note that these four themes are not relevant to (the performance of) *all* populist parties. I nevertheless expect that the breeding ground for populist parties is especially fertile where related issues are salient and where established parties are considered unresponsive or incapable of dealing with them.

The first theme of **culture and ethnicity** is relevant for many populist parties, since populism's anti-pluralist character and homogeneous portrayal of 'the people' is very compatible with a culturally exclusivist vision of society. Indeed, it is this vision that characterises the many populist parties in Europe that can be placed in the populist radical right (PRR) category (Mudde 2007). Following Mudde (2007: 22), the key ideological feature of these parties is 'nativism', meaning 'an ideology, which holds that states should be inhabited exclusively by members of the native group ("the nation") and that non-native elements (persons and ideas) are fundamentally threatening to the homogeneous nation-state'. The PRR's nativism is related to different themes across Europe. While in Western European countries nativism is primarily expressed by an anti-immigration attitude – and, more recently, hostility towards Islam – immigration has hardly played a role in the political debates of post-communist countries. Here, the PRR tends to target ethnic minority groups, and in some countries the Roma population in particular (e.g. Minkenberg 2002; 2013; Mudde 2005; Bustikova and Kitschelt 2009; Pirro 2014a).

As far as the electoral performance of radical right parties is concerned, scholars have previously considered the inflow of immigrants or the size of ethnic minority groups as independent variables. Studies have yielded mixed results. Some scholars found that higher levels of immigration, or a large number of foreign citizens, stimulated support for the radical or extreme right (Knigge 1998; Lubbers et al. 2002; Golder 2003; Swank and Betz 2003; Arzheimer 2009; Smith 2010). Others found no (significant) correlation (Kitschelt and McGann 1995; Norris 2005; Van der Brug et al. 2005; Arzheimer and Carter 2006; Messina 2007). Rather than considering objective numbers of immigrants and minorities in trying to explain PRR performance, in any case, it might make more sense to focus on subjective indicators: the prevalence of nativist attitudes within a given electorate, and the salience of issues such as immigration and multiculturalism (see Van der Brug et al. 2005; Lubbers et al. 2002; Ivarsflaten 2008; Oesch 2008). Populist parties with a nativist ideology are likely to perform better if a large number of voters actually care about issues related to immigration and minorities, and subscribe to cultural protectionist ideas.

Not all populist parties, however, have a nativist character. Radical left-wing populist parties are defined primarily by their socio-economic policies and their aim to promote the rights of the underprivileged (March and Mudde 2005; March 2011). For these parties, **economic hardship**, the second theme identified here, is likely to be more relevant to their electoral performance. Particularly in periods of mass unemployment, left-wing populists can make the case that the political establishment is more concerned with the interests of the capitalist elite than those of the ordinary worker. Yet economic hardship can be expected to benefit populist parties without a left-wing ideology as well, if the economic situation instigates a more general mood of dissatisfaction with the political establishment.

Variables such as unemployment, economic growth, and inflation have actually often been included in studies on the performance of the radical *right*. Again, results have been mixed: some scholars found that high levels of unemployment (under certain conditions) facilitated the vote for extreme right parties (Jackman and Volpert 1996; Golder 2003; Arzheimer 2009), whereas others found a *negative* relationship between levels of unemployment and extreme right support (Knigge 1998; Lubbers et al. 2002; Arzheimer and Carter 2006). Arzheimer and Carter (2006: 434) speculated that 'people may turn (back) to the more established and experienced mainstream parties in times of economic uncertainty rather than to the parties of the extreme right that lack such experience'. Others have argued that the state of the economy is unlikely to be a key driver behind electoral success of radical right parties, because these parties tend to concentrate more on cultural, rather than economic, issues (Mudde 2007; Bornschier 2010). Several studies, indeed, indicated that radical right parties have mobilised primarily on the basis of cultural grievances (e.g. Oesch 2008; Ivarsflaten 2008; Spies 2013). What is more, a study on the broader category of anti-political establishment parties also found little evidence that levels of unemployment are related to APE party performance (Abedi 2004).

In my study, economic hardship is nevertheless considered to serve as a potential catalyst for populist party success for two reasons. First, the economic situation may not be relevant for the performance of all populist parties, but it may be for some. March and Rommerskirchen (2012), for instance, found that radical left parties performed better in times of high unemployment. For those populist parties that juxtapose the people (the *plebs*) with economic elites and their political allies, economic malaise may well provide a favourable opportunity structure. Furthermore, the demand for populist parties in post-communist countries has actually often been related to the dismantling of communist welfare states and the subsequent growth of economic inequality (Bustikova and Kitschelt 2009).

Second, the financial and economic crisis that broke out in 2008 is likely to have increased the salience of issues such as unemployment and welfare state reforms across the whole of Europe. This may not only have benefited left-wing populist parties, but may also have encouraged PRR parties to revise and prioritise their economic policies, in an attempt to appeal to the 'losers of globalisation' who not only oppose immigration, but also feel challenged economically (see Kriesi et al. 2006; 2008). Indeed, Van der Brug and Van Spanje (2009) showed that there are a substantial number of people in Western Europe who are left-leaning on socio-economic matters and right-leaning on immigration. In times of crisis, economic protectionism and 'welfare chauvinism' – the idea that welfare entitlements should be reserved for the native population – may become more central to PRR party programmes.

Related to the economic crisis in Europe is the third theme of **European integration**. The EU's complex and opaque institutional set-up is something which populist parties are prone to oppose (Taggart 2004). In view of the populist love for transparency and hatred of backroom deals, shady compromises and complicated technicalities, Canovan (1999: 6) argued that European Union politics resembles a 'sitting duck' for populist attacks. Indeed, European integration is a process which is opposed by populist parties across the board. PRR parties tend to see the European Union as a 'foreign' threat to the sovereignty of their nation, while left-wing populists often portray the EU as a neo-liberal project that encourages a 'race to the bottom' in terms of welfare entitlements and working conditions (see Hooghe et al. 2002; De Vries and Edwards 2009). The bailouts for financially troubled countries and proposals to pool more sovereignty to the European level in response to the Eurocrisis can be expected to have fuelled Eurosceptic sentiments, and possibly also the electoral salience of European integration (see March and Rommerskirchen 2012; Werts et al. 2012). Populist parties thus had an incentive to emphasise their opposition to Europe even more than before the crisis (Albertazzi and Mueller 2013: 365).

The fourth theme that is likely to feature in the anti-establishment rhetoric of populist parties is **corruption**. This issue relates to the populist ideology very closely, since it links in directly with the normative distinction between the 'pure' people and the mendacious elites. Populist parties can be expected to perform well if there is a perception that the political establishment is corrupt, or characterised by patronage and cronyism (see Kitschelt and McGann 1995). As discussed, these themes have been particularly salient in the post-communist context; in many Central and Eastern European countries corruption has been considered an endemic problem (Mudde 2002a; Rupnik 2007; Pop-Eleches 2010; Pirro 2014a). Here, populist party performance may be related not only to voters' judgements about the established parties' policy record, but also to perceptions about the more fundamental trustworthiness of the political elite (see Hanley and Sikk 2014).

It is worth mentioning that the four selected themes may overlap to a certain extent in the discourse of populist parties. For example, the theme of European integration may be related to economic as well as cultural grievances, and 'gravy train-riding Eurocrats' are also regularly accused of being corrupt. The interrelatedness of the themes is not necessarily a problem for the analysis, however, as it is assumed that the electoral fortune of populist parties depends on a *combination* of explanatory conditions. This will be further discussed in the final section of this chapter.

To summarise, in this study I consider three fundamental conditions in the aim to explain the electoral performance of populist parties: the electoral system; the responsiveness of the established parties; and the supply of credible populist parties (see Figure 1.1). Populist parties are expected to be more successful in an environment characterised by a proportional electoral system, a widespread perception that established political parties are unresponsive, and a presence of credible populist challengers. I expect the absence of these conditions to be conducive to the failure of populist parties. In addition, I identified four themes that typically feature in the discourse of populist parties, and that may therefore also be relevant to their electoral performance: culture and ethnicity; economic hardship; European integration; and corruption. If these themes are salient, populist parties can be expected to perform better at the polls, particularly when established parties are perceived to be unresponsive with regard to these themes, and when populist parties present themselves as credible political alternatives. This is not to argue that *all* four themes are relevant for *all* populist parties. The relevance of the themes is largely dependent on the political context and the ideological features of a given populist party.

One final point to raise about this explanatory model is that similar variables can arguably be identified to explain the electoral performance of new 'challenger' parties in general. Other non-populist parties that are critical of the establishment are equally likely to thrive when there is widespread dissatisfaction with mainstream parties (see, for instance, Kitschelt 1988 and Müller-Rommel 1998 on left-libertarian parties and green parties, respectively). All parties, moreover, are likely to fail if they do not present themselves as credible actors. For populist

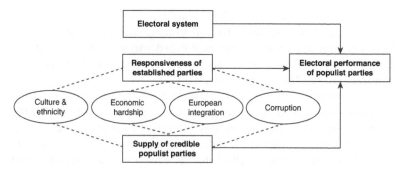

Figure 1.1   Explanatory model concerning the electoral performance of populist parties

parties, however, the perceived failure of the established parties is of particular importance, as they are defined by their anti-establishment appeal and their supposed aim to make politics responsive to the ideas and interests of the ordinary people. For this research, in addition, the concept of 'credibility' is operationalised so that it applies to populist parties in particular. These parties are credible insofar as they manage to voice a convincing, yet not overly extremist, anti-establishment rhetoric. Organisational cohesion, furthermore, is especially relevant for populist parties, as they are often weakly institutionalised and therefore more vulnerable if internal conflicts occur. Finally, as explained, the four selected themes relate to issues that are typically central to the appeals of populist parties.

Whether the electoral performance of populist parties truly relies on a different logic compared with the performance of other parties, however, has to become clear from the analyses in this study. The final section of this chapter outlines in more detail how the study is designed.

Research design, methodology and plan of the book

Two aims are central in this book: to identify populist political parties in contemporary Europe (between 2000 and 2013) and to explain their electoral performance. In order to fulfil the first aim, I studied relevant literature on specific countries and parties. There was not an abundance of secondary literature to rely on for all 31 countries under consideration. Where required and possible, therefore, primary party literature was also examined. In addition, I consulted country experts in order to validate the selection and description of cases, and to fill in missing pieces of information. The list of country experts consulted is provided in Appendix A, and Appendix B includes a template of the questionnaire that was sent to them.[10] Election results were mainly derived from the website Parties and Elections in Europe (Nordsieck 2013).

In order to explain the identified populist parties' performance in national elections, the study triangulates a broad analysis of 31 countries with three in-depth case studies. Both parts of the analysis take the explanatory framework outlined in Figure 1.1 as a starting point, although they have a different focus. The first part, in which Qualitative Comparative Analysis (QCA) techniques are applied, focuses mainly on the breeding ground for populist parties across a wide range of European countries. The three case studies that follow are primarily meant to unravel the causal mechanisms underneath populist party performance, and focus more specifically on the party competition between populist and established parties. This mixed-methods approach is also taken in order to increase the validity of the study's findings. The two parts are complementary, as the QCA analysis is aimed at identifying broad causal patterns, whereas the case studies assess the plausibility of these patterns by considering certain cases in detail (Lieberman 2005).

Instead of using conventional statistical approaches, such as regression analysis, this study turns to QCA techniques for the first part of the analysis (see e.g. Ragin 1987; 2000; 2008; Rihoux and Ragin 2009; Schneider and Wagemann 2012). QCA is a comparative approach, geared to demonstrating causal complexity and 'multiple conjunctural causation'. This means, first, that the QCA approach assumes that it is often a *combination* of conditions that induces a certain outcome. Consequently, in QCA terminology the term 'condition' is used instead of 'independent variable', as QCA steps away from the 'additivity' assumption that single variables have their own independent impact on the outcome. QCA, in addition, departs from the 'uniformity of causal effects' notion that a single condition has the same effect across contexts. The effect of one single condition may, instead, vary across cases, depending on the presence or absence of other conditions.

Relatedly, QCA is based on the assumption that different combinations of explanatory conditions may induce the same outcome. This notion of 'equifinality' is of particular importance in my study, since various different contextual factors and political issues are likely to be relevant for the wide variety of populist parties across Europe. The proportionality of an electoral system, for example, may be of greater importance to new and small populist parties than to older and sizeable populist parties, such as the Austrian Freedom Party and the Swiss

People's Party. As discussed, corruption and economic hardship may play a larger role for populist parties in post-communist countries than they do for their counterparts in some longer-established democracies in Western Europe. It may thus be possible to discern different 'paths' to populist success and failure, depending on the relevance of certain conditions and issues in a given country. QCA provides the appropriate techniques to identify those paths.

Several more specific features and potential drawbacks of QCA will be discussed in Chapter 3, which presents the fuzzy set QCA analysis (the fsQCA). One issue important to mention here is that countries are taken as the units of analysis in the QCA, since in this part of the study I am mainly interested in the breeding ground for populist parties across European countries. The analysis is therefore primarily based on country-level data. The four identified themes play a central role in the aim of assessing whether there are various paths leading to populist success or failure. Can we, for instance, observe a better performance of populist parties where people hold nativist and Eurosceptic views, where the economy is in a bad shape, and where there are high perceived levels of corruption? And do we observe different outcomes in countries where one or more of these conditions are absent?

The QCA will thus focus specifically on the socio-cultural, socio-economic and socio-political conditions related to the four selected themes, but also the three more general explanatory factors are taken into consideration: the electoral system; the responsiveness of established parties; and the supply of credible populist parties. In this medium-N research design it is challenging to assess precisely whether established parties have been responsive to voters with regard to specific issues. As a proxy for the established parties' responsiveness in a given country, citizens' more general perceptions of the quality of democracy and political institutions will be used (see Chapter 3). The credibility of populist parties is similarly difficult to operationalise quantitatively. In view of the assumed importance of this condition, however, a rudimentary assessment of the credibility of populist parties across Europe is made in Chapter 2. The outcomes of this assessment will be used in the QCA in the subsequent chapter.

A final note concerning the time-span of the QCA is that the period of study ranges from 2000 to 2013. Since party systems in many post-communist countries were still in flux in the years after the transition to democracy, analysing elections since the turn of the 21st century is assumed to lead to a more meaningful pan-European comparison. In the selected period, furthermore, new parties in Central and Eastern Europe broke through, which voiced criticism of the mainstream political camps that had been in government after the fall of communism (Pop-Eleches 2010; Hanley and Sikk 2014). As the QCA is aimed at assessing cross-national, and not cross-temporal variation, the average percentage of the vote for populist parties in each country across this period is taken as a measurement for the outcome variable. Similarly, average figures are used for the operationalisation of the conditions, most of which are expected to have remained rather stable during the period of study (see Chapter 3 for more details). Yet, since the financial and economic crisis at the end of the 2000s may have influenced the conditions and the performance of populist parties, a separate analysis is performed using data from more recent years only. This additional analysis also serves to assess the robustness of the findings from the first analysis.

After the QCA, the book will continue with the three in-depth case studies. In this part of the study, particular emphasis will be placed on the responsiveness of established parties concerning the issues central to the appeal of the populist challengers, as well as the credibility of populist parties themselves. The three chapters will also seek to explain cross-temporal variation in the electoral performance of individual populist parties. The selected cases are the Netherlands, Poland and the United Kingdom. The case selection is, first of all, based on the need to include cases from both Western and post-communist Europe. In this way, the performance of populist parties can be compared across countries with a fundamentally different political background, in which different issues are likely to rank high on the political agenda.

The Netherlands and Poland are selected because both countries provide an ideal 'laboratory' environment for learning about the electoral performance of populist parties. Both countries have witnessed the rise and fall of populist parties since the start of the 21st century, and in both countries populist parties have entered government. The Netherlands and Poland are thus countries in which successful and unsuccessful manifestations of populism can be compared, which makes the two cases especially suitable in order to gain understanding of the electoral performance of populist parties in general. The United Kingdom is selected as a third, 'negative', case. The UK is one of the countries in Europe where populist parties have thus far been unsuccessful in national elections. The British case, in addition, is characterised by the Single Member Plurality electoral system that is applied in general elections. The UK thus lends itself particularly well to studying the effect of a disproportional electoral system on the fortunes of populist parties.

The case studies rely on a variety of methods and data sources. In order to identify the populist parties in the three countries and to learn about their ideological characteristics, qualitative content analyses of party manifestos and other party documents were performed. In addition, several semi-structured interviews with country experts and politicians were carried out (see Appendix D for the list of interviewees). Besides providing information about the characteristics of the various populist parties, these interviews also shed light on the factors relevant to their electoral performance. In addition, expert surveys were composed and sent out to country experts in the three selected countries (see Appendix E for an example of the survey). Findings from these surveys substantiated the identification of populist parties and were also used to validate the analysis of the populist parties' electoral performance. I finally made use of existing opinion poll and election study data, as well as insights from the secondary literature.

Having outlined the conceptual, theoretical and methodological starting points of the study, the next chapter of this book proceeds with identifying the populist parties in the 31 countries under consideration. It will become clear that this is not a straightforward exercise, for instance because populism is not always a lasting attribute of political parties, and is sometimes only expressed sporadically. Many borderline cases can be found in post-communist countries in particular. After having selected the 'full' cases of populism, Chapter 3 presents the design and results of the QCA. The outcomes indicate that the credibility of populist parties is of vital importance to their electoral performance, while contextual conditions and dominant public attitudes alone cannot account for populist success or failure. The three case studies are presented in Chapters 4, 5 and 6. They confirm the importance of the credibility condition: established parties may create a favourable opportunity structure when they neglect certain salient social issues or ruin their own reputation as trustworthy representatives of the people, but populist parties are to a large extent responsible for their own success or failure. This logic also applies to populist parties competing under unfavourable electoral rules, as the analysis of the British case suggests. Chapter 7, finally, revisits and reflects on the findings of the study, and touches on their implications and avenues for further research.

2
Populist Parties across Europe

In this chapter the aim is to identify the populist parties in Europe that have gained parliamentary representation at least once between 2000 and 2013. As discussed in the previous chapter, I assume that certain parties have populism at the very core of their appeal; these parties cannot be properly characterised without considering their populist discourse. These populist parties (1) portray 'the people' as virtuous and essentially homogeneous; (2) advocate popular sovereignty, as opposed to elitist rule; and (3) define themselves against the political establishment, which is alleged to act against the interest of 'the people'. The previous chapter has already indicated that there are certain challenges when it comes to identifying a clearly circumscribed set of populist parties. This chapter will confirm that there are a substantial number of parties that can be seen as borderline cases of populism. As will be shown, one of the difficulties of using the concept as a tool of classification is that populism is not always a stable core attribute of certain political parties only. Populist rhetoric can in theory be voiced by all parties, and political actors may also modify their degree of populism over time. Particularly in post-communist countries, furthermore, anti-establishment rhetoric tends to be a feature of many (new) parties, making a distinction between populist and non-populist parties arguably less meaningful.

In the end, however, parties are identified that can, at least for a certain period of their existence, be considered as genuine cases of populism. In addition, the chapter provides a rudimentary assessment of the credibility of populist parties in the various European countries, in order to provide the data for one of the conditions in the QCA presented in the next chapter. As outlined in Chapter 1, in order to determine whether a populist party has been credible, its electoral appeal and organisational cohesion are considered. Regarding the former element, the electoral appeal of populist parties, I will consider the visibility and persuasiveness of the party leadership, and the party's ability to dissociate itself convincingly from extremism as well as from the political establishment. Some of these indicators are not directly relevant for all populist parties in this study, and they are therefore not all discussed for each individual case. Some populist parties, for instance, never came close to participating in government, and it has thus not been difficult for them to distance themselves from the political mainstream. Others, in turn, never had significant problems in dissociating themselves from extremism. On the basis of the assessment of credibility, it is determined whether a country has been characterised by a substantial, reasonable, limited or no supply of credible populist parties during the period of study.[1] In the next chapter, these categories will be turned into quantitative values in order to conduct the QCA.

The analysis in this chapter mainly relies on a study of secondary and party literature, and the assistance of country experts (see Appendices A and B). Countries in which no populist parties have won seats in national parliaments are disregarded, unless borderline cases have surfaced that require discussion. The countries which are not discussed here are Cyprus, Malta, Portugal, Spain and the United Kingdom – the last country, however, will be discussed in detail in Chapter 6. It is worth noting that the QCA in the next chapter covers all 31 countries, including those in which populist parties have failed to break through. Further, in order to avoid tautological reasoning as regards the assessment of credibility ('the parties that did not manage to win any seats must have lacked credibility'), the country experts were asked whether there have been any credible yet electorally unsuccessful populist parties (see Appendix B). The responses indicated that there were no such cases that would influence the judgement about the supply of credible populist parties in a given country.

After a description of the populist (borderline) cases in the various countries, and an assessment of their credibility, the concluding section of this chapter touches on the general observations that can be made on the basis of this exercise.

The populist parties and their credibility[2]

Austria

The Austrian Freedom Party (*Freiheitliche Partei Österreichs*, FPÖ) is one of the best-known populist parties in Europe. The FPÖ was founded in the

1950s, but it could only truly be characterised as a populist radical right party after Jörg Haider took over the leadership in 1986. Since then, the party has intensified its criticism of the grand coalitions between the Social Democrats and Christian Democrats, and 'aimed to convince the public that Austrians were sustaining a corrupt and wasteful system that catered exclusively to the special interests of political insiders' (Heinisch 2008: 80; see also Müller 2002). The party later added more explicit xenophobic, Eurosceptic, nationalistic and welfare chauvinistic elements to the core of its appeal. The FPÖ became increasingly successful in the 1990s; at its height in 1999 it won 26.9 per cent of the vote in the parliamentary election and entered government in coalition with the Christian Democratic ÖVP. Resignation of FPÖ cabinet members led to the fall of the coalition, after which the party suffered a big loss in the following election of 2002, receiving 10 per cent of the vote.

A new Christian Democrat–Freedom Party coalition was nevertheless formed, intensifying intra-party conflicts within the FPÖ (Luther 2011; Fallend 2012; Heinisch 2013). The party eventually split in 2005 and the Alliance for the Future of Austria (*Bündnis Zukunft Österreich*, BZÖ) was formed, of which Haider initially became the leader. The BZÖ took over the Freedom Party's position in the governing coalition. Afterwards, the Freedom Party, under the leadership of Heinz-Christian Strache, and the Alliance both competed in the subsequent parliamentary elections of 2006, 2008 and 2013. In 2008, the FPÖ and BZÖ made a particularly strong appearance, winning 17.5 per cent and 10.7 per cent of the vote, respectively. Yet, while the FPÖ increased its vote share to 20.5 per cent in the election of September 2013, the BZÖ failed to cross the electoral threshold. By this time, the BZÖ had watered down its populist appeal significantly, and it will therefore not be considered as a populist party in the 2013 election. In its stead, the party *Team Stronach*, launched by 80-year-old millionaire businessman Frank Stronach, entered the *Nationalrat* after having received 5.7 per cent of the vote. The party of the Austro-Canadian entrepreneur campaigned on a Eurosceptic, anti-bureaucracy and anti-tax platform and called for a democratisation of the Austrian political system. Unlike its Austrian populist counterparts, immigration was not a central issue for Team Stronach. The party did show ample disdain for 'professional politicians' (*Berufspolitiker*), who were accused of cronyism and corruption, and alleged to have little regard for the problems and interests of Austria's citizens (Team Stronach 2013).

In the period since 2000, Austrian voters have thus been supplied with various populist contenders, even though these have not always been entirely credible. Jörg Haider appealed to many voters with his stylish and unconventional manner of campaigning. In Heinisch's (2008: 80) words, 'Haider's use of imagery, exaggeration and simplification was disarmingly effective.' Internal conflict arose, however, after the Freedom Party entered government, in which it played a rather ineffective role (Fallend 2012). Disagreements cropped up between pragmatists willing to promote an image of respectability and grass-root hardliners, who favoured maintaining a populist anti-establishment course (Heinisch 2008; Luther 2011). After the party split, however, the 'renewed' Freedom Party in opposition could return to 'the successful formula of racial identity-oriented populism and all-out opposition' on the road to the new election in 2006 (Heinisch 2008: 83). After the departure of Haider, the FPÖ furthermore benefited from 'having in Strache a young, telegenic leader once again', whose debating skills could be seen as a 'considerable asset for the party' (Heinisch 2013: 68). Having remained in office, the BZÖ failed to construct an equally strong anti-establishment profile, even though it raised its electoral appeal under the renewed leadership of Haider at the time of the 2008 national election. For the BZÖ, the death of Haider in a car crash soon after the election signified not only the loss of a visible leader, but also the trigger for new tensions about the ideological course of the party. As for the – at the time of writing – new party of Frank Stronach, it remains to be seen to what extent it can remain a credible force after its first eye-catching campaign and entrance into parliament. Despite a diminished appeal at the time of the 2002 election, it can be concluded that since 2000 there has been a *substantial supply* of credible populist parties in Austria, particularly taking into consideration the enduring appeal of the Austrian Freedom Party.

Belgium

The most successful populist party in Belgium has been the Flemish Block (*Vlaams Blok*, VB), renamed Flemish Interest (*Vlaams Belang*) in 2004 after a Belgian court's verdict that indicted the party for violating the racism and xenophobia law. The party was founded in 1978, as an amalgamation of various radical Flemish nationalist factions. The party's predominant aim was Flemish independence, but in the mid-1980s the VB's electoral strategy shifted more towards opposing immigration and criticising the alleged corruption of the established parties (Swyngedouw 1998). In its populist discourse, the VB essentially contrasted the (morally just) Flemish people with francophones and immigrants, as well as the political elite (De Lange and Akkerman 2012; Pauwels 2013). In the 1990s the vote share of the VB rose steadily, and the party won 11.6 per cent of the nationwide vote in 2003 and 12.0 per cent in 2007.[3]

In the 2010 federal election the party suffered a loss, receiving 7.7 per cent of the popular vote. Up until today the party has been subject to a *cordon sanitaire* erected by the mainstream parties, which has prevented the party from entering office. As opposed to Flemish Interest, the less successful National Front (*Front National*, FN) in Wallonia has been a proponent of a united Belgium. The sister party of the French National Front has been driven more by xenophobia than by territorial issues (Mudde 2007: 42). In 2003 and 2007 the party's vote share was about 2 per cent. The party disappeared from parliament in 2010 after receiving just 0.5 per cent of the vote. A somewhat more successful populist party, List Dedecker (*Lijst Dedecker*, LDD), entered parliament in 2007 after winning 4 per cent of the vote. This 'neo-liberal' populist party did not so much focus on issues related to immigration, but targeted its criticism more against big government and the Belgian 'particracy', which supposedly denied citizens political influence (Pauwels 2010). Dedecker won a mere 2.3 per cent of the vote in 2010.

A final, borderline, case is the largest winner of the 2010 national election on the Dutch-speaking side of the border: the New Flemish Alliance (*Nieuw-Vlaamse Alliantie*, N-VA). The party has favoured an independent Flemish state and criticised the, allegedly dominant, francophone elite. Although Teun Pauwels (2011a: 110) described the N-VA's discourse as 'moderately populist' after having measured populist rhetoric in the party's literature, the N-VA considerably lagged behind the Flemish Interest and List Dedecker as far as populism in its election manifesto was concerned. In addition, Pauwels (2013: 86) more recently argued that, despite its use of anti-establishment rhetoric, the N-VA should not be classified as a genuine populist party in view of its elitist character-istics and lack of appeal to the *vox populi*. The party will therefore be excluded from this study.

Belgium has thus also been a country in which various populist parties have emerged. The most notable of these, the Flemish Block/Interest, has been described by Carter (2005: 88) as a well-led and well-organ-ised party, whose leader Filip Dewinter, who had become the dominant leading figure by 1987, improved the party organisation 'until it became well structured and efficient'. Dewinter himself has been described as a 'charismatic' (Carter 2005: 88) and 'popular' politician (Van Assche 2003: 4). Since the party has always been excluded from assuming office, furthermore, the VB has never had to compromise its anti-establishment discourse. In more recent years, however, this may have become a curse rather than a blessing: voters have apparently begun to doubt the point of voting Flemish Interest in view of the enduring *cordon sanitaire*, and have been tempted to switch to the more centrist NV-A instead (Pauwels 2011b).

Besides losing its hold among Flemish nationalists, the VB has also witnessed growing tensions inside its organisation, and critical questions have arisen about the party leadership (Abts and Swyngedouw 2012).

Turning to the other Belgian populists, Jean-Marie Dedecker, founder and leader of his own party, has been described as a charismatic leader and as 'a powerful speaker, [who] always provokes discussion and is also able to react in a sharp and humorous way' (Pauwels 2010: 1024). Prior to the 2010 federal elections, however, several incidents divided the party and internal disputes arose (Pauwels 2013). On the Walloon side of the border, finally, the National Front has lacked charismatic leadership (Mudde 2007: 42) and suffered from several splits throughout its existence (Carter 2005: 75). In terms of credibility, then, the party with the best record has been the Flemish Block/Interest. In view of the declining electoral attraction of the ostracised VB, and the fact that its appeal is limited to Flanders only, it can be concluded that the Belgian case has been characterised by a *reasonable supply* of credible populist parties overall.

Bulgaria

Various anti-establishment forces have emerged in recent Bulgarian politics. In the period after 2000, the Attack Party (*Partiya Ataka*) became the most notable party on the populist radical right. Ataka gathered between 7.3 and 9.4 per cent of the vote in the parliamentary elections of 2005, 2009 and 2013. The party has been populist in its anti-establishment rhetoric and its appeal to the common Bulgarians. A 2005 campaign poster, for example, read 'To take our Bulgaria back for the Bulgarians', and in his first parliamentary speech party leader Volen Siderov denounced previous governments as 'national traitors complicit in a "genocide" against the Bulgarian people' (Ghodsee 2008: 30, 32). Like many other PRR parties in Central and Eastern Europe, *Ataka* adhered to orthodox Christianity and has combined a nationalist message with anti-Semitic and anti-Roma rhetoric (Mudde 2007: 82, 85; Pirro 2014a). In addition, the party has deployed a radical left-wing socio-economic agenda (Ghodsee 2008). Another case of populism is the Law, Order and Justice party (*Red, zakonnost i spravedlivost*, RZS), which entered the Bulgarian parliament with 4.1 per cent of the vote in 2009, to disappear again in 2013. This party campaigned on the basis of an anti-corruption message and stressed 'the huge differences between those in power and the ordinary Bulgarians' (Novinite 2009).

Two other parties, which both experienced a spectacular rise, have also regularly been associated with populism: the National Movement Simeon the Second (NDSV) (later renamed National Movement for Stability and Progress) and the party Citizens for European Development of Bulgaria (GERB) (e.g. Ghodsee 2008; Cholova 2012; Karasimeonov and Lyubenov 2013). The first party was built around its namesake: the former exiled Bulgarian tsar. In 2001 it won no less than 42.7 per cent of the vote on the basis of a programme that promised to 'quickly improve living standards and eliminate corruption' (Učeň 2007: 57). After its first term in government, these goals were not met and the party lost half of its support in the election of 2005 (Ghodsee 2008; Cholova 2012). After another term in office, the party disappeared from parliament in 2009. In this year's election many disappointed voters instead turned to the newly founded GERB. This party experienced a similar meteoric rise, winning 39.7 per cent of the vote in its first national election on the basis of an anti-corruption and crime-fighting platform. The party of ex-bodyguard and then mayor of Sofia, Boyko Borissov, went on to form a government which also could not live up to expectations. Several anti-government demonstrations were organised towards the end of Prime Minister Borissov's term, leading to the resignation of the government, yet GERB still gathered 30.5 per cent of the vote in the early 2013 election.

Bulgaria has thus seen the swift rise of parties that were characterised by their anti-establishment rhetoric. This is not entirely surprising in a country where the issue of political corruption ranked high on the political agenda. Whether there are sufficient reasons to classify the NDSV and GERB as *populist* parties is a moot point, certainly in view of the waning of their anti-establishment rhetoric in office. This applies in particular to the NDSV, which had very much lost its populist anti-elite appeal by the time of its second campaign in 2005 (Cholova 2012). Furthermore, it is questionable whether the notion of popular sovereignty has been truly central to the discourse of the two parties, even if GERB leader Borissov, unlike Simeon II, portrayed himself as 'a man of the people fighting against the corrupt elite' (Karasimeonov and Lyubenov 2013: 415). It is mainly on the basis of country expert assessments that I will treat both the NDSV and GERB as populist parties, but the former only at the time of its first parliamentary election campaign in 2001.

Concerning electoral credibility, both the NDSV and GERB (initially) benefited from well-known and popular figureheads. Following Ghodsee (2008: 29), 'Simeon II embodied the possibility of national salvation', while Borissov's crime-fighting reputation made him 'one of the most popular Bulgarian politicians' (Cholova 2012: 85). Ataka, in turn, has been able to rely on 'the charismatic appeal of an outspoken and seemingly ubiquitous leader' (Ghodsee 2008: 36). At the same time, the party's radical anti-Semitic and anti-Roma rhetoric did not truly hamper the credibility of the party, since such nativist sentiments were shared by a considerable number of Bulgarian voters (Ivanov and Ilieva 2005). RZS leader Yane Yanev, finally, built up credibility as a prominent anti-corruption figure. All parties, however, have been plagued by serious internal disputes after entering parliament, and NDSV and GERB were, in addition, not able to steer clear of corruption scandals after forming governments (Cholova 2012). Taking into consideration, however, that these damaging incidents often occurred *after* successful elections, it can be argued that there has been a *reasonable supply* of credible populist parties throughout the period of study.

Croatia

Several Croatian parties have been associated with populism. One of these is the Croatian Democratic Union (HDZ) under the leadership of the late president Franjo Tuđman (Mudde 2007: 54). Yet after Tuđman's death in 1999 the party moderated its rhetoric substantially and turned into a centrist mainstream party. Another ambiguous case is the Croatian Party of Rights (*Hrvatska stranka prava*, HSP), which claimed to be the direct continuation of the historical party with the same name, and initially showed extreme right characteristics. The party had modest electoral success in the 1990s and early 2000s, after which the party leadership advanced attempts to make the HSP an acceptable coalition partner (Čular 2004; Henjak 2007). The HSP disappeared from parliament in 2011. In view of its overall ideological moderation, the HSP is not classified as a populist party during the period relevant to this study.

A more radical anti-establishment and nativist splinter party founded in 2009, the HSP dr. Ante Starčević (HSP-AS), managed to win one seat in 2011 after having formed an electoral coalition with the far right Croatian Pure Party of Rights (HČSP). Bearing in mind its more radical populist character, the HSP-AS splinter is included in this study. This also applies to the Croatian Labourists – Labour Party (*Hrvatski laburisti – Stranka rada*, HL-SR), which entered parliament in 2011 with 5.2 per cent of the vote. The party, led by Dragutin Lesar, has been characterised by anti-establishment rhetoric and a left-wing populist discourse (Henjak et al. 2013). The HL-SR distinguished between, on the one hand, the 'working people' it represented and, on the other, mischievous entrepreneurs, capitalists and bankers, as well as their political allies.

Since both radical parties remained in the margins during the campaign, their modest breakthrough came as something of a surprise. The main assets of the parties were their leaders, who gained popularity on the basis of their image as crime fighter (Ruža Tomašić, HSP-AS) or defender of workers' rights (Dragutin Lesar, HL-SR) (Antić 2012). In view of the lack of credible populist contenders prior to the 2011 election, it is concluded that there was a *limited supply* of credible populist parties in Croatia during the period between 2000 and 2013, but a *reasonable supply* during the last election campaign.

Czech Republic

After the disappearance from parliament of the populist radical right Association for the Republic-Republican Party of Czechoslovakia (SPR-RSČ) in 1998, populist parties did not have a real nationwide presence in the Czech Republic. The Public Affairs party (*Věci Veřejné*, VV) was founded in 2001, but initially remained active at the local level only. In 2010 it successfully participated in the parliamentary election, receiving 10.9 per cent of the vote. Central issues to the party were fighting corruption, improving transparency in politics and promoting direct democracy. Lacking clear additional ideological features, the party presented itself mainly as 'a pure alternative to all established political parties and as an advocate of the people's interests' (Havlík 2012: 103). The pledge to 'whip out political dinosaurs' became a particularly well-known campaign slogan (Hloušek and Kaniok 2010: 5). After its electoral victory, VV joined a coalition government. This did not turn out to be a success for the party, and Public Affairs did not even stand in the parliamentary election of 2013.

Two other new political parties entered the Czech parliament in 2013 with 18.7 and 6.9 per cent of the vote, respectively: ANO 2011 and Tomio Okamura's Dawn of Direct Democracy (*Úsvit přímé demokracie Tomia Okamury*). The former party, whose name means 'yes' and is also the acronym of 'Action of Dissatisfied Citizens', was founded by billionaire tycoon Andrej Babiš in 2011. Its main aim was to end the political corruption that was alleged to stifle Czech business (HBS 2013; Hloušek and Kaniok 2014). While ANO is a clear case of an anti-establishment party, its populist credentials have been somewhat less apparent. Relying on the experts' assessments, in this study ANO is given the benefit of the doubt and included in the category of populist parties. Úsvit, on the other hand, had a clearer populist radical right profile in the campaign, and its leader, Japanese-Czech businessman Tomio Okamura, became known for his outspoken nativist and Eurosceptic views. The party further proposed direct democracy as a solution for 'the corruption, nepotism, clientelism and kleptocracy' within Czech politics (Hornát 2013).

As far as the Czech populist parties' credibility is concerned, Public Affairs could rely on the popularity of its campaign figurehead Radek John, who had become a well-known TV personality and investigative journalist (Havlík 2012). John regularly reported about corruption and government malfunctioning and built up a credible image with regard to these issues (Hloušek and Kaniok 2010). Once in office, however, the party suffered from internal disputes, and party members, including de-facto leader Vít Bárta, became tainted due to their involvement in corruption scandals. The party eventually dissolved, even though a section of the party split off and remained part of the coalition. The events had created a very favourable environment for anti-establishment parties in the run up to the 2013 election, from which ANO and Úsvit could evidently profit. The former party could attract ample attention with a well-funded campaign and the (tacit) support of newspapers owned by leader Babiš (Hloušek and Kaniok 2014). Meanwhile, besides appealing to voters tired of corruption, Úsvit's leader Okamura attracted attention with widely publicised, yet controversial, anti-Roma remarks. In view of the absence of populist parties before 2010, it can be concluded that there has been only a *limited supply* of credible populist parties in the Czech Republic during the whole period of study, even though this grew to be a *substantial supply* in the election campaigns of 2010 and 2013.

Denmark

Denmark saw the early rise of a right-wing populist party: the Danish Progress Party (FRP) was one of the Scandinavian populist anti-tax parties that achieved notable success in the 1970s. The party, which began to focus on the issue of immigration in later years, gradually lost support and disappeared from the Danish parliament in 2001. By this time the FRP was overshadowed by the Danish People's Party (*Dansk Folkeparti*, DF), led by Pia Kjærsgaard. This party was founded in 1995 after Kjærsgaard and her allies broke away from the Progress Party. Following Jens Rydgren, the DF can be seen as a typical radical right-wing populist party, as it has combined ethno-nationalist xenophobia with anti-political establishment populism (Rydgren 2004). Similarly to other populist parties in Western Europe, the party has been characterised by an anti-immigration stance, Euroscepticism and welfare chauvinism (Klein 2013). In the four elections between 2001 and 2011, the People's Party received between 12 and 14 per cent of the vote and provided parliamentary support for three successive minority governments. By doing so, the DF has been able to influence government policy, most notably by inducing the implementation of stricter immigration laws (Akkerman and De Lange 2012).

Unlike the Progress Party, the People's Party managed to steer clear of publicly visible internal strife, largely due to a strictly enforced party discipline (Zaslove 2012). Pia Kjærsgaard, who led the party until 2012, has furthermore been described as an appealing, able and talented party leader (Widfeldt 2000: 490; Carter 2005: 91). In the 2005 parliamentary election, 'charismatic party "mother"' Kjærsgaard even became the second most popular politician in terms of personal votes (Knudsen 2005: 3). The affiliation with the various minority governments was not a great issue as far as the credibility of the DF's anti-establishment criticism was concerned; since it was never officially part of the coalition, the party 'could fairly easily follow a strategy of remaining committed to a radical opposition role on the one hand, while claiming policy results on the other' (Akkerman and De Lange 2012: 591; see also Zaslove 2012). Irrespective of the party's first modest loss in the 2011 election, the People's Party has proven to be one of the more durable populist parties in Europe, and it can be concluded that there has been a *substantial supply* of credible populist parties in Denmark.

Estonia

In Estonia, the party *Res Publica* has been labelled a 'new centrist populist' party by Peter Učeň (2007). The party received no less than 24.6 per cent of the vote in its first parliamentary election in 2003, and subsequently joined a coalition government. The party showed typical populist features in demanding political reforms, calling for a replacement of 'old politics' and criticising traditional parties for being corrupt (Balcere 2012; Lagerspetz and Vogt 2013). However, the party did not unequivocally appeal to the 'common people' (Sikk 2009: 7), and was not a defender of pure popular sovereignty. In office, Res Publica was not able to fulfil the promised reforms, and it lost its anti-establishment appeal (Taagepera 2006; Balcere 2012). The party ended up merging with the Pro Patria Union in 2006, forming a mainstream conservative party. All in all, there are insufficient reasons to treat Res Publica, in 2003 or thereafter, as a genuine populist party, and the conclusion is that there has been *no supply* of credible populist parties in Estonia. That said, Res Publica appeared to benefit from a political climate of distrust and disillusion, in an election that was marked by a large anti-establishment vote (Lagerspetz and Vogt 2013). It is therefore questionable whether it is always possible to distinguish between the grounds for the success of populist parties, on the one hand, and essentially non-populist anti-establishment parties, on the other.

Finland

The True Finns party (*Perussuomalaiset*, PS) was founded in 1995 and can be seen as the successor of the agrarian populist Finnish Rural Party (*Suomen Maaseudun Puolue*, SMP). Timo Soini, PS party leader since 1997, has projected 'a form of "responsible populism" directed at the "small man"' (Arter 2007: 1155). True Finns has actually adopted the label of populism itself, 'distinguishing the "populist" version of democracy advocated by the party from the more elitist or bureaucratic version that characterises modern democracies' (Raunio 2013: 134). The party showed disdain for 'old politics' in Finland and its consensual nature (Arter 2010). As regards more concrete policy proposals, True Finns has followed a nationalist, morally traditionalist, Eurosceptic, and ambivalent socio-economic course. Although the party increasingly applied anti-immigration rhetoric throughout the years, True Finns has remained more moderate than some of its European populist counterparts (Arter 2010). The party did not make a great impression in the 1999 and 2003 parliamentary elections, but improved its vote share in 2007, receiving 4.1 per cent of the vote. Partly on the basis of Soini's successful criticism of the European bailout packages for Greece and Ireland during the Eurozone crisis, True Finns won no less than 19 per cent of the vote in the 2011 parliamentary election (Raunio 2013).

True Finns' leadership has been a great asset for the credibility of the party: Tapio Raunio (2007: 5) described Timo Soini as 'a very charismatic figure with excellent debating skills'. Up until the election of 2011, the party witnessed hardly any internal criticism of his leadership (Raunio 2013). David Arter (2010: 488) furthermore argued that:

> It was Soini's performance as his party's candidate at the 2006 presidential election [...] that raised PS' profile, gave it electoral credibility and enabled it to recruit support away from the urban 'deep south' [...] Soini, who has attracted substantial media interest, has been the PS' 'trump card' ever since.

Since the party's profile only truly rose in 2006, it can be argued that there has been a *reasonable supply* of credible populist parties in Finland during the whole period relevant to this study, but a *substantial supply* during the last two campaigns.

France

One of the oldest populist radical right parties in Western Europe is the French National Front (*Front National*, FN), which was founded in 1972, uniting various radical right factions. The ideology of the party, until the start of 2011 headed by Jean-Marie Le Pen, has been somewhat 'elastic' throughout the decades (Hainsworth and Mitchell 2000). The party shifted its emphasis from anti-communism in the 1970s to anti-immigration and the preservation of French identity in the 1980s, and to anti-globalisation and Euroscepticism in the 1990s. Ethno-nationalism has remained a core element of the party's appeal, which is illustrated by the FN's anti-immigration and, later, anti-Islam discourse, and its support for welfare chauvinist policies (Rydgren 2008a; Balent 2013). The party has been populist in vehemently criticising the political elites and identifying a rift between the establishment and the French people. In a speech in 2002, for instance, Le Pen described his electorate as those who were 'often referred to as "ordinary folk", the "rank and file", and the "excluded"' (Balent 2013: 177).

The party attracted considerable electoral support in the 1980s and 1990s, at its height winning 14.9 per cent of the vote in the first round of the 1997 parliamentary election. This never translated into more than one parliamentary seat (in 1988 and 1997), due to the winner-takes-all principle in French parliamentary elections. The notable exception was the parliamentary election of 1986, when a proportional representation system was applied: that year the Front National won 35 seats. In 1999 the party survived a split, initiated by leading party figure Bruno Mégret and his allies, and Le Pen reached the second round of the French presidential election of 2002. In the three parliamentary elections since 2000, FN's first-round results were erratic; it received 11.3 per cent of the vote in 2002, a mere 4.3 per cent in 2007 and, after Le Pen's daughter Marine took over the helm of the party, 13.6 per cent in 2012. In that year, the party also re-entered parliament with two seats, and Marine Le Pen received no less than 17.9 per cent of the vote in the French presidential election.

In terms of credibility, Carter (2005: 83) has classified the Front National as a well-organised and well-led party, Le Pen being a strong charismatic leader who rallied the disjointed French radical right together. Despite the serious split in 1999, the party managed to survive. According to Mudde, this was related to the fact that the party was already older and well institutionalised (Mudde 2007: 273). By 2007, however, the FN reached a low ebb and the ageing Le Pen (born in 1928) seemed ready to be replaced (Marthaler 2007). This happened in 2011, and daughter

Marine has proven to be a more than worthy successor. Following Magali Balent (2013: 170), 'Marine Le Pen inherited her father's charisma and media savvy' and 'developed something of an argumentative streak, making her a favourite with the media'. At the same time, she has been able to dissociate the FN from political extremism by adopting 'a more restrained and respectable rhetoric that adheres more closely to the expectations of the electorate' (Balent 2013: 168). Up until the election of 2012, furthermore, Marine Le Pen managed to prevent desertions of more radically minded party members. Taking the above developments into consideration, it is concluded that France has seen a *reasonable supply* of credible populist parties in the period since 2000, but a *substantial supply* in 2012.

Germany

Populist radical right parties have also appeared in contemporary Germany, although none of them broke through at the federal level. Parties such as the Republicans (*Republikaner*), the German People's Union (DVU) and the National Democratic Party of Germany (NPD) have been hindered by the legacy of the Nazi past, which materialised in legal hurdles against, and a strong stigmatisation of, radical right parties (Decker 2008). What is more, the radical right has long failed to present itself as a united block, and the Republicans in particular have been haunted by internal dissent throughout the years (Backes and Mudde 2000; Carter 2005: 70–72). Even though the NPD managed to build up a more cohesive organisation, its adherence to a neo-Nazi programme, also after its merger with the DVU in 2011, limited its electoral appeal (Decker 2008).

As its current name, 'The Left' (*Die Linke*), already suggests, the only German populist party to have gathered seats in the *Bundestag* has adhered to a different ideology. Die Linke has its roots in the former ruling communist party of the German Democratic Republic, and entered the federal parliament of united Germany in 1990 under the name Party of Democratic Socialism (*Partei des Demokratischen Sozialismus*, PDS). The PDS never received more than 5.1 per cent of the nationwide vote (in 1998), until it formed a coalition with the new Labour and Social Justice Party (WASG). The latter party was founded in 2005 by disgruntled left-wingers, some of whom were former members of the large Social Democratic Party (SPD). As a result, the alliance, named The Left Party.PDS (*Die Linkspartei. PDS*), expanded its appeal in western Germany and won 8.7 per cent of the vote in the federal election of 2005. The official merger between the parties led to the foundation of Die Linke, which gathered 11.9 per cent of the vote in 2009. In the federal election of September 2013 the party suffered a loss and received 8.6 per cent of the vote.

As a transformed communist party, the PDS in the 1990s has already been described as a 'social-populist' party (March and Mudde 2005: 36). In more recent years, Die Linke has also consistently voiced populist rhetoric, in addition to its anti-capitalist and pacifist discourse. In the words of Hough and Koß (2009: 78), the party 'regularly talks in the language of elites betraying the population at large, and it is frequently disdainful of the wider political process'. Following Luke March (2011: 125), Die Linke's 'anti-capitalism is presented very much as the "good" people's battle against "bad" big business'.

Another non-radical right party regularly associated with populism is the Alternative for Germany (AfD) party, which was founded in 2013 and nearly crossed the 5 per cent threshold in the federal election of the same year. European integration has been the primary theme for the party; the AfD favoured abolishing the Euro as we know it and voiced opposition against Eurozone bailouts and further transfers of sovereignty (AfD 2013). Despite more general criticism of political parties and calls for direct democracy, the AfD was not a genuine populist party at the time of the 2013 election – its founding members were actually part of the academic and journalistic elites. It remains to be seen whether the party will take a more populist (radical right) direction in the future.

The most credible populist party in Germany has thus been Die Linke, even though the appeal of its predecessor PDS was limited to the post-communist eastern part of Germany (March 2011: 123–124). In the election year of 2002, moreover, the party suffered from 'continued internal ideological and strategic disagreements under the lacklustre leadership of Gabi Zimmer' (March 2011: 126). The party has been internally divided between, broadly speaking, more ideologically oriented '*fundis*' and pragmatic '*realos*' (Hough 2010). When the alliance with WASG was formed in 2005, however, the party members managed to create a 'harmonious status quo' (Hough and Koß 2009: 77). The party further benefited from its leading figures Gregor Gysi and Oskar Lafontaine, the latter a former SPD heavyweight. March (2011: 126, 128) described the two men as 'effective and charismatic media stars', and argued that Lafontaine contributed to the party's improved image in western Germany as well as its internal cohesion (see also Hough 2010). The party has since established itself as a serious force on the left, even though Lafontaine retired in early 2010 due to health reasons, and internal disputes intensified again. It can, then, be argued that there has been a *reasonable supply* of credible populist parties at the German federal level.

Greece

The country central to the Eurozone crisis in 2009 is a challenging case if one aims to distinguish between populist and non-populist parties. Takis Pappas (2014a), in fact, argued that Greece, following the electoral victory of the Panhellenic Socialist Movement (PASOK) in the early 1980s, turned into a 'populist democracy', with both dominant parties (PASOK and New Democracy) engaging in clientelistic and polarising politics. It is questionable, however, whether Pappas' approach to populism is entirely compatible with the one applied in this book, and whether PASOK and New Democracy neatly fit the definition of populist parties presented here. Even if the use of populist rhetoric has been a more general feature of politics in Greece, I will aim to distinguish those populist parties that have railed against the two large established parties since 2000. This is still not a straightforward task, taking into consideration the recent rise of several anti-establishment parties in the crisis-riven country.

Populist parties were already present in the Greek parliament before the global economic recession of 2008. The Popular Orthodox Rally (*Laïkós Orthódoxos Synagermós*, LAOS) entered the Greek parliament in 2007 with 3.8 per cent of the vote. The party was founded in 2000 by Georgios Karatzaferis, who had been expelled from the centre-right party New Democracy (ND) earlier that year. LAOS can be seen as a clear populist case – the abbreviation LAOS in fact means 'people' in Greek. Its leader presented the party as 'an anti-establishment voice and himself as a man of the people, in contrast to the elites who allegedly dominated political life' (Verney 2004: 21). The party further adopted anti-immigration and Eurosceptic rhetoric and expressed irredentist desires (Dinas 2008). LAOS increased its vote share to 5.6 per cent in 2009, but disappeared from parliament in 2012.

The Coalition of the Radical Left (SYRIZA), which entered parliament in 2004 but only became a real political force after the two 2012 elections, can be included as a left-wing case of populism. In the (second) election of June 2012 the party received 26.9 per cent of the vote, becoming the second largest party in parliament and effectively replacing PASOK as the main left-wing party. Similarly to Die Linke in Germany, SYRIZA has adopted the concept of a 'non-privileged' people, exploited by capitalist or neo-liberal elites (Pappas 2014b; Stavrakakis and Katsambekis 2014). In his statements, Alexis Tsipras, the leader of SYRIZA since 2009, has railed against bankers and the Greek oligarchy, as well as the corrupt (pro-austerity) political establishment and its foreign allies – not least German Chancellor Angela Merkel. The Communist Party of Greece

(KKE) has been associated with populism as well (Marantzidis 2008; Gemenis and Dinas 2010), but, since its ideology is primarily rooted in Marxism, the KKE is not considered here to be a populist party (see March 2011: 52–6).

Finally, two parties on the cultural right side of the political spectrum appeared after the advent of the crisis: the Independent Greeks (*Anexártitoi Éllines*, ANEL) and Golden Dawn (*Chryssí Avgí*). The latter received 7 per cent of the vote in both 2012 elections and attracted widespread controversy, for instance due to racially motivated attacks on ethnic minorities. In view of its essentially anti-democratic neo-Nazi character, it is not considered to be a populist party. ANEL, on the other hand, has shunned the extreme language of Golden Dawn, even though it clearly applies an ethnic definition of 'the people' (Pappas 2014b). ANEL is here considered to be a populist party, since leader Panos Kammenos, another ex-ND MP, explicitly contrasted the victimised Greeks with the devious established parties and foreign enemies, such as representatives of the 'global financial order', Germany and the European Union. ANEL has further been characterised by a conservative and traditionalist position on cultural issues, hostility towards immigration, and an ambiguous protectionist economic programme. The party won 10.6 and 7.5 percent of the vote in the two elections of 2012.

Especially in recent years, Greece has thus seen the mobilisation of populist parties on the left as well as the right. Before the crisis years, the Popular Orthodox Rally was able to market itself rather effectively to the disaffected part of the electorate, due largely to party leader Karatzaferis' ownership of several media outlets. LAOS largely lost its credibility as an anti-establishment party, however, when it supported the caretaker government that was formed in 2011. ANEL was subsequently able to fill the vacuum on the right, and its leader Kammenos was successful in his attempts to portray himself as an outsider to the corrupt political class (Pappas 2014b). At the same time, PASOK, the governing party at the time of the outbreak of the global financial crisis, was vulnerable to a challenge from the radical left SYRIZA, led by the young and energetic Alexis Tsipras. It can, then, be concluded that there has been a *substantial supply* of credible populist political parties in contemporary Greece.

It must be noted that electoral credibility was perhaps easily obtained in a context where the two traditionally dominant parties, ND and PASOK, were very unpopular and distrusted. Greece is, furthermore, another case where one might question the empirical relevance of distinguishing between populist and non-populist challengers, since it is likely that also essentially non-populist parties, such as the Golden Dawn, have benefited from a widespread anti-establishment mood among citizens struggling to cope with harsh austerity measures.

Hungary

More borderline cases can be found in Hungary. Two parties can be identified as members of the populist radical right. The Justice and Life Party (*Magyar Igazság és Élet Pártja*, MIÉP) was founded in 1993 by István Csurka and claimed to stand for 'the defence of the Hungarian people from foreign, "oppressing powers" and its own political elite' (Batory 2008: 59). The party further championed the irredentist goal of a Greater Hungarian state and voiced xenophobic rhetoric. MIÉP was represented in parliament between 1998 and 2002 only, and again failed to enter parliament in 2006, when it formed an electoral alliance with the Movement for a Better Hungary (*Jobbik Magyarországért Mozgalom*, Jobbik). The latter party was more successful in the parliamentary election of 2010, when it competed independently and received 16.7 per cent of the vote. Jobbik has claimed to be 'the only party that "genuinely" stands up for the interests of "the people"' (Batory 2010: 6), and became known for its anti-Roma rhetoric, as well as its clericalism and opposition to European integration (Batory 2010; Pirro 2014a).

The party FIDESZ (an acronym for Alliance of Young Democrats) has been associated with populism as well, but mainly after the turn of the 21st century. The party started out as a youth-based anti-communist movement in the 1980s, then became a liberal political party, but remarkably transformed itself into a nationalist conservative party under the long leadership of Viktor Orbán (see Tóka and Popa 2012). FIDESZ became the leading centre-right force after the election of 1998, and adopted the name FIDESZ-Hungarian Civic Alliance (FIDESZ-MPSZ) in 2003. After an electoral defeat in 2002, FIDESZ was ousted from government and subsequently adopted a more radical anti-establishment discourse. This seemed ever more rewarding in view of the growing unpopularity of the scandal-prone centre-left government (see Tóka and Popa 2012). At the same time, the party had started to pronounce more strongly its idealised conception of the Hungarian community and created a discourse 'built on a metaphorical polarization between the communist past and present, the clash of national and international interests, and the opposing interests of the ruling "elites of luxury" and the "working citizens"' (Rajacic 2007: 650). In an alliance with the Christian Democratic People's Party (KDNP) – which had more or less become FIDESZ's satellite party – Orbán's party ended up winning an absolute majority of the vote (52.7 per cent) in the election of 2010.

In view of its non-populist roots and the flexibility of its ideology, classifying FIDESZ as a populist party remains somewhat debatable. Authors have noted the more widespread use of populism in contemporary Hungarian politics (Rajacic 2007; Pappas 2014a), and Hungary may thus be another case where populism lacks real discriminatory power as far as party classification is concerned. Hungary is also a case where anti-establishment rhetoric should not be confused with populism. The newly founded social liberal party Politics can be Different (LMP), for instance, also rode the anti-establishment wave in the 2010 election campaign, but cannot be seen as a populist party. Be that as it may, there are sufficient reasons to treat FIDESZ as a populist party at the time of the 2006 and 2010 parliamentary elections.

In the context of widespread disillusionment with the centre-left government, FIDESZ's active opposition against the ruling politicians, and the apparent cohesiveness of its organisation, made the party a credible electoral option in both elections. The Hungarian populist radical right parties were not always equally credible. MIÉP failed to rejuvenate ideologically and eventually fell apart after several intra-party conflicts and defections. Jobbik's star began to rise after 2006, when its anti-government and anti-Roma demonstrations attracted substantial attention. At the end of the decade, Jobbik had recruited 'young charismatic intellectuals as leaders' and the party ran effective campaigns, extending its appeal to 'youth and the people living in the countryside' (Halasz 2009: 493). Similarly to the Bulgarian case, the rather extremist rhetoric of the Hungarian populist parties cannot be considered to have acted as a serious curb on their credibility, taking into consideration the prevalent xenophobic sentiments among certain parts of the Hungarian population (Bernáth et al. 2005). Given the absence of a credible (genuinely) populist contender in 2002, it is concluded that there was a *reasonable supply* of credible populist parties in Hungary during the whole period of study, but a *substantial supply* in 2006 and 2010.

Iceland

Following the global financial crisis in 2008, Iceland was hit by a severe banking crisis and economic crash, and the government was widely blamed for its failure to accept responsibility (Hardarson and Kristinsson 2010). Distrust of the political elite had risen in the run up to the April 2009 parliamentary election, and a new party, the Citizens' Movement (*Borgarahreyfingin*, BF), received 7.2 per cent of the vote. The party had voiced populist anti-establishment criticism in the campaign and held 'the system, politicians and banksters' responsible for the crisis;

'[t]hey were not thinking about us, but about protecting and maximizing their stake in "the booming economy"', the party claimed (Reykjavik Grapevine 2009). The party's general agenda was summarised as: 'Let's bring the people to parliament' (Reykjavik Grapevine 2009).

BF was able to benefit from the widespread anti-establishment mood in the country and an effective grass-root organisation at the time of the 2009 election, but soon fell apart once represented in parliament. Other small parties that emerged in recent Icelandic political history cannot be considered as genuine populist parties. Even though it added anti-immigration rhetoric to its discourse in its later years, the small conservative Liberal Party (FF), represented in parliament between 1999 and 2007, was essentially a single-issue party, known for its opposition against the fisheries management system and its more general anti-statism. The Icelandic branch of the Pirate Party, which, unlike its sister organisations in other countries, managed to enter parliament in 2013, should also not be seen as a populist party. The Pirate Party 'franchise' is a transnational organisation and does not subscribe to the notion of a 'homogeneous people'. There has thus been a *limited supply* of credible populist parties in Iceland (and *no supply* in 2013), even though, again, it cannot be ruled out that anti-establishment motives played an important role in the vote for essentially non-populist challenger parties.

Ireland

Since its foundation in 1905, the main aim of the Irish party 'We Ourselves' (*Sinn Féin*, SF) has been to strive for a single independent Irish state. The party has nevertheless changed significantly throughout the decades after major political developments in Ireland and several party splits. In the UK territory of Northern Ireland Sinn Féin has eventually become a governing party, but in the Republic of Ireland the party has been much less dominant, also in terms of electoral performance. The latter branch of the party can be defined as a socio-economically left-wing populist party. As Duncan McDonnell (2008: 204) has argued, 'not only does SF already exploit discontent regarding mainstream parties, the economy, Irish sovereignty and the EU, but it explicitly puts itself forward as a "clean", anti-Establishment party which is close to the common people in local communities'. Even though the party has not opposed multiculturalism and social heterogeneity, it developed a clear notion of Irish identity through its nationalism, which was itself rooted in its historical struggle for independence. Sinn Féin has also clearly been the most Eurosceptic of the main Irish parties. The party entered the national parliament in 1997 and saw its vote share increase in the subsequent elections of 2002, 2007 and 2011 (from 6.5 to 9.9 per cent of the vote). Sinn Féin has been able to portray itself as a representative of the poor in deprived rural and inner-city areas (the 'real' Ireland). The party also retained a credible anti-establishment appeal, since all three traditionally dominant Irish parties refused in public to consider entering a government with Sinn Féin. Despite defections in the past, the party has also remained relatively united in more recent years. In 2011, the political environment appeared particularly conducive to populist success in view of the widespread dissatisfaction with the economic mismanagement of the coalition government led by the Fianna Fáil party (Little 2011). The electoral appeal of Sinn Féin has nevertheless been somewhat limited. The party remained stigmatised due to its association with past paramilitary action and terrorist attacks. Taking this into consideration, it is concluded that there has been a *reasonable supply* of credible populist parties in the Republic of Ireland.

Italy

Italy has been dubbed 'a country of many populisms' (Tarchi 2008: 84), and there are indeed several cases that require discussion here. A first case is the regionalist populist Northern League (*Lega Nord*, LN), which came into being as a result of the merger between the Lombard League and other regionalist movements in 1991 (Albertazzi and McDonnell 2005; McDonnell 2006). Its original trademark aim was an autonomous 'Padania', an area without a historical referent consisting of the northern Italian provinces. Padania has been alleged to serve as an economic 'milk cow' for the central government in Rome. Since the turn of the 21st century, the party has campaigned for less far-reaching territorial devolution. Further characteristics of the party have been its anti-immigration and – in more recent years – anti-Islam position, its tough line on law and order, and its moral–cultural conservatism. In terms of populism, the League has constructed an idealised notion of the Padanian community, where '[t]he people are a genuine, healthy and natural entity, free of the vices that contaminate the ruling class' (Tarchi 2008: 92). The party explicitly targeted the political establishment and condemned the dominant parties' practices of corruption and clientelism (Tarchi 2008). After some more successful electoral results in the 1990s, the Lega Nord only received 3.9 per cent of the vote in 2001, but nevertheless took part in the second governing coalition headed by Prime Minister Silvio Berlusconi. Afterwards, the party received 4.6 per cent of the vote in 2006 and 8.3 per cent in 2008, upon which it joined another Berlusconi-led government that survived until November 2011. A technocratic government headed by Mario Monti was subsequently formed that aimed to implement reforms and austerity measures in response to the Eurozone crisis and the concomitant financial and economic problems of Italy. In the new parliamentary election of February 2013, the Lega Nord suffered a loss, receiving 4.1 per cent of the vote.

This latter election was marked by the spectacular performance of the Five Star Movement (*Movimento 5 Stelle*, M5S) of comedian and political activist Beppe Grillo. Formally established in 2009, the M5S made a substantial impact in the 2012 local elections and went on to win no less than 25.6 per cent of the vote in the 2013 parliamentary election. The movement had an unmistakable anti-establishment character: political parties were criticised for their corruption and economic mismanagement, most notably via online communities and local rallies throughout the country (Bordignon and Ceccarini 2013). Bankers, large industrial firms and the news media were also targeted by Grillo, and portrayed as part of the same ruling class. As a replacement for the current political system, M5S advocated an internet-based bottom-up form of democracy. Despite the lack of an explicit homogeneous portrayal of 'the people', the M5S can be considered as a case of populism; in Grillo's rhetoric, a clear-cut line was drawn 'between the morality of ordinary people, uncorrupted by power, and an elite that is by definition separate and self-referential' (Bordignon and Ceccarini 2013: 435). M5S's substantive programme touched on various issues and expressed, for instance, political reformist and environmentalist desires (see Bartlett et al. 2013). It is difficult to pin down the ideology of the M5S, however, which is partly the result of the movement's refusal to associate itself with traditional ideologies.

A more disputed case of populism is the party of the longest-serving post-war prime minister of Italy, and also billionaire media tycoon, Silvio Berlusconi. His party was founded in 1993 under the name of – and is currently again known as – 'Come on Italy' (*Forza Italia*, FI). Forza Italia has often been associated with populism (e.g. Raniolo 2006; Pasquino 2007; Ruzza and Fella 2009). Berlusconi, even while in office, has indeed been known for his anti-establishment rhetoric and his appeal to 'the ordinary public of shoppers and television viewers' (Tarchi 2008: 94). Throughout his career, Berlusconi has aimed to present himself as a businessman more than a politician, and continued his supposed battle against corrupt elites and their communist allies, including intellectuals and members of the judiciary. It is questionable, however, whether the term 'populism' should be used for the centre-right Forza Italia as a whole or just for Berlusconi personally. In the words of Marco Tarchi (2008: 86), the party's expression of populism was 'entirely delegated to the leader, who has made it a trademark of his political style, but not a source of ideological inspiration'. In March 2009 Forza Italia merged with other, non-populist, parties to form the People of Freedom party (*Il Popolo della Libertà*, PdL). The most notable other party merging into the PdL was the National Alliance (AN), a party with neo-fascist roots that turned itself into a mainstream conservative party (Ruzza and Fella 2009: 181).

Both FI and the PdL are nevertheless considered populist parties, in view of Berlusconi's enduring dominance, both in election campaigns as well as inside the parties' organisations. Following McDonnell (2013), the People of Freedom party and Forza Italia could even be seen as Berlusconi's 'personal parties'.[4] Berlusconi's parties had been dominant forces ever since the foundation of Forza Italia, and also the parliamentary election of 2013 was a relative success for Berlusconi and his PdL. With 21.6 per cent of the vote, the party lost compared with the previous election of 2008 (when it gained 37.4 per cent of the vote), and the vote shares of Forza Italia in 2001 and 2006 had also been higher (29.4 and 23.7 per cent, respectively). Nevertheless, despite the numerous charges against Berlusconi for corruption, fraud and sex offences, and despite the economic crisis that hit Italy under his last prime ministership, the septuagenarian politician could still attract a surprisingly large number of voters. Berlusconi's personal appeal, facilitated by his control of the most important media outlets, had not yet waned at the time of the 2013 election, and he again struck a chord with his anti-tax policy position in particular (Garzia 2013).

Beppe Grillo, in turn, has been described as 'a great showman', who knew 'all the rhetorical techniques to enthuse his audience' (Bordignon and Ceccarini 2013: 435). In the years prior to the 2013 election, Grillo mobilised a growing group of supporters and representatives (Bartlett et al. 2013) – even though building a stable and efficient party organisation afterwards was one of the main challenges for the M5S. Finally, former Lega Nord leader Umberto Bossi, who resigned in 2012, has been described as a charismatic leader, who was 'held to possess extraordinary personal qualities and a *fiuto politico* (political sixth sense) which put his actions and U-turns beyond reproach' (McDonnell 2006: 130). At the same time, while in government, the party 'succeeded in presenting itself simultaneously as both "the opposition within government" and a driving force behind high-profile areas of government policy' (Albertazzi and McDonnell 2005: 953; see also Albertazzi and McDonnell 2010). In this way, the League's anti-establishment credibility was long preserved, until a corruption scandal hit the party and Bossi personally in 2012, leading to the party leader's resignation. Yet, all things considered, the conclusion is that there was a *substantial supply* of credible populist parties in Italy between the elections of 2001 and 2013.

Latvia

Identifying populist parties in Latvia is complicated, not only due to the fact that the party system has remained very changeable and characterised by numerous splits and mergers, but also because various parties have emerged that claimed to 'rejuvenate' politics (Auers 2013; see also Sikk 2012). After 2000, one such party was New Era (JL), which entered parliament after winning 24 per cent of the vote in 2002. New Era combined neo-liberal with conservative positions, but was above all characterised by its anti-incumbency and anti-corruption message (Balcere 2012: 51). While New Era could thus evidently be described as an anti-establishment party, it will not be considered as a populist case because, similarly to Res Publica in Estonia, it 'failed to make prominent references to the "common people"' (Sikk 2009: 7; 2012: 475; cf. Lang 2005; Učeň 2007; Balcere 2012). In 2011 JL merged into the mainstream liberal-conservative Unity party.

Again – and this argument has also been made for several previously discussed cases – one may suspect that JL voters in 2002 were driven by the same (anti-establishment) motives as voters for typical populist parties, particularly taking into consideration the salience of corruption as a political issue and the widespread public distrust of political parties (Auers 2013). The same is likely to apply if we look at the performance of the more recently founded Reform Party (ZRP) of former president Valdis Zatlers, which received 20.8 per cent of the vote in 2011. In the run up to the early parliamentary election – which was provoked by President Zatlers himself – the ZRP criticised several 'oligarch parties' for their corruption, and proposed to introduce mechanisms of participatory democracy (Ikstens 2012). It is not quite correct, however, to perceive the ZRP as a populist party, since it did not portray the (Latvian) people as homogeneous – the party actually favoured extended rights for minorities in ethnically heterogeneous Latvia – and because its criticism was primarily directed towards specific parties, more than the political establishment as a whole.

The party All for Latvia! (*Visu Latvijai!*, VL) will be considered as a case of populism. In the 2006 parliamentary election VL still only received 1.5 per cent of the vote, but it improved its performance in 2010, in an alliance with the national-conservative For Fatherland and Freedom/ LNNK – a party itself having populist radical right roots (Mudde 2007: 54). In 2010 this National Alliance (*Nacionālā Apvienība*, NA) won 7.7 per cent of the vote. The parties merged officially in 2011, after which the NA party lost its radical populist rhetoric. Prior to the merger, All for Latvia could still be seen as a nativist populist party, which adhered to conservative social values and aimed to protect Latvian national identity by restricting citizenship rules and reinforcing the status of the Latvian language (Auers 2010). In its campaign, the party visited rural Latvian towns and villages – often by horse and cart – because here the 'real' Latvians were supposed to live (Auers 2010: 6). The VL politicians claimed to be truly different from the other, corrupt, political actors.

In terms of credibility, All for Latvia became more visible in the run up to the 2010 parliamentary elections, when its, many young, candidates ran an active campaign with visits to local communities and an innovative use of new social media (Auers 2010). If All for Latvia (2006–2010) is considered to be the only genuine populist party in Latvia, there has only been a *limited supply* of credible populist parties in Latvia since 2000 (and *no supply* in 2011). It must be reiterated, however, that Latvia is another difficult case if one seeks to use the concept of populism to distinguish between parties in a meaningful way. This issue is also evident in the following case.

Lithuania

As in the case of neighbouring Latvia, a large number of new parties have emerged (and disappeared) in post-communist Lithuania. Several of those, such as the National Revival Party (TPP) or New Union Party (NS), have voiced anti-establishment and anti-corruption rhetoric, but failed to truly meet the other definitional criteria of populist parties. A clearer case of populism is the Order and Justice Party (*Tvarka ir teisingumas*, TT), formerly named the Liberal Democratic Party (LDP), founded in 2002 and headed by former prime minister Rolandas Paksas. The party was not least a vehicle for Paksas' presidential campaign (Duvold and Jurkynas 2013). In February 2003 Paksas indeed managed to become elected as president, although he was impeached again in April 2004 after the revelation of an illicit donation by a Russian businessman. Paksas' party had a clear anti-establishment appeal. In the 2008 election campaign, for instance, the film 'The Pilot' was aired, in which the hero was modelled on Paksas and the enemies on other Lithuanian politicians. The party explicitly contrasted the self-enriching, oligarchic elite with the Lithuanian people (Balcere 2012; Ramonaitė and Ratkevičiūtė

2013). The more substantive programme of the party has been relatively vague, but included elements of nationalism, moral conservatism, and strict law and order policies. Order and Justice won 11.4 per cent of the vote in the parliamentary election of October 2004 and 12.7 per cent in 2008. It suffered a loss in the 2012 election, receiving 7.3 per cent of the vote.

The Labour Party (*Darbo Partija*, DP) has also been identified as a populist party. Founded by Russian-born millionaire Victor Uspaskich, months before the parliamentary election of 2004, the party stressed the corrupt nature of the elite and claimed to defend underprivileged Lithuanians. The party further supported the introduction of direct forms of democracy, but its more general ideological profile has been rather ambiguous (Duvold and Jurkynas 2013). The party won no less than 28.4 per cent of the vote in 2004, upon which it entered government. Once in office, the party faced charges of fraudulent accounting, leading to the resignation of Uspaskich as minister and the party's departure from office. The DP suffered a great loss in the subsequent 2008 election, gathering just 9 per cent of the vote. In 2012 the party again received almost 20 per cent of the vote, but by this time the party had largely lost its populist, anti-establishment character. The DP will therefore only be considered as a populist party in 2004.

In 2012, another new party entered parliament: Way of Courage (DK). Although the party claimed to fight 'clans of bankers and oligarchs, corrupt officials and paedophile groupings', it was founded primarily in a specific response to a rather bizarre string of interrelated paedophilia and murder cases (Davoliute 2012). In view of its idiosyncratic character, it will not be included here as a populist party.

What is clear, in any case, is that corruption scandals have contributed to a widespread distrust of politicians (Duvold and Jurkynas 2013). As discussed, the two populist parties themselves have also not steered clear of scandals. In the case of the DP, however, these only erupted after the party entered government and lost its populist credentials. TT figurehead Paksas' reputation, in turn, was obviously tainted after his impeachment, even though the events gave him the opportunity to 'establish his profile as somebody stigmatised by the Lithuanian political elite' (Balcere 2012: 61). Despite being a controversial figure, Paksas remained one of the most popular politicians in the country (Krupavicius 2004). In view of the lack of true populist contenders in the 2000 election, it is concluded that there has been a *reasonable supply* of credible populist parties in Lithuania. Yet again, it must be noted that the question of whether or not parties were populist may not have been of crucial importance to explain electoral results in the fluid Lithuanian party political context. Discontented voters may primarily have been attracted to new parties – populist or not – because they were 'new, untried and different' (Duvold and Jurkynas 2013: 130).

Luxembourg

In the much more tranquil political environment of Luxembourg, one populist party can be identified: the Alternative Democratic Reform Party (*Alternativ Demokratesch Reformpartei*, ADR). As a former single-issue pensioners' party founded in 1987 – the name of the party between 1992 and 2006 was Action Committee for Democracy and Pensions Justice – the ADR had to reinvent itself after the government implemented most of its desired policies (Dumont and Poirier 2005). The party subsequently developed an eclectic anti-establishment programme, including critical comments about European integration and public sector corruption. The party described itself as 'a populist party that is neither right nor left' (Dumont et al. 2011: 1059), and has appealed to the disillusioned 'ordinary' citizens – the Luxembourg nationals in particular – who were allegedly ignored by the traditional governing parties. The party received between 6.6 and 10 per cent of the vote in the three elections between 2004 and 2013.

The ADR has received attention with its confrontational stance in parliamentary debates, and could count on the endorsement of local celebrities to boost its appeal. The party did not suffer from any notable internal disputes until the prominent MP Aly Jaerling left the party in 2006, dissatisfied with the ADR's ideological course. Afterwards, tensions remained between, notably, the party's liberal and conservative wings (Huberty 2009; Dumont et al. 2012). Taking these skirmishes in more recent years into account, Luxembourg has seen a *reasonable supply* of credible populist parties.

The Netherlands

Having long lacked a presence of truly successful populist parties, the Netherlands has seen the rise of several populist contenders since 2002, of which Chapter 4 of this book will provide a more detailed analysis. The List Pim Fortuyn (*Lijst Pim Fortuyn*, LPF) entered parliament in 2002 with 17 per cent of the vote. The party's flamboyant leader was assassinated close to the end of the campaign, but his populist anti-establishment appeal and hard line on immigration and cultural integration nonetheless convinced many voters to cast their ballot for his party (Van Holsteyn and Irwin 2003). Fortuyn's former party, Liveable

Netherlands (*Leefbaar Nederland*, LN), also crossed the threshold with 1.6 per cent of the vote. The LPF suffered a blow in the subsequent parliamentary election of 2003 (it received 5.7 per cent of the vote), and failed to enter parliament in 2006. 'Liveable' already disappeared in 2003.

In 2006 a new populist party entered the Dutch parliament with 5.9 per cent of the vote: Geert Wilders' Freedom Party (*Partij voor de Vrijheid*, PVV). Compared with Fortuyn, Wilders appealed to the 'ordinary people' more explicitly and took a more radical stance against Islam (Vossen 2011). In the election of 2010 the PVV increased its vote share, winning 15.5 per cent, and subsequently provided parliamentary support for a minority government. The Freedom Party's vote share declined to 10.1 per cent in the early 2012 election. Finally, the Socialist Party (*Socialistische Partij*, SP), a party with a Maoist past, is a borderline case of populism. The SP will not be considered as a populist party in the period relevant to this study, since it moderated its populist anti-establishment rhetoric at the end of the 1990s (De Lange and Rooduijn 2011; Lucardie and Voerman 2012).

As will be discussed in more detail in Chapter 4, the credibility of populist parties in the Netherlands has fluctuated over the past decade. Pim Fortuyn received a significant amount of attention when he entered the political stage towards the end of 2001, largely thanks to his flamboyant personality and confrontational style (Kleinnijenhuis et al. 2003). Fortuyn was an eloquent speaker and formulated an effective anti-establishment rhetoric, but his party largely lost its appeal after Fortuyn's assassination. Just as Liveable Netherlands, the party also fell victim to continuous infighting. In the years that followed, Geert Wilders reached the centre of attention with provocative statements. The PVV's support for the minority coalition between 2010 and 2012 did not truly harm its anti-establishment credibility, as the party was, like the Danish People's Party, able to keep 'one foot in and one foot out' of government. In comparison with the LPF, the Freedom Party has also remained more cohesive since its breakthrough, even though it suffered from several defections in the run up to the 2012 election. It can, then, be concluded that the Netherlands has seen a *reasonable supply* of credible populist parties since the election of 2002.

Norway

As in Denmark, the Norwegian version of the Progress Party (*Fremskrittspartiet*, FrP) initially agitated against state involvement – when it was founded in 1973, the party was officially named 'Anders Lange's

Party for a Strong Reduction in Taxes, Duties and Public Intervention'.
The party adopted a clearer anti-immigration profile by the mid-1980s,
even though it remained 'more liberal, less authoritarian and less
nativist' in comparison with its Danish counterpart (Jupskås 2013: 205).
The FrP can, nonetheless, also be identified as a populist party, as it has
presented itself as 'the party which speaks the ordinary people's case in
ordinary people's language in opposition to a political establishment'
(Hagelund 2005: 149–150). By the time of the 2001 parliamentary election, the party had become a substantial political force: it received 14.6
per cent of the vote that year, and more than 22 per cent in 2005 and
2009. The party saw its popularity decline in the election of September
2013, when it gathered 16.3 per cent of the vote. The Progress Party
nevertheless entered a governing coalition afterwards.

Carl I. Hagen was the face of the FrP between 1978 and 2006, and
has been described as an appealing leader, able to limit the damage
from internal strife (Carter 2005: 80–81; Hagelund 2005). According to
Anders Widfeldt (2000: 490), Hagen was an 'effective media performer',
'photogenic and articulate', and able to communicate directly 'to the
"common man" with a "common sense" message'. Prior to the 2001
election, however, divisions within the party became publicly visible,
and the rival populist radical right party Democrats was founded in 2002,
mainly consisting of former FrP members. After this, the Progress Party
became more cohesive again and clearly overshadowed the Democrats in
electoral competition. After Hagen's departure in 2006, new party leader
Siv Jensen, nicknamed the 'Norwegian Margaret Thatcher', has proven
to be a worthy successor. Being a more professional, 'less confrontational and more even-keeled' leader than Hagen, Jensen has contributed
to cementing the FrP's position as an important political party (Jupskås
2013: 2008). In conclusion, there has been a *substantial supply* of credible populist parties in the Norwegian context.

Poland

As will be discussed in detail in Chapter 5, after a period of party system
instability two radical parties entered the Polish parliament in 2001. The
first of these, Self Defence (*Samoobrona*, SO), turned itself from a farmers'
trade union and social movement into a populist political party with a
rather vague, yet predominantly left-wing and nationalist, programme.
The course of the party was mainly determined by its leader, Andrzej
Lepper, who did not object to being called a populist, if, as he said,
'populism means an uncompromising struggle against a corrupt establishment in defence of ordinary people and national interests' (quoted in

Jasiewicz 2008: 14). The party entered the Polish parliament in 2001 with 10.2 per cent of the vote, and increased its vote share slightly in 2005. Between May 2006 and August 2007 the party was part of the governing coalition. Self Defence disappeared from parliament in the early parliamentary election of 2007.

The League of Polish Families (LPR), the other junior coalition partner in 2006 and 2007, can be considered a borderline case of populism. Although the party can certainly be seen as a radical anti-establishment party, it based its policy positions more on its conservative interpretation of Catholic teachings than on the 'popular will'. The party followed a similar electoral trajectory as Self Defence, but will not be included in the QCA in the next chapter.

Another, somewhat ambiguous, case is the party Law and Justice (*Prawo i Sprawiedliwość*, PiS), the former senior coalition partner of Samoobrona and the LPR. The party, founded in 2001, primarily focused on the issues of crime and corruption in its first campaign. Although the party's general ideology has not changed dramatically over the years, it can be classified as a genuine populist party from the 2005 parliamentary election campaign onwards, when it largely incorporated the radical populist and nationalist discourse of the two smaller radical parties (Stanley 2013). While PiS entered parliament in 2001 with 9.5 per cent of the vote, it saw its vote share increase during its populist phase. In the elections of 2005, 2007 and 2011 the party gathered between 27 and 32 per cent of the vote.

Concerning electoral credibility, Self Defence lacked a professionally developed party organisation, but in 2001 party leader Lepper 'made an efficient transition from streetwise thug to persuasive spokesman for the poor and alienated' (Millard 2003: 78). The party broadened its appeal beyond the most radical protest-voters, and benefited from the general anti-establishment mood that had surfaced at the time of the election. Once represented in parliament, Self Defence MPs were regularly involved in scandals, and many defected or were expelled from the parliamentary group. Law and Justice gradually seized the electoral support of Self Defence as well as the League of Polish Families. The figureheads of Law and Justice, twin brothers Jarosław and Lech Kaczyński, successfully managed to present themselves as political outsiders, even though they had undeniably played important roles in Polish post-communist politics (Markowski 2006). PiS was well organised for most of the period, and, after its period in power, successfully claimed credit for implementing anti-corruption measures, as well as for the relatively favourable economic conditions (Szczerbiak 2008). Since 2001, then, there has been a *substantial supply* of credible populist parties in Poland.

Romania

Romania is another difficult case when it comes to using ideological labels, such as 'populism', to describe political parties: many parties have been leader-centred, driven by short-term tactical considerations, and did not develop consistent ideological profiles (Crowther and Suciu 2013). Nevertheless, one rather clear case of populism is the Greater Romania Party (*Partidul România Mare*, PRM), which was founded in 1991. It has been one of the more extreme populist radical right cases; following Mudde (2007: 45), '[i]ts discourse regularly crosses into the realm of antidemocracy and racism, even if the core ideology remains within (nominally) democratic boundaries'. In addition to its anti-Hungarian, anti-Roma, anti-Semitic and irredentist appeals, the party of Vadim Tudor presented itself as 'the party of the excluded outsiders' (Crowther and Suciu 2013: 275), and targeted the corrupt political establishment, using slogans as 'Down with the Mafia, Up with the Motherland!' (Andreescu 2005: 189). The party celebrated a large victory in the parliamentary election of 2000 – several members of another radical right party, the Romanian National Unity Party (PUNR) had joined the PRM by this time – winning 19.5 per cent of the vote. In 2004 the party still received 13 per cent of the vote, but in 2008 it disappeared from parliament.

In the national election of December 2012, the new People's Party (*Partidul Poporului*, PP-DD) of former journalist, presenter and lowbrow TV station owner Dan Diaconescu fared better; it received 14 per cent of the vote on the basis of a loose populist, nationalist and socio-economically left-wing programme. The party sketched a 'dichotomy between the people who are affected by the economic crisis and the established elite, which is unable to resolve the crisis, or even caused it' (Smrčková 2012: 207). Appeals against corruption and clientelism further characterised the PP-DD's anti-establishment discourse (Gherghina and Soare 2013).

There are a few borderline cases that will be excluded from the analysis, but which exemplify the wider presence of populism in Romanian politics. A political figure regularly associated with populism is Romanian President Traian Băsescu, who, in the face of continuous conflicts between him and the government, has played the role of 'people's delegate' in his attacks against the 'Romanian political class' (Crowther and Suciu 2013: 388). However, it is questionable whether the centre-right mainstream parties associated with the officially non-aligned Băsescu, the Democratic Liberal Party (PD-L) and its predecessor PD, can be seen as real cases of populism (Smrčková 2012). The dominant centre-left communist successor party, the Social Democratic Party of Romania (initially called FDSN, later PDSR, and after 2001 PSD), has also been associated with populism, but mainly in the period before 2000 (March 2011: 143; Smrčková 2012). It is, finally, worth mentioning another populist and xenophobic party, the New Generation Party-Christian Democrats (PNG-CD), which relied mainly its leader, businessman George 'Gigi' Becali. The party failed to present good candidates for legislative elections, however, and did not manage to enter the Romanian parliament.

As far as the credibility of the Romanian populist parties is concerned, Vadim Tudor, the leader of the Greater Romania Party, ended up second in the 2000 presidential election with 'effective and colourful anti-establishment rhetoric' (Pop-Eleches 2008: 472). In the parliamentary election campaign, as well, 'Tudor and the PRM were successful in shaping the dialogue of the campaign and ultimately the tenor of opposition in Parliament' (Sum 2010: 21). Extremist discourse has not seriously damaged the credibility of the PRM; as in Bulgaria and Hungary, xenophobic attitudes were shared by a considerable proportion of the Romanian electorate (Andreescu 2005). The profile of the PRM became somewhat unclear in later years, when its protest appeal gradually waned, and when Tudor unsuccessfully attempted to join the mainstream European People's Party (EPP) group in the European Parliament in 2005 (Smrčková 2012). The party also suffered from several defections after this attempt. In a highly personalised 2012 election campaign, well-known TV personality Dan Diaconescu used his popular TV station as his 'main vehicle for visibility and popularity' (Gherghina and Soare 2013: 11), and presented himself as a problem-solver and spokesperson of the ordinary Romanian people. Diaconescu has nevertheless been a controversial figure, as illustrated by his arrest in 2010 on the charge of extortion – even though Diaconescu was able to use this incident to claim that the establishment was conspiring against him. All in all, it can be concluded that Romania has seen a *reasonable supply* of credible populist parties between 2000 and 2012.

Slovakia

Slovakia is another post-communist country where populism has arguably had a widespread presence across the party system (Učeň et al. 2005; Deegan-Krause and Haughton 2009; Spáč 2012). Several parties formed in the 1990s, such as the Association of Workers of Slovakia (ZRS) and the Party of Civic Understanding (SOP), criticised the political elite for being unresponsive and corrupt. Both said parties disappeared from parliament after one term, not having lived up to expectations after they entered office. The Communist Party of Slovakia (KSS), in parliament between 2002 and 2006, also voiced anti-establishment criticism, but should essentially be treated as a non-populist communist party (March 2011: 74). The Alliance of the New Citizen (ANO) was present in parliament (and government) during the same years, even though its populist anti-establishment rhetoric was somewhat less pronounced (Učeň et al. 2005; Deegan-Krause and Haughton 2009; Spáč 2012). Populism has arguably also characterised the more durable mainstream parties in Slovakia. Kevin Deegan-Krause (2012) described the populist nature of the governments headed by Vladimír Mečiar, leader of the the national-conservative Movement for a Democratic Slovakia (*Hnutie za demokratické Slovensko*, HZDS), in the 1990s. During his first spell in office (1992–1994), Mečiar continued to convey his perception of a fundamental conflict between the Slovak people and the anti-Slovak elite. Even though the HZDS arguably lost its populism to a certain degree in its second period in power between 1994 and 1998 (Spáč 2012), the party revived its populist discourse afterwards (Deegan-Krause and Haughton 2009). Since then, its electoral performance has gradually deteriorated. The HZDS received 19.5 per cent of the vote in the parliamentary election of 2002, 8.8 per cent in 2006, and 4.3 per cent in 2010, which was not enough to enter parliament. The party disbanded in early 2014.

In its last period of parliamentary representation (2006–2010), the HZDS was a junior coalition partner of the party Direction (*Smer*). The latter party was founded in 1999 by Robert Fico, after he broke away from the Party of the Democratic Left (SDĽ). Smer became the dominant party in Slovakia, gradually increasing its vote share from 13.5 per cent of the vote in the 2002 parliamentary election to 44.4 per cent in 2012, which was sufficient for an absolute majority in the Slovak parliament. Smer voiced populist rhetoric from the outset, and continued to blame the (past) elites for 'their lack of concern for the ordinary citizen' during its first period in office (2006–2010) (Deegan-Krause 2012: 197). It has been observed, however, that Smer toned down its populist rhetoric somewhat throughout the years (Učeň et al. 2005; Spáč 2012). Therefore, taking a conservative approach, Smer will be treated here as a populist party in the election campaigns of 2002 and 2006 only.

Another party in power between 2006 and 2010 was the populist radical right Slovak National Party (*Slovenská národná strana*, SNS). The party has claimed to defend the rights of native Slovaks, has opposed extending ethnic minority rights, and has further been characterised by a protectionist, welfare chauvinist and Eurosceptic profile. In the 1990s its discourse was mainly targeted against Czechs, Jews and especially

Hungarians, but the party also became increasingly 'Romaphobe' (Mudde 2007: 87). Its parliamentary election results have been erratic. In 1998 the SNS received 9.1 per cent of the vote, but, after a split, the party disappeared from parliament in 2002. In 2006 the SNS made an impressive comeback with 11.7 per cent of the vote, followed by a loss in 2010 (5.1 per cent). In 2012 the party failed to cross the electoral threshold once more, receiving 4.6 per cent of the vote.

Finally, the party Ordinary People and Independent Personalities (*Obyčajní Ľudia a Nezávislé Osobnosti*, OĽaNO), founded in 2011, can be added to the list of Slovak populist parties. Even though the party, as a platform for non-partisan candidates, has thus far lacked a clear ideological identity, it 'assumed the role of representative and defender of ordinary people', and blamed the established politicians for their corruption and clientelism (Spáč 2012: 247). OĽaNO received 8.6 per cent of the vote in the 2012 parliamentary election.

In Slovakia, then, a whole range of political parties have emerged in the past decades that campaigned on the basis of a populist anti-establishment platform. Most of these parties were characterised by a visible and popular leader who managed to successfully tap into the widespread distrust of the political elite among the Slovakian population (Spáč 2012). Their credibility as anti-establishment actors was often damaged after a disappointing period in office, in which the parties became tangled up in corruption scandals themselves (Deegan-Krause and Haughton 2009). However, sufficient new, or revamped, populist parties were available to replace them in subsequent elections. It can, therefore, be concluded that there has been a *substantial supply* of credible populist parties in Slovakia. It must be noted, however, that the Slovakian case again shows that identifying a stable and unambiguous 'canon' of populist parties in countries with a remarkably fluid party system is easier said than done.

Slovenia

In Slovenia, another radical right SNS was founded in 1991, which has been led by Zmago Jelinčič Plemeniti ever since: the Slovenian National Party (*Slovenska Nacionalna Stranka*, SNS). In its first decade, the party voiced irredentist desires and took a welfare chauvinist position and a hostile stance towards immigrants from other Yugoslav republics (Krašovec 2012). After 2000, the party added Euroscepticism to its agenda, and also became more explicitly hostile towards Roma. The changes in the SNS programme have been interpreted as an attempt to find niches unoccupied by the established parties, in order 'to present itself as the only party which cares about ordinary people' (Krašovec 2012: 275). The SNS has, nevertheless, become marginal; it received between 4.4 and 6.3 per cent of the vote in the three parliamentary elections of 2000, 2004 and 2008, and disappeared from parliament in 2011 after having polled 1.8 per cent of the vote. The new parties that entered parliament after the 2011 election, Civic List (DL) and Positive Slovenia (PS), had a non-populist and essentially socially liberal character (Krašovec 2012; Zajc 2013). The SNS suffered from several incidents damaging its electoral credibility. After a previous split in 1993, several more MPs, who disagreed with the party's course, broke away in 2008. In addition, party leader Jelinčič has faced several charges due to fraudulent behaviour, and one SNS MP was sentenced to jail for corruption and blackmail (Krašovec 2012: 269). Also taking into consideration Jelinčič's lacklustre performance during the campaign of 2011, it is concluded that there has been a *limited supply* of credible populist parties in Slovenia.

Sweden

In the parliamentary election of 2010, the populist radical right Sweden Democrats (*Sverigedemokraterna*, SD) won 5.7 of the vote and finally crossed the electoral threshold, after having won only 1.4 per cent and 2.9 per cent in 2002 and 2006, respectively. The party's increased electoral fortunes went hand in hand with attempts to create a more respectable ideological image. This process started in the second half of the 1990s, when the party gradually moved away from its neo-fascist roots (Rydgren 2008b; Widfeldt 2008; Klein 2013). The Sweden Democrats were still staunchly opposed to immigration – especially of Muslims – arguing that this caused unemployment and threatened both Swedish culture and the country's welfare state. The party has also voiced its aversion to European integration, globalisation and (American) cultural imperialism, and has taken a culturally traditionalist line. In addition, the SD has expressed populist anti-establishment rhetoric: the party has targeted the purported left-wing elites in particular and claimed to 'say what the common people think' (Rydgren 2008b: 148).

Calls for changing the ideological course of the party had previously led to tensions inside the Sweden Democrats, resulting in several defections and expulsions (Carter 2005: 74–75; Widfeldt 2008). Despite its attempts to appear more respectable, the party remained stigmatised due to its fascist past (Rydgren 2008b). Leading Swedish media outlets have, for instance, refused to publish and broadcast Sweden Democrats campaign adverts (Klein 2013). Gradually, however, the party's more moderate rhetoric started to pay off, and since 2005 the party has benefited from having a young and dynamic new leader: Jimmie Åkesson. As Widfeldt (2008: 271) noted, 'His smart appearance, his low-key but confident and reasoned style and his "clean" background belied any accusations of extremism or quirkiness'. Considering the entire period between the elections of 2002 and 2010, however, it can be argued that there has been only a *limited supply* of credible populist parties in Sweden.

Switzerland

Various populist parties have entered the Swiss federal legislature, the National Council, in the past decades. The Swiss People's Party (in German: *Schweizerische Volkspartei*, SVP), also known as the Democratic Union of the Centre (in French: *Union Démocratique du Centre*, UDC), even became the largest party from 2003 onwards. Being a party with long historical roots, the SVP had its greatest successes in more recent times; its vote share expanded gradually from 15 per cent in 1995 to 29 per cent in 2007. The party suffered a minor loss in the 2011 election, receiving 26.6 per cent of the vote. The growth of the SVP in the 1990s was accompanied by an ideological radicalisation of the formerly agrarian-conservative party (Albertazzi 2008; Mazzoleni 2013). The Zürich branch, led by Christoph Blocher, became dominant at the national level, and steered the party in a more populist, xenophobic and Eurosceptic direction. Under Blocher, the party began to accuse the political class explicitly of conspiring behind the backs of the people, identified the negative side effects of immigration more frequently, and called for the preservation of Swiss culture, against the supposed threat of Islam in particular.

Several other populist parties have entered the Swiss National Council as well (see Albertazzi 2008). Although some of these became important parties at the cantonal level, they have remained rather marginal in the federal parliament. The populist radical right Swiss Democrats, for instance, long occupied a handful of seats prior to its gradual decline, and disappeared from parliament in 2007. The regionalist populists of the League of Ticinesians (*Lega dei Ticinesi*, LdTi), which was founded in 1991, have been represented in the National Council with one or two seats throughout their existence. In the election of 2011, the Geneva Citizens' Movement (*Mouvement citoyens genevois*, MCG) also managed to win one seat in the National Council.

In the past decade, the main populist party at the national level has clearly been the Swiss People's Party, which eclipsed smaller radical right parties in terms of visibility and funding (Bornschier 2010: 133). Under Blocher's leadership, the SVP has been able to improve its communication strategies and to professionalise its organisation (Albertazzi 2008; Zaslove 2012). At the same time, self-made businessman Blocher personified the alleged ' "Swiss" virtues of determination and hard work', and has been able 'to address people's concerns by using simple and media-friendly language' (Albertazzi 2008: 116). Notwithstanding the increased appeal of the party, more moderate SVP members split from the party in 2008 to form the mainstream Conservative Democratic Party of Switzerland (BDP). New parliamentary elections were still far away, however, and the SVP was able to find 'a new internal cohesion' (Mazzoleni 2013: 251). The party also managed to retain its anti-establishment character once it took part in the Swiss Executive Council (Zaslove 2012). The SVP could claim credit for fulfilling its policy promises in government (Bornschier 2010: 164), while Blocher remained the 'enfant terrible of national politics' (Mazzoleni 2013: 245). Switzerland has, all in all, seen a *substantial supply* of credible populist parties since the start of the 21st century.

Conclusion

In this chapter I aimed to identify the populist parties in 31 European countries that have won at least one seat in national parliaments between 2000 and 2013. As the preceding pages have shown, distinguishing between populist and non-populist parties is not always a straightforward exercise. This is, first of all, related to the fact that populism is not an attribute of a clearly circumscribed universe of political parties only (see Van Kessel 2014). In theory, all political parties can resort to populist rhetoric – even though some are clearly more inclined to do so than others, depending on their ideology and potential to convincingly portray themselves as outsiders. There is no clear-cut rule for determining how much populist rhetoric a party should voice in order for it to be classified as a 'genuine' populist party. In this regard, cases such as the New Flemish Alliance in Belgium and the Dutch Socialist Party are difficult to pin down; they used populist rhetoric, but not always to the same degree as more unambiguous cases. Thinking of Silvio Berlusconi's parties in Italy in particular, ambiguity may also arise if populism is a trait of a party leader more than of the party as a whole. Throughout the chapter, I have provided reasons for either treating or not treating individual cases as populist parties, but it is hard to deny the inevitable existence of borderline cases.

Another issue is that populist parties do not necessarily stay populist throughout their existence. At the same time, non-populist parties may turn themselves into populist parties, FIDESZ in Hungary, the Austrian Freedom Party and the Swiss People's Party being good examples. The populist thin ideology is arguably easier to adopt or to shed than more comprehensive ideologies, which are more clearly associated with concrete policy proposals. It has often been argued that parties are especially likely to lose their populist anti-establishment appeal once they enter government. This is related to the notion that populism has a self-limiting and 'episodic' character (Taggart 2000). As Mény and Surel (2002: 18) have argued, a populist party's eventual fate 'is to be integrated into the mainstream, to disappear, or to remain permanently in opposition'. Cases such as the Swiss People's Party, the Polish Law and Justice and the Italian Northern League, however, have indicated that populist discourse can be retained in office (see Albertazzi and McDonnell 2005; Stanley 2010; Akkerman and De Lange 2012; Zaslove 2012). Providing support for a minority government while formally remaining in opposition, as the Dutch Freedom Party and the Danish People's Party have done, has proven a good way to keep 'one foot in and one foot out of office' in particular.

Still, the ability of parties to adopt or discard populist rhetoric relatively easily poses a challenge when it comes to using populism as a 'classifier'. This, as well as the borderline problem, is especially pertinent in the post-communist countries in Central and Eastern Europe. In several of these countries, party systems have remained fluid and characterised by the quick rise and demise of political parties (see e.g. Casal Bértoa 2013). As a result, it is more difficult than in Western European cases to distinguish between a political establishment and (populist) outsiders challenging it.

In addition, few countries in the region have experienced an entirely smooth transition towards democracy, and in many post-communist countries corruption scandals have undermined the credibility of parties in government. As we have seen in this chapter, a large number of parties, some more successful than others, have aimed to capitalise on a more general anti-establishment mood (see also Učeň 2007; Sikk 2012; Hanley and Sikk 2014). These parties have often been associated with populism, even though not all of them also explicitly defended popular sovereignty or treated the people as a homogeneous body. Not all these anti-establishment parties, therefore, should be treated as cases of populism. Yet, in view of the widespread disillusion with mainstream parties in several post-communist countries, and the related salience of corruption as a political issue, it is questionable whether the distinction between populist and strictly non-populist challengers is entirely relevant concerning the electoral performance of these parties, or the motives of their voters. This is something which should be taken into consideration in the remainder of this book.

Bearing in mind the widespread use of anti-establishment rhetoric in much of Central and Eastern Europe, it is no surprise that scholars sceptical about using populism as a concept of classification often refer to problematic cases in post-communist Europe (e.g. Deegan-Krause and Haughton 2009; Sikk 2009). Be that as it may, there are sufficient parties across Europe that could not truly be characterised without taking their populist anti-establishment discourse into account. These include rather short-lived cases such as Self Defence in Poland and the List Pim Fortuyn in the Netherlands, but also long-standing and resilient parties such as the Front National in France and the Flemish Interest in Belgium. Table 2.1 presents these cases, which can, at least for a particular period in time, be considered as genuine 'populist parties'.

Table 2.1 Populist parties in Europe that gained parliamentary representation after national elections between 2000 and 2013

Country	Party	Elections*
Austria	Freedom Party (FPÖ)	2002–2013
	Alliance for the Future of Austria (BZÖ)	2006–2008
	Team Stronach (TS)	2013
Belgium	Flemish Interest (VB)	2003–2010
	National Front (FN)	2003–2010
	List Dedecker (LDD)	2007–2010
Bulgaria	National Movement Simeon the Second (NDSV)	2001
	Attack Party (Ataka)	2005–2013
	Citizens for European Development of Bulgaria (GERB)	2009–2013
	Law, Order and Justice (RZS)	2009–2013
Croatia	Croatian Labourists – Labour Party (HL-SR)	2011
	Croatian Party of Rights dr. Ante Starčević (HSP-AS)	2011
Cyprus	–	
Czech Republic	Public Affairs (VV)	2010
	ANO 2011 (ANO)	2013
	Dawn of Direct Democracy (Úsvit)	2013
Denmark	Danish People's Party (DF)	2001–2011
Estonia	–	
Finland	True Finns (PS)	2003–2011
France	National Front (FN)	2002–2012
Germany	Party of Democratic Socialism/ The Left (PDS/Linke)	2002–2013

Continued

Table 2.1   Continued

Country	Party	Elections*
Greece	Popular Orthodox Rally (LAOS)	2004–2012
	Coalition of the Radical Left (SYRIZA)	2004–2012
	Independent Greeks (ANEL)	2012
Hungary	FIDESZ-Hungarian Civic Alliance (FIDESZ-MPSZ)	2006–2010
	Movement for a Better Hungary (Jobbik)	2006–2010
Iceland	Citizens' Movement (BF)	2009
Ireland	Sinn Féin (SF)	2002–2011
Italy	Forza Italia (FI) / People for Freedom (PdL)	2001–2013
	Northern League (LN)	2001–2013
	5 Star Movement (M5S)	2013
Latvia	All For Latvia! (VL)	2006–2010
Lithuania	Labour Party (DP)	2004
	Order and Justice Party (TT)	2004–2012
Luxembourg	Alternative Democratic Reform Party (ADR)	2004–2013
Malta	–	
Netherlands	List Pim Fortuyn (LPF)	2002–2006
	Liveable Netherlands (LN)	2002–2003
	Freedom Party (PVV)	2006–2012
Norway	Progress Party (FrP)	2001–2013
Poland	Self Defence (SO)	2001–2007
	Law and Justice (PiS)	2005–2011
Portugal	–	
Romania	Greater Romania Party (PRM)	2000–2012
	People's Party – Dan Diaconescu (PP-DD)	2012
Slovakia	Movement for a Democratic Slovakia (HZDS)	2002–2012
	Direction (Smer)	2002–2006
	Slovak National Party (SNS)	2002–2012
	Ordinary People and Independent Personalities (OLaNO)	2012
Slovenia	Slovenian National Party (SNS)	2000–2011
Spain	–	
Sweden	Sweden Democrats (SD)	2002–2010
Switzerland	Swiss People's Party (SVP)	2003–2011
	League of Ticinesians (LdTi)	2003–2011
	Swiss Democrats (SD)	2003–2011
	Geneva Citizens' Movement (MCG)	2007–2011
UK	–	

*This column indicates in which elections between 2000 and 2013 an individual party has participated as a populist party. This does not mean that the party also won seats in the given election years. See Table A.1 in Appendix C for election results.

It was clear from the case descriptions that many of these populist parties built their programme around one or more of the four themes identified in the previous chapter: culture and ethnicity; economic hardship; European integration; and corruption. The next chapter, which presents the results of the QCA, assesses whether (public attitudes towards) these themes relate to the levels of support for populist parties across countries.

In addition to identifying populist parties, and thereby contributing to the academic debate about applying the concept of populism to party politics, this chapter has aimed to provide an assessment of these parties' electoral credibility. This assessment provides input for the QCA, in which the supply of credible populist parties is selected as one of the conditions. Even though it lay beyond my powers to provide an in-depth analysis of the credibility of each and every populist party, it was clear from my study of the case-oriented literature that the success or failure of populist parties has often been related to their own agency: in particular, the appeal of their leadership and their ability to remain united. The next four chapters, presenting results from the QCA and the three in-depth case studies, will assess more closely the impact of electoral credibility, as well as the other conditions identified in Chapter 1, on the electoral performance of populist parties.

3
Paths to Populist Electoral Success and Failure: fsQCA Analysis

Having discussed the way populism has manifested itself in contemporary European party systems, I will now turn to the electoral performance of the populist parties identified in the previous chapter. This chapter presents the results of the fuzzy set Qualitative Comparative Analysis (fsQCA). As its name suggests, QCA is essentially a research approach and technique of comparison. As explained in Chapter 1, the approach is primarily chosen because QCA is able to demonstrate how an outcome can be based on different combinations of explanatory conditions across contexts. Following this notion of 'equifinality', there can be different paths towards the same outcome. Since populist parties are not all similar in terms of the issue positions they take and the themes they emphasise, this principle appears crucial to the aim of explaining their electoral performance across countries.

In addition to the principle of equifinality, some further features of the QCA approach are worth mentioning (see e.g. Ragin 1987; 2000; 2008; Rihoux and Ragin 2009; Schneider and Wagemann 2012). First, it is assumed that it is the *combination* of conditions (a configuration) that relates to a certain outcome. This principle is known as 'conjunctural causation'. Conditions are not automatically assumed to affect the outcome independently. Instead of the term 'independent variable', therefore, the term 'condition' is preferred. The QCA approach further adheres to the notion that causality is not always symmetrical: different (combinations of) conditions may be relevant when explaining either the presence or the absence of a particular outcome (in this case, either electoral success or failure of populist parties).

My analysis first focuses on the electoral performance of populist parties in the entire period of study (2000–2013), and then on their results in the latest national elections. This latter analysis is meant to test the robustness of the previous findings as well as to assess whether the financial and economic crisis has affected the conditions underlying populist party success or failure. The two analyses each consist of two main parts, following roughly the two-step approach introduced by Schneider and Wagemann (2006). The first part considers the three more fundamental conditions that are expected to relate to the electoral performance of populist parties: the proportionality of the electoral system, the responsiveness of established parties, and the supply of credible populist parties (see Chapter 1). The notion of equifinality is especially relevant for the second part of the analyses, which assesses whether we can observe different paths to populist success and failure across European countries, depending on the relevance of the four more specific themes identified: culture and ethnicity; economic hardship; European integration; and corruption. It is expected that when these themes, which are particularly compatible with the populist thin ideology, arouse strong views among voters in a certain country, populist parties have a greater potential to mobilise support.

The first chapter of this book has already outlined the theoretical expectations in more detail. In this chapter I will therefore begin by discussing more practical and technical issues related to the operationalisation of the outcome variable and conditions, before moving to the results of the fsQCA.

Operationalisation of conditions and outcome

The first QCA technique that was developed is now referred to as 'crisp set QCA' (csQCA) (Ragin 1987). csQCA makes use of Boolean algebra, which is based on binary language. The data related to the individual conditions and outcome variable are, consequently, expressed in dichotomous values (1 or 0) only. In more recent years, the 'fuzzy set QCA' (fsQCA) technique has been developed, which removes the drawbacks of 'crude dichotomisation' of data (Ragin 2000; 2008). With fsQCA, the method used in this chapter, the data can be expressed in fuzzy set 'membership scores' ranging anywhere from 0 to 1. Critics have likened the process of transforming raw data into these fuzzy set scores (the 'calibration' of data) to the manipulation of 'objective' data (see De Meur et al. 2009). Calibration should, however, never happen in an arbitrary way and must be based on theoretically and substantively informed choices. The process actually forces the researcher to make sense of the data and the distribution of cases prior to 'pushing the button' and focusing on the outcomes.

Another critique of QCA is that it is a 'case-sensitive' approach, in the sense that including or excluding a few cases may produce different outcomes. This study, however, circumvents this problem by taking a pan-European approach and including all 31 'comparable' European countries. A related issue is that applying QCA to small- and medium-N studies has a drawback; when more explanatory conditions are included in the analysis, the number of possible configurations increases exponentially. It then becomes much less likely that all these configurations have empirical referents (i.e. cases that are 'covered' by a particular configuration). Yet the problem of 'too many variables, too few cases' is not specific to QCA techniques, and using QCA obliges the researcher to make well-informed decisions about selecting explanatory conditions (De Meur et al. 2009: 158).

In the analyses presented in this chapter, a total of seven conditions and one outcome variable (populist party electoral performance) are considered. This section discusses the data sources used to operationalise these conditions, as well as the choices made concerning the calibration of the data. For most of the conditions and the outcome, the 'direct method' of calibration is applied. Accordingly, three qualitative anchors are defined: one for full membership (1), one for full non-membership (0) and one indicating the crossover point (0.5). By means of a logarithmic function, the FSQCA 2.5 software used in this study then calculates for all cases the fuzzy set membership scores in a particular condition or the outcome (Ragin and Davey 2012). Table 3.1 presents the thresholds that were chosen for the fsQCA, and in the following paragraphs I substantiate the choices made. These were based on theoretical and substantive grounds: that is, by making sense of the theoretical meaning of the values, and also by considering the distribution of the cases in the individual conditions. The tables in Appendix C (A.1–A.5) provide more detailed information about the data and calibration process with regard to individual conditions.

Electoral success of populist parties (POPSUC)

The outcome variable, first of all, is the electoral performance of populist parties. For the first part of the analysis, this variable is operationalised by calculating the average vote share of populist parties in the parliamentary elections in each country between 2000 and 2013 (see Appendix C, Table A.1). If there has been more than one populist party in a single country, the vote shares of these parties are aggregated. In almost all countries, three or four national elections have been held throughout this period; only in the Netherlands (five) and Greece (six)

Table 3.1 Conditions in the fsQCA

Conditions	Description	Calibration
POPSUC	Average (combined) vote share of populist parties in national elections between 2000 and 2013.	1 = 20 per cent 0.5 = 10 per cent 0 = 0 per cent
PR	Proportionality of electoral system. Higher values imply a higher degree of proportionality.	1 = 16.78 0.5 = 10 0 = 0
UNRESP	Perceived unresponsiveness of established parties, measured through indicators related to satisfaction with democracy and confidence in parliament and parties.	See Appendix C: Table A.3
CREDIB	Supply of credible populist parties.	1 = substantial 0.67 = reasonable 0.33 = limited 0 = no
NATIV	Levels of nativist sentiments.	See Appendix C: Table A.4
ECOHARD	Economic hardship, measured through levels of unemployment.	1 = 15 per cent 0.5 = 8 per cent 0 = 4 per cent
EURSCEP	Levels of Euroscepticism, measured through survey questions on evaluations of European Union membership.	1 = 27.8 per cent 0.5 = 14.1 per cent 0 = 7.3 per cent
CORRUP	Levels of perceived public sector corruption.	1 = 6.6 0.5 = 3.5 0 = 0.6

have there been more. For the second part of the analysis, only the latest election results are considered. The main data source used is the website Parties and Elections in Europe (Nordsieck 2013).

A country is considered to have obtained full membership in the outcome if populist parties have won 20 per cent of the vote on average. If this provision is met, it can be argued that populist parties have become an important political force in a given country. There have been countries in which individual populist parties gained a (much) higher vote share in the past: examples include the Austrian Freedom Party, the Bulgarian GERB, FIDESZ in Hungary, Forza Italia, the Lithuanian Labour Party, Poland's Law and Justice, and Slovakia's Smer. However, given that populist parties are often still radical outsiders, an average (combined) vote share of more than 20 per cent for these parties is observed in only a handful of countries. Percentage points exceeding this upper limit are considered as 'extraneous variation'; a 20 per cent average vote share already signifies very substantial and stable support for populist parties in a given country. The chosen crossover value is 10 per cent of the vote. This means that countries with an average 'populist vote share' of more than 10 per cent are considered to be 'more in than out' of the category of populist electoral success, and cases where this percentage is lower 'more out than in'. Practice has shown that populist parties gaining just over 10 per cent become potential coalition or 'government support' partners, examples from the past being the Czech Public Affairs (2010), the Danish People's Party (for the first time in 2001), Self Defence in Poland (2005) and the Slovak National Party (2006). When the average vote share of populist parties lies below 10 per cent, however, they generally remain relatively marginal members of the opposition – notwithstanding exceptions to the rule, such as the Italian Lega Nord. The point at which a country reaches full non-membership is, straightforwardly, set at 0 per cent of the average vote, signifying the virtual absence of support for populist parties at the national level.[1]

A look at the distribution of cases after determining these anchors reveals that 17 cases fall below the 10 per cent crossover point and 14 above, if the entire period between 2000 and 2013 is considered (see Table 3.2). France is the most 'ambiguous' case, with an average populist vote share of 9.7 per cent. If only the last election in each country is considered, 13 cases fall below the crossover point and 18 above – the Netherlands and Ireland being the most ambiguous cases, with 10.1 and 9.9 per cent of the vote, respectively. This is an indication of an increase in populist party success in several countries' most recent elections.

Proportionality of the electoral system (PR)

The first condition relates to electoral system proportionality. Instead of considering specific electoral formulae, district magnitude or thresholds, this analysis uses the least squares index to gauge the proportionality of the electoral system (Gallagher 1991). This index reflects the actual disproportionality between the distribution of votes and seats, and, as such, provides a good measure for the combined mechanical effects of the electoral rules in a given country (see e.g. Carter 2005: 199). The analysis uses the average least squares index figure of the relevant elections in each country. Since a proportional electoral system is expected to be conducive to the electoral success of populist parties, the scores are inverted, allocating a 0 to the country with the highest average disproportionality over the past elections (France, see Table A.2).

The determination of the full membership and full non-membership values is based on to the most extreme cases in the distribution. The upper threshold is set at 16.78, equalling the inverted least squares index score of the Netherlands. With no artificial threshold and a district magnitude of 150, the electoral system in this country could hardly be more proportional. A party is only required to win 0.67 per cent of the vote in order to receive a seat in parliament. The non-membership value is 0, equalling the score of France. This country has about the same average proportionality figure as the UK, where a single member plurality system is used in general elections. In the French two-tiered single-member majority system, only candidates who receive at least 12.5 per cent of the first-round vote proceed to the second run-off round – that is, if no candidate has already won an absolute majority in the first round.[2] As a result, many votes cast in the first round are 'wasted'.

Since there is no obvious gap between the values of more proportional systems, on the one hand, and less proportional systems, on the other, there is no apparent crossover point for the proportionality (PR) condition. It makes sense, however, to use the value of 10, as this places cases with evident proportionality-decreasing electoral mechanisms in the 'less proportional' category. The single-member district electoral systems of the UK and France clearly belong to this latter category. Lithuania and Hungary, in turn, have used relatively disproportional mixed-member systems, while Italy and Greece have applied large majority or winner bonuses. Croatia, finally, has used a sizeable 5 per cent threshold at the constituency level.[3] The remainder of the countries have applied fairly ordinary PR, single transferable vote (Ireland and Malta) or mixed-member systems (Bulgaria, Germany and Romania) with a more proportional character. When using the crossover value of 10, clearly fewer cases (7) belong to the 'less proportional' than to the 'more proportional' (24) category (see Table 3.2). This is a simple reflection of the fact that most countries in Europe use a relatively proportional electoral system.

Unresponsiveness of the established parties (UNRESP)

In order to come to a general assessment of the (un)responsiveness of established parties, four sets of data are combined that, taken together, roughly cover the period of this study. The first two sets relate to the satisfaction levels with the way democracy works in a particular country, for which data from the 2004 and 2009 waves of the European Election Study are used (Schmitt et al. 2009; Van Egmond et al. 2013). As an indicator of the perceived unresponsiveness of established parties in each country, the percentage of respondents who were 'not at all satisfied' with the way democracy worked is taken.[4] The latter two sets of data relate to levels of confidence in parliament and political parties, and stem from the fourth wave of the European Values Survey of 2008 (EVS 2011). For each country, the selected percentage relates to the respondents who had no confidence at all in these political institutions.

The four sets of data are combined in order to construct an, admittedly rough, proxy for the perceived (un)responsiveness of established parties in each country. For each of the four individual items, the data have been calibrated using the direct method of calibration. Since it is difficult to determine theoretically meaningful anchors with regard to each of the survey questions – for instance, what percentage of people should be dissatisfied with the way democracy is functioning, in order to consider a case a full member of the set? – the data were calibrated based on the distribution of cases within the sets. In order to avoid the fuzzy set scores being influenced too much by outlier cases, the full-membership value relates to the case with the second largest percentage in a particular item (see Table A.3). Following the same logic, the lower threshold is equal to the value of the case with the second lowest percentage. The crossover point was determined by calculating the mean score for each item (after having omitted the highest and lowest percentages). Following this procedure, each case received a fuzzy set membership score for each of the four items (unless data were missing). The final UNRESP score of each case represents the average of these (available) fuzzy set scores.

Credibility of populist parties (CREDIB)

The third condition relates to the electoral credibility of the populist parties. This condition has effectively been operationalised in Chapter 2, in which I assessed whether countries have been characterised by a substantial, reasonable, limited or no supply of credible populist parties. For the fsQCA, each country received a score of 1, 0.67, 0.33 or 0, depending on which of the respective categories it fell into: a score of 1 corresponded to a substantial supply, a score of 0 to no supply. It is relevant for the second part of the analysis that for some cases the score at the time of the latest election differs from the average CREDIB value across the entire period (see Table A.5).

Theme 1: Culture and Ethnicity (NATIV)

Similarly to the responsiveness condition, the first of the more specific themes, culture and ethnicity, is operationalised through a combination of data sources. My aim was to select data that reflected 'nativist sentiments' in the 31 European countries under consideration. Since the issue of immigration has been less important in post-communist countries than in Western European ones, I attempted to use survey questions dealing with more general fears of the demise of national culture or ethnic homogeneity. In the end, data were selected from Eurobarometer (European Commission 2009), the European Values Survey (EVS 2011), the European Election Study (Van Egmond et al. 2013) and the European Social Survey (ESS 2006). The four selected items relate to evaluations concerning the presence of people from other ethnic groups; the importance of national ancestry; the requirement of immigrants to adapt to national customs; and the question of whether more immigrants from a different race or ethnic group should be allowed to enter the country (see Table A.4). Even in countries with low levels of immigration, it can be assumed that nativist respondents were likely to provide a 'restrictive' response to the specific questions about immigration. The NATIV condition is operationalised in a similar way as the UNRESP condition: a final average fuzzy set score is calculated, based on the calibration of the four individual sets of survey data (see, again, Table A.4).

Theme 2: Economic hardship (ECOHARD)

With regard to the theme of economic hardship, unemployment figures from Eurostat (2014) are used (see Table A.2).[5] Since unemployment is a politically sensitive issue, it is here considered to be the best proxy for economic distress in general (see March and Rommerskirchen 2012). Taking into consideration the unemployment figures in the period between 2000 and 2012, an unemployment rate of 4 per cent is a sensible value to use for the lower threshold; only the very prosperous countries Norway (3.5 per cent) and Switzerland (3.7 per cent) had lower average unemployment figures. This stands in contrast to countries such as Poland, Slovakia and Spain, where average unemployment figures have been closer to 15 per cent, the value used as the upper threshold. An 8 per cent unemployment rate is used as a crossover value; this figure is close to the median (7.7 per cent) as well as the average unemployment rate of all 31 countries across the period of study (8.2 per cent). Note that in recent crisis-marred years unemployment figures in some countries have shot up, which is why the analysis of populist party performance in the most recent elections takes into consideration the unemployment rates in the countries' latest election year (or the 2012 figure if the election year was 2013; see Table A.5). There are no good theoretical grounds for altering the calibration values for this latter analysis.

Theme 3: European integration (EURSCEP)

For the theme of European integration, I am interested in the levels of Euroscepticism in a given country. The EURSCEP condition is constructed using Eurobarometer Survey data related to the recurring item asking respondents to evaluate the EU membership of their country (European Commission 2013b). The percentage of respondents who considered their country's membership a 'bad thing' is taken as an indicator of the level of Euroscepticism in a country. The average figure over the (available) years between 2000 and 2011 is used as the basis for a country's fuzzy set score (see Table A.2). As regards the calibration, the value corresponding to the traditionally most Eurosceptic long-term member, the United Kingdom, is taken as the upper limit (27.8 per cent). Only Croatia, which was included in surveys from 2004 onwards, has recorded a slightly higher average figure (29.6 per cent). In view of the latter country's short membership period, the UK value is preferred. The value of the traditionally most Europhile country, founding member Luxembourg (7.3 per cent), is taken as the lower limit. The average figure of 14.1 across the 28 EU members, which also lies close to the median (12.6), is taken to mark the crossover point.

Similarly to developments in unemployment, levels of Euroscepticism have increased dramatically in several countries in more recent years (again, the latest figures available will be used in the analysis concerning the most recent populist party performance; see Table A.5). Notable examples include the crisis-stricken countries Greece, Portugal, Slovenia and Spain. A final note is that the EURSCEP condition is not very relevant to the non-EU countries Iceland, Norway and Switzerland. Comparable Eurobarometer data on these countries are also lacking, but, since the three non-EU countries have been characterised by a markedly Eurosceptic population (see Skinner 2013), the countries are given a fuzzy set score of 1 in this condition.

Theme 4: Corruption (CORRUP)

For the final condition, Transparency International (TI) data are used, which reveal perceived levels of public sector corruption (TI 2014). The data may not be suitable to determine how much actual corruption there is within a certain country, but this is not a problem for this analysis, as it is assumed that populist parties may benefit from the *perception* that there is widespread corruption. TI places countries on a 0 to 10 scale as regards their perceived corruption levels. Data from 2000 until 2013 are considered, and for each country the mean figure for this period (or the years available) is calculated (see Table A.2). Since higher levels of perceived corruption are assumed to stimulate populist party success, the TI data is reversed, so that low values represent 'cleanliness' and high values corruption.[6]

The distribution of cases was again considered in order to determine the calibration anchors. Judging from the TI data, the public sector does not get much cleaner than in Finland and Denmark; both countries have an average perceived corruption value of 0.6, which is used as the lower limit. Romania has the highest average corruption perception score (6.6), which marks the upper limit for the QCA. The average value across all countries within the period of study (3.5) is used to determine the crossover point.

Having determined all calibration anchors for the analysis, Table 3.2 presents the membership scores of the countries in each of the conditions and in the outcome.

fsQCA results

The remainder of the chapter presents the results of the fsQCA. The first main analysis focuses on the entire period of study and effectively considers the conditions related to the prolonged presence or absence of populist electoral success. A two-step approach is taken, which is akin to the one introduced by Schneider and Wagemann (2006), even though my analysis does not involve an entirely similar distinction between 'remote' and 'proximate' factors. In the first step, I seek to discover whether the electoral performance of populist parties can be related to the more general conditions identified: the electoral system; the responsiveness of established parties; and the supply of credible populist parties. Even though the relative importance of the three individual conditions may well differ from case to case, they are deemed important for the performance of populist parties in general. After assessing whether this is indeed the case, the second step of the analysis investigates whether it is possible to provide a more comprehensive explanation for populist party success and failure by taking more specific contextual factors into account. It focuses on the four more specific themes of culture and ethnicity; economic hardship; European integration; and corruption. Since the electoral relevance of these themes is presumed to vary across countries, I expect different paths to populist success and failure to appear after the second step in particular.

In order to observe potential effects of the financial and economic crisis and to cross-validate the results from the first two-step analysis,

Table 3.2   Calibrated data for the fsQCA (period: 2000–2013)

Country	Conditions							Outcome
	PR	UNRESP	CREDIB	NATIV	ECOHARD	EURSCEP	CORRUP	POPSUC
Austria	0.9	0.35	1	0.43	0.06	0.86	0.19	0.95
Belgium	0.83	0.26	0.67	0.38	0.44	0.13	0.33	0.77
Bulgaria	0.53	0.99	0.67	0.67	0.83	0.06	0.93	1
Croatia	0.42	0.95	0.33	0.57	0.89	0.97	0.92	0.08
Cyprus	0.93	0.21	0	0.86	0.12	0.76	0.6	0
Czech Rep.	0.62	0.72	0.33	0.77	0.34	0.37	0.87	0.43
Denmark	0.95	0.03	1	0.10	0.12	0.61	0.05	0.7
Estonia	0.84	0.60	0	0.62	0.73	0.07	0.57	0
Finland	0.89	0.23	0.67	0.33	0.53	0.82	0.05	0.37
France	0.05	0.39	0.67	0.24	0.61	0.66	0.37	0.48
Germany	0.81	0.43	0.67	0.32	0.54	0.35	0.21	0.38
Greece	0.44	0.64	1	0.82	0.82	0.33	0.9	0.82
Hungary	0.46	0.78	0.67	0.85	0.48	0.65	0.79	1
Iceland	0.86	0.15	0.33	0.06	0.07	1	0.07	0.08
Ireland	0.57	0.28	0.67	0.40	0.41	0.04	0.28	0.34
Italy	0.39	0.65	1	0.51	0.52	0.34	0.85	1
Latvia	0.81	0.86	0.33	0.45	0.86	0.65	0.89	0.09
Lithuania	0.41	0.62	0.67	0.44	0.84	0.18	0.84	0.82
Luxembourg	0.82	0.08	0.67	0.33	0.05	0.05	0.11	0.37
Malta	0.94	0.21	0	0.83	0.3	0.66	0.64	0
Netherlands	0.95	0.09	0.67	0.10	0.05	0.09	0.08	0.59
Norway	0.89	0.06	1	0.05	0.03	1	0.09	0.94
Poland	0.68	0.69	1	0.35	0.92	0.05	0.87	1
Portugal	0.73	0.70	0	0.48	0.6	0.45	0.55	0
Romania	0.73	0.91	0.67	0.38	0.32	0.05	0.95	0.7
Slovakia	0.53	0.39	1	0.56	0.96	0.03	0.89	0.99
Slovenia	0.87	0.31	0.33	0.62	0.25	0.21	0.6	0.16
Spain	0.73	0.25	0	0.32	0.92	0.09	0.47	0
Sweden	0.93	0.08	0.33	0.06	0.32	0.92	0.06	0.12
Switzerland	0.89	0.08	1	0.07	0.04	1	0.08	1
UK	0.07	0.55	0	0.64	0.18	0.95	0.15	0

Notes: The fuzzy set scores represent the data across the complete period of study (2000–2013). Tables A.1–A.4 in Appendix C provide the raw data and more information about the data sources, as well as about the calibration of the UNRESP and NATIV conditions. Most scores have been recalculated for the analysis concerning the latest electoral performance of populist parties. See Table A.5 in Appendix C for more information.

an additional analysis is performed which follows a similar route, but only focuses on the performance of populist parties in each country's latest national election. For the latter analysis, most of the conditions are operationalised using only more recent data (see Table A.5 for more details). All analyses were performed using the FSQCA 2.5 software (Ragin and Davey 2012).

Populist party performance in the period 2000–2013

An fsQCA is structured around the search for necessary and sufficient conditions for a certain outcome to occur (see e.g. Schneider and Wagemann 2012). I first assess whether there are any single explanatory conditions that can be considered necessary for the presence (or absence) of populist electoral success. Afterwards, I consider whether there are any (combinations of) conditions whose presence is sufficient for populist success or failure.

Assessment of necessity

In this study, a necessary condition is a condition that needs to be present in order for populist electoral success (or failure) to occur. The presence of this condition alone, however, does not automatically imply the presence of the outcome, since additional factors may be relevant as well. In order to determine whether a particular condition is necessary, it is considered whether populist electoral success or failure is a 'subset' of this condition. If this is the case, the membership values of the cases in the condition (X) are equal to or higher than the corresponding values in the outcome (Y). If a condition is necessary, after all, X should be present whenever Y is present. The degree to which a subset relation has been approximated is calculated by means of a 'set theoretic consistency' formula (Ragin 2006: 291).[7]

Taking populist electoral success as the outcome, the analysis provided the following consistency scores for each of the conditions: CREDIB (0.931); PR (0.748); CORRUP (0.619); ECOHARD (0.586); UNRESP (0.567); NATIV (0.537); EURSCEP (0.495). No high scores were found when the conditions were negated (that is, when it was assessed whether the *absence* of certain conditions was necessary for the electoral success of populist parties). As the scores show, there is no perfect subset relationship between one of the conditions and the outcome, as all consistency values are below 1. With a very high score of 0.93, however, the supply of credible populist parties (CREDIB) is considered a necessary condition for the presence of populist party success. The measure for the coverage of necessary conditions, yielding a value of 0.815, provides a first indication that CREDIB can be also seen as a *relevant* necessary condition.[8]

The relationship between the supply of credible populist parties and populist party electoral performance is portrayed in Figure 3.1. Neither the POPSUC set (Y) nor the CREDIB set (X) is skewed towards high membership, which is another indication that CREDIB is not a trivial necessary condition (see Schneider and Wagemann 2012: 233–237).

The fact that the consistency score is below 1 is due to the cases in which populist parties have been successful, even though these parties have not always been optimally credible. These are the cases above the diagonal line in Figure 3.1; Bulgaria, for instance, has a CREDIB score of 0.67 and a POPSUC score of 1. It must be borne in mind, however, that the measurement of the populist parties' credibility was relatively crude, providing reason to be relatively relaxed about these 'outliers'.

I also assessed whether there were any conditions necessary for the *absence* of populist party success. This analysis did not produce consistency values close to 1. Thus, while the supply of credible populist parties can be considered as a necessary condition for the electoral success of populist parties, it cannot be concluded that the absence of credible populist parties is a necessary condition for the electoral failure of populist parties (the related consistency score was 0.80). In some countries, as we will see, populist parties have been reasonably credible, yet also reasonably unsuccessful.

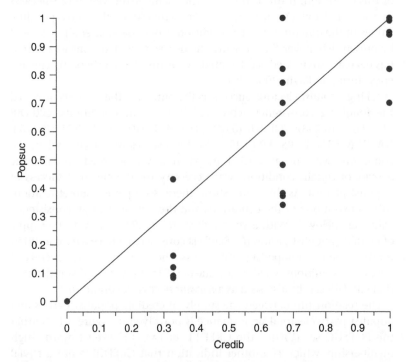

Figure 3.1 Plot of cases' membership in POPSUC against their membership in CREDIB

Assessment of sufficiency: Three general conditions

The next objective in the analysis is to determine which (combinations of) conditions are sufficient for the presence (or absence) of populist electoral success. This again involves a search for subset relationships, yet, contrary to the consistency test for necessary conditions, the consistency test for sufficient causal configurations assesses whether a given configuration (that is, a combination of conditions) is a subset of the outcome.[9] When a sufficient configuration is present, the outcome must also be present. Accordingly, the membership values of the cases in the given configuration (X) need to be equal to or lower than the corresponding values in the outcome (Y).

To assess the sufficiency of configurations, the first step is to calculate the membership of each case in these configurations. By means of the data calibration process outlined in the first part of this chapter, each case has previously received a fuzzy set membership score between 0 and 1 in each of the conditions. Cases can also be given a score in each of the possible *combinations* of conditions (the configurations). The membership of a case in a particular configuration is determined by taking the lowest membership score across the individual component conditions, following a 'weakest link reasoning' (see Ragin 2009: 96).[10] Following this procedure, each case has a fuzzy set membership score of more than 0.5 in one ideal typical configuration only (see for instance Schneider and Wagemann 2012, Chapter 4). Each case, in other words, is best characterised by one combination of dichotomously expressed conditions. Table 3.3 presents a 'truth table', which provides an overview of all the possible configurations when the three general conditions (PR, UNRESP and CREDIB) are included in the analysis. The last two columns show how many and which cases have a membership score of more than 0.5 in a given configuration.

Based on the fuzzy set scores of the cases, the consistency column of Table 3.3 reports to what extent a subset relationship has been approximated (that is, whether the given configuration is a subset of the outcome variable). In other words, the consistency scores indicate whether the configuration is sufficient for the outcome (in this case, populist electoral success). For this analysis, it is determined that configurations with a consistency value of higher than 0.81 are considered sufficient for the populist success outcome. Since there is a large gap between the fourth and fifth truth table rows in terms of consistency values, it makes sense empirically to include the configurations in the first four rows among the configurations leading to a positive outcome (see Schneider and Wagemann 2012: 127–129). Furthermore, as the

Table 3.3 Truth Table

Conditions				Outcome		
PR	UNRESP	CREDIB	POPSUC	Consistency	N	Cases
0	1	1	1	0.936728	4	GRE; HUN; ITA; LIT
0	0	1	1	0.935421	1	FRA
1	1	1	1	0.897849	3	BUL; POL; ROM
1	0	1	1	0.814781	11	AUS; BEL; DEN; FIN; GER; IRE; LUX; NET; NOR; SLK; SWI
0	1	0	0	0.620301	2	CRO; UK
1	1	0	0	0.513708	4	CZR; EST; LAT; POR
1	0	0	0	0.419903	6	CYP; ICE; MAL; SLV; SPA; SWE
0	0	0	–		0	

operationalisation of the CREDIB condition has been relatively rough, a somewhat 'lenient' threshold seems appropriate. Accordingly, a value of 1 in the POPSUC outcome is allocated to the first four configurations, which cover 19 out of the 31 cases. The configurations that yield lower consistency scores, or which lack empirical referents (see final row), are not considered sufficient for populist electoral success.

After the fuzzy set truth table has been created and the consistency threshold set, a Boolean minimisation process is carried out to discard conditions in a particular configuration that are irrelevant for the outcome. This leads to minimised configurations or 'prime implicants'. A typical analysis by means of the FSQCA software produces three different results: a complex, a parsimonious and an intermediate solution. Regarding the latter two solutions, simplifying assumptions have been made about the configurations without empirical referents (the logical remainders). For a parsimonious solution, a hypothetical outcome is allocated to the configurations without empirical referents if this leads to a more parsimonious solution. For the intermediate solution, only theoretically plausible simplifying assumptions are made.[11]

When the analysis is performed with only the PR, UNRESP and CREDIB conditions, all three solutions showed the same results: the supply of credible populist parties alone is a sufficient condition for the electoral success of populist parties. This outcome can be described in the following formula: CREDIB → POPSUC. The solution has a consistency value of 0.815, however, indicating that some cases have a higher score in the credibility condition than in the populist electoral success outcome. Five cases with a CREDIB score of 0.67, denoting a reasonable supply of credible populist parties, even have a value lower than 0.5 in the outcome: France (0.48), Finland (0.37), Germany (0.38), Ireland (0.34) and Luxembourg (0.37). Strictly speaking, these cases are 'true logically contradictory cases', for they violate the notion that CREDIB alone is a sufficient condition for populist success (see Schneider and Wagemann 2012: 123–129). These cases are also important in explaining why the lack of credible populist parties did not emerge as a necessary condition for the failure of populist parties.

It is, nevertheless, clear that the credibility of populist parties comes out as a remarkably dominant condition. This is also suggested by the coverage value, which indicates how much of the outcome is covered by the paths in the solution (in this case, the single condition CREDIB only).[12] With a value of 0.931, the 'empirical relevance' of this solution can also be deemed high (see Ragin 2006). There is some reason to be sceptical about these results. As mentioned before, it is difficult to provide a precise quantitative measurement of electoral credibility across a relatively large amount of cases. There is a risk, moreover, that a post-hoc assessment of electoral credibility is influenced by the electoral results of a given party, effectively leading to a tautological argument. Even then, the finding that the electoral credibility of populist parties is crucial to their performance is plausible, and it emphasises the need for comparative studies to take this factor into account.

The first analysis shows that the two other conditions (PR and UNRESP) do not appear in a sufficient configuration for populist party success. As regards the electoral system condition, this should not come as a great surprise, taking into consideration that populist parties in Greece, Hungary, Italy and Lithuania have performed well despite relatively disproportional systems. It should be noted, however, that the disproportionality of the electoral systems in Italy and Hungary was actually likely to benefit the large populist parties in these two countries (Berlusconi's Forza Italia and PdL, and FIDESZ, respectively). Furthermore, the electoral systems in the four said countries are still much more proportional than systems with only single-member constituencies. Then again, the case of the French Front National shows that it is possible for an outsider to win a substantial amount of votes under a very disproportional electoral system, indicating that the influence of the electoral system should not be overestimated.

Following the results, established parties' unresponsiveness is also not a key ingredient for the success of populist parties. As could be seen in

Table 3.3, 12 countries have a relatively low score in this condition, but nevertheless saw populist parties doing at least reasonably well. It must be borne in mind that the indicators used for this condition dealt with people's general perceptions of the state of democracy and satisfaction with political actors, and not directly with established parties' perceived responsiveness with regard to specific issues. This is an important point, which will be further discussed below. It is, nevertheless, interesting to see that populist parties can be successful in countries, such as Denmark, Norway and Switzerland, where general political satisfaction levels are very high.

The analysis dealing with the *failure* of populist parties followed the same procedure with a consistency threshold of 0.84. The complex solution shows that populist parties have been unsuccessful in countries that combine a lack of credible populist parties with either a proportional electoral system or an unresponsive political establishment (thus, ~CREDIB*(PR+UNRESP) → ~POPSUC).[13] The results point out that populist party success is not guaranteed, even if a proportional electoral system is applied and even if there is widespread dissatisfaction with political developments and actors. It makes little theoretical sense, however, to assume that these two conditions have also been the *cause* of populist party failure. The more parsimonious solutions actually indicate that the lack of credible populist parties alone is sufficient for the electoral failure of populist parties (consistency: 0.923810; coverage: 0.797092).

Assessment of sufficiency: Four themes

Having considered the more general conditions related to electoral institutions and the agency of both established and populist parties, the next part of the analysis considers whether the relative importance of four specific themes (culture and ethnicity; economic hardship; European integration; and corruption) relates to the performance of populist parties across Europe. When a sufficiency analysis is run with just these four contextual conditions, no consistent solutions are found. Since the previous analysis has pointed out that the supply of credible populist parties is a necessary condition for populist success, this is no great surprise. This condition is therefore added to the four specific contextual themes and the analysis is rerun with a consistency threshold of 0.83 (based on the consistency values in the truth table). Proceeding as such leads to parsimonious and intermediate solutions which are equal to the ones in the previous analysis: the supply of credible populist parties alone is a sufficient condition for populist success. It is worthwhile, however, to take a closer look at the complex solution, which consists of the four paths depicted in Table 3.4.[14] Without having made

Table 3.4 Paths implying POPSUC (period: 2000–2013)

	CREDIB*			
	NATIV* ~ECOHARD* EURSCEP* CORRUP +	ECOHARD* ~EURSCEP* CORRUP +	~NATIV* ~EURSCEP +	~NATIV* ~CORRUP
Consistency	0.962428	0.955284	0.847926	0.778330
Raw Coverage	0.219368	0.464427	0.484848	0.515810
Unique Coverage	0.011199	0.108037	0.019763	0.183794
Covered cases*	Hun (0.52, 1.00)	Bul (0.67, 1.00); Gre (0.67, 0.82); Ita (0.52, 1.00); Lit (0.67, 0.82); Pol (0.87, 1.00); Slk (0.89, 0.99)	Bel (0.62, 0.77); Lit (0.56, 0.82); Net (0.67, 0.59); Pol (0.65, 1.00); Rom (0.62, 0.70)	Aus (0.57, 0.95); Bel (0.62, 0.77); Den (0.90, 0.70); Nor (0.91, 0.94); Net (0.67, 0.59); Swi (0.92, 1.00)
True logically contradictory cases**	–	–	Ger (0.65, 0.38); Ire (0.60, 0.34); Lux (0.67, 0.37)	Fin (0.67, 0.37); Fra (0.63, 0.48); Ger (0.67, 0.38); Ire (0.60, 0.34); Lux (0.67, 0.37)
Solution Cons.	0.834887			
Solution Cov.	0.826087			

*Cases with membership in configuration and outcome > 0.5. The values correspond to the cases' membership scores in the configuration and outcome, respectively.

**Cases with membership in configuration > 0.5 and outcome < 0.5.

any assumptions about logical remainders, the table shows the combinations of conditions that were present in the countries where populist parties have been (reasonably) successful.

The results show that the supply of credible populist parties is a condition present in all paths, but it is more daunting to interpret meaningfully the remaining parts of the four configurations. The first path, combining the supply of credible populist parties with high levels of nativist and Eurosceptic sentiments, an absence of economic hardship and high levels of perceived corruption, covers only the case of Hungary (although its membership in the configuration (0.52) is relatively low). Six cases are covered by the second path combining CREDIB with economic hardship, low levels of Euroscepticism and high levels of perceived corruption (Slovakia, Poland, Bulgaria, Lithuania, Greece and Italy). It makes sense that credible populist parties have been successful in certain Eastern European and Mediterranean countries with – at least up until the crisis – generally Europhile populations, which were further characterised by high levels of unemployment and a pervasive air of corruption. The latter two paths, covering also more prosperous Western European countries (including the five 'borderline cases'), show that credible populist parties can perform well in contexts with low levels of nativist sentiments, combined with either low levels of Euroscepticism or low levels of perceived corruption. Although this finding is interesting, the latter two paths do not truly provide a theoretically plausible explanation as to why populist parties in these countries have been successful. If, for instance, there is a general sense in a country that corruption levels are low and that people from other cultures cause little harm, why would populist parties still receive substantial support?

One reason could be that different social issues have played a role in the success of these parties. Yet it should also be considered that indicators reflecting the opinion of a population at large are insensitive to the possibility that there is a small but electorally relevant section of the electorate that is concerned about a particular issue. As the next chapter will actually discuss, irrespective of the country's low scores in the UNRESP and NATIV conditions, the breakthrough of populist parties in the Netherlands can largely be explained by considering the dissatisfaction among certain voters with the established parties' handling of issues related to immigration and multiculturalism. A lesson from this QCA is, then, that neither the more general political climate, nor dominant attitudes concerning certain issues, are always crucial in explaining the electoral success of populist parties.

Concerning the analysis of the electoral failure of populist parties (ran with a consistency threshold of 0.82), it is again worthwhile to discuss the complex solution, as it points out that contextual factors are also not always crucial in explaining the *absence* of populist party success (see Table 3.5). For reasons of space, I will not discuss the outcomes in detail, but it is clear that the lack of credible populist parties was in most cases a key ingredient for the failure of populist parties.[15] As the second and fourth causal paths further indicate, countries marked by high levels of perceived corruption, combined with either high levels of nativism or economic hardship, do not necessarily see strong populist parties. It is worth highlighting that this does not mean that these themes were also absent from the political debate in these countries. As shown in the previous chapter, for instance, countries such as Estonia and Latvia have seen (multiple) parties campaigning on the basis of an anti-corruption platform. Themes such as corruption are thus not necessarily relevant to populist parties only, as will be discussed further in the concluding section.

Populist party performance in the last elections

The previous analyses have suggested that the performance of populist parties is largely a matter of their own agency, more so than structural or contextual factors. In this section I discuss whether different patterns can be observed if only the most recent, crisis-affected elections are considered in the analysis.[16] The same procedures are followed as in the analyses above, and I will only touch on findings that genuinely differ from those presented before. Most of the results are actually very similar. Unsurprisingly, the supply of credible populist parties has also been of crucial importance in the latest national election in each country. The presence of credible populist parties again turns out as a necessary condition for populist party success (consistency: 0.966; coverage: 0.829), while the absence of credible populist parties cannot be considered a necessary condition for populist party failure (consistency score: 0.786). The analyses of sufficiency that include only the three more general conditions (PR, UNRESP and CREDIB) also yielded virtually the same results.

When the four more specific themes are entered into the analysis together with the CREDIB condition, the complex solution related to the presence of populist electoral success does show some differences. The third and fourth paths in Table 3.6 have also appeared in the previous analysis (see Table 3.4), but paths one and two are different. These paths combine a supply of credible populist parties and high

Table 3.5 Paths implying ~POPSUC (period: 2000–2013)

	~CREDIB*			
	~ECOHARD* EURSCEP* ~CORRUP +	NATIV* CORRUP +	~NATIV* ECOHARD* ~EURSCEP +	ECOHARD* CORRUP +
Consistency	0.953287	0.866496	0.865832	0.863836
Raw Coverage	0.348293	0.426675	0.305942	0.372946
Unique Coverage	0.127686	0.070796	0.016435	0.022124
Covered cases*	Ice (0.67, 0.92); Swe (0.67, 0.88); UK (0.82, 1.00)	Cyp (0.60, 1.00); Cro (0.57, 0.92); Czr (0.67, 0.57); Est (0.57, 1.00); Mal (0.64, 1.00); Slv (0.60, 0.84)	Por (0.52, 1.00); Spa (0.68, 1.00)	Cro (0.67, 0.92); Est (0.57, 1.00); Lat (0.67, 0.91); Por (0.55, 1.00)
True logically contradictory cases**	–	–	–	–
Solution Cons.	0.905282			
Solution Cov.	0.628319			

*Cases with membership in configuration and outcome > 0.5. The values correspond to the cases' membership scores in the configuration and outcome, respectively.

**Cases with membership in configuration > 0.5 and outcome < 0.5.

Table 3.6 Paths implying POPSUC (last election)

	CREDIB*			
	NATIV* EURSCEP* CORRUP +	ECOHARD* CORRUP +	~NATIV* ~EURSCEP +	~NATIV* ~CORRUP
Consistency	0.908116	0.881670	0.881333	0.835176
Raw Coverage	0.369701	0.473815	0.412095	0.518080
Unique Coverage	0.026808	0.081671	0.018703	0.176434
Covered cases*	Czr (0.75, 0.99); Gre (0.82, 1.00); Hun (0.55, 1.00); Ita (0.51, 1.00)	Bul (0.67, 1.00); Gre (0.94, 1.00); Hun (0.80, 1.00); Ita (0.76, 1.00); Pol (0.67, 1.00); Slk (0.86, 0.77)	Bel (0.62, 0.54); Net (0.67, 0.51); Pol (0.65, 1.00); Rom (0.62, 0.84)	Aus (0.57, 0.99); Bel (0.62, 0.54); Den (0.90, 0.67); Fin (0.67, 0.94); Fra (0.65, 0.75); Net (0.67, 0.51); Nor (0.90, 0.87); Swi (0.92, 1.00)
True logically contradictory cases**	Cro (0.57, 0.35)	Cro (0.67, 0.35); Lit (0.67, 0.31)	Ire (0.60, 0.49); Lux (0.62, 0.27)	Ger (0.67, 0.40); Ire (0.60, 0.49); Lux (0.67, 0.27)
Solution Cons.		0.848523		
Solution Cov.		0.841646		

*Cases with membership in configuration and outcome > 0.5. The values correspond to the cases' membership scores in the configuration and outcome, respectively.

**Cases with membership in configuration > 0.5 and outcome < 0.5.

levels of perceived corruption, either with high levels of nativism and Euroscepticism, or with economic hardship. Three cases (Greece, Hungary and Italy) are covered by both paths. The paths differ from the first analysis as the ~ECOHARD condition has vanished from the first path – which now also covers more cases – and the ~EURSCEP condition from the second path. Both changes reflect the higher scores of certain countries in ECOHARD and EURSCEP in more recent years. This is a likely consequence of the financial and economic crisis that hit several European countries in particular, and which also fuelled Eurosceptic sentiments.

It is important to note that one must be careful in assuming that the presence of certain conditions in a given path is always meaningful in explaining the performance of individual populist parties. The Italian Five Star Movement of Beppe Grillo, for instance, has not been known for tapping into nativist sentiments; the second path may, therefore, be more relevant to this party's performance. Nevertheless, the first and second configurations provide the basis for a plausible account as to why populist parties in the associated countries have been successful. The remaining two paths, however, again show that, when the environment is apparently unfavourable to the rise of populism, populist parties can still be (very) successful. The reverse argument can also be made concerning the failure of populist parties. The analysis with ~POPSUC as outcome again indicates that populist party success was absent in some cases, despite an ostensibly favourable opportunity structure.[17] The crisis-affected countries Spain and Portugal provide good examples. The absence of credible populist contenders again appears to be one key reason for this.

Conclusion

Several main observations can be made on the basis of the analyses presented in this chapter. For one, the results suggest that the credibility of populist parties themselves is of vital importance to their electoral performance. The results suggested that the supply of credible populist contenders is a necessary, and almost sufficient, condition for the electoral success of populist parties. The lack of credible populist parties has in most cases also been crucial in explaining the electoral failure of such parties. There is reason to treat these findings with some caution. As discussed, the measurement of electoral credibility has been unavoidably rough, and there was a danger of tautological reasoning when post-hoc assessments of parties' credibility were made ('successful

populist parties must have been credible', and *vice versa*). Still, the evaluation of credibility has been performed with care, and the results of the fsQCA are likely to demonstrate the vital importance of this condition for the performance of populist parties.
The results also indicated that other (contextual) factors had far less explanatory power. Populist parties have performed well under proportional, but also under more disproportional, electoral systems (examples include Hungary, Italy, Greece and, above all, France). This is not to deny that a disproportional electoral system can pose a hurdle for small populist parties, but electoral rules did not turn out to be a key ingredient for the success or failure of populist parties (as a necessary condition or part of a sufficient configuration). The condition related to the (un)responsiveness of established parties was also absent in the solutions. Populist parties have done well in low-trust countries such as Bulgaria, Poland and Romania, but also in countries such as Denmark, the Netherlands, Norway and Switzerland, where people have been relatively satisfied with the way democracy works and where trust in parliament and political parties has been relatively high. In order to explain the performance of populist parties in these latter countries, it seems necessary to assess the responsiveness of established parties more precisely, by looking more specifically at the salience of individual societal issues, and the way established parties were perceived to handle them.

Several such issues were expected to be particularly relevant for populist parties, and these are issues related to the four themes identified: culture and ethnicity; economic hardship; European integration; and corruption. Some discovered paths provided a plausible clue as to why populist parties have been successful in certain (crisis-stricken) countries. In the analysis of populist success in the latest election, the results showed paths combining a supply of credible populist parties and high levels of perceived corruption with either economic hardship, or high degrees of nativist sentiments and Euroscepticism. At the same time, however, the analyses showed that the relevance of the four themes could not always be easily related to populist party performance. For instance, rather counterintuitively, successful populist parties were found in contexts where, broadly speaking, low levels of nativism were combined with a relatively Europhile population or low levels of perceived corruption. It was interesting to observe that populist parties can do well under apparently unfavourable conditions, but these results also indicate that a more precise analysis is required to explain what *did* cause populist electoral success in these countries.

The same goes for explaining the electoral failure of populist parties, beyond an assessment of their own credibility. In some countries the environment for populism seemed favourable, for instance due to high levels of unemployment and perceived corruption, but these countries nevertheless did not see the breakthrough of populist parties. Besides the failure of populist parties to mobilise on the basis of a credible platform and organisation, this is likely to relate to the actions of competitors who were able to seize the ownership of electorally salient themes. Essentially non-populist outsiders can also benefit from a mood of dissatisfaction with established parties. The logic behind the performance of populist parties is not necessarily that different compared with parties such as the anti-corruption challengers that have appeared in many post-communist countries (see Hanley and Sikk 2014). As has been discussed in Chapter 2, particularly in countries in Central and Eastern Europe, it is often difficult to distinguish clearly between populist and non-populist parties in the first place. Mainstream parties, at the same time, may also be able to win back the confidence of voters by stealing the thunder of populist challengers (see Bale 2003: Meguid 2008).

Besides looking at contextual factors or widely held opinions in society, it thus seems necessary to consider the specific party political context in which populist parties operate, in order to make sense of their electoral performance. This is what I will do in the next three chapters, in which I discuss the success and failure of populist parties in the Netherlands, Poland and the United Kingdom. After discussing the, sometimes thorny, issue of populist party identification, the chapters concentrate more specifically on the responsiveness of established parties with regard to salient issues. As will become clear, these issues were often related to the four 'populist themes' that were included in this analysis, even though not all themes were relevant in all three cases. The electoral credibility of the populist parties will also be studied in more detail, in order to assess whether this factor is indeed as important as the QCA suggested.

4
Populist Parties in the Netherlands

The first case study presented in this book covers the Netherlands. This chapter seeks to identify the populist parties that have appeared in contemporary Dutch politics, to describe their ideological characteristics and to explain their electoral performance on the basis of the explanatory model outlined in Chapter 1. I will thus discuss the role of the electoral system, the responsiveness of established parties with regard to the issues central to the appeal of the populist challengers, and the electoral credibility of the populist parties themselves. The four themes central to the appeal of many populist parties (culture and ethnicity; economic hardship; European integration; and corruption) are discussed insofar as they have been relevant to the electoral competition between the populist parties and their mainstream competitors.

While Dutch populist parties never achieved much electoral success in the decades after the Second World War, this changed in more recent years. Two populist parties in particular obtained a considerable share of the vote: the List Pim Fortuyn (*Lijst Pim Fortuyn*, LPF) in 2002, and the Freedom Party (*Partij voor de Vrijheid*, PVV) from 2006 onwards. Various other populist parties have made less successful attempts. The Netherlands thus presents itself as a case in which successful and unsuccessful manifestations of populism can be compared, providing an ideal 'laboratory environment' for learning about the electoral performance of populist parties in general.

As I will argue in this chapter, the electoral success of the Dutch populist parties has been facilitated by the proportionality of the Dutch electoral system, which has been conducive to the breakthrough of small parties competing for the support of a largely dealigned and volatile electorate. To understand the actual breakthrough of populist parties and their subsequent success or failure to survive, the agency of political actors must also be considered. This relates, in the first place, to the responsiveness of established political parties. As will be shown, by the turn of the 21st century none of the mainstream parties were sufficiently responsive to concerns related to immigration and cultural integration of, most notably, the Muslim minority population. This provided a favourable opportunity structure for Dutch populist parties that placed these issues at the core of their appeal. In addition, the credibility of the populist parties themselves has proven crucial to their breakthrough and electoral persistence. Although Pim Fortuyn was able to generate ample media attention and support for his political project, his party soon lost credibility after Fortuyn was assassinated and no new leader with the same magnetism stood up. The LPF, furthermore, fell victim to numerous internal struggles. Geert Wilders has since emerged as the most able populist radical right politician representing culturally conservative, and later also more explicit welfare protectionist and Euroreject, opinions. Despite the fact that his PVV also suffered from several defections, it was not plagued by the organisational chaos that had marked the party of the late Fortuyn.

The following section provides an overview of the populist parties that have appeared on the Dutch political scene and discusses in particular the two most notable cases: the LPF and the PVV. The remainder of the chapter focuses on the question of how the electoral performance of populist parties in the Netherlands can be explained. The concluding section summarises the findings and draws implications from the Dutch case for the broader study.

Identifying the populist parties in the Netherlands[1]

In the past, several new parties with populist characteristics entered the Dutch Lower House (*Tweede Kamer*) (see Lucardie and Voerman 2012). For a long time these parties remained rather marginal. The Farmers' Party (*Boerenpartij*) entered parliament in 1963, but would never receive more than 4.8 per cent of the vote (in 1967) and disappeared from the *Tweede Kamer* in 1981. The ethno-nationalist parties led by Hans Janmaat in the 1980s and 1990s (the Centre Party, *Centrumpartij* (CP), and Centre Democrats, *Centrumdemocraten* (CD)) only achieved limited and short-lived electoral success.

A party that did see its support levels increase considerably in later years was the radical left Socialist Party (*Socialistische Partij*, SP), which entered parliament in 1994 with 1.3 per cent of the vote. In the 1990s the party, which had a Maoist past, could be described as a 'populist socialist' party (see March 2011: 128–133), but the party softened its populist anti-establishment rhetoric over the years. This is illustrated by the content analysis performed by De Lange and Rooduijn (2011: 324); in 1994 anti-elite references were found in 17 per cent of the SP's election manifesto paragraphs, but this percentage dropped to a mere 1.5 per cent in 2006 – the year in which the SP secured its largest victory in parliamentary elections, with a vote share of 16.6 per cent. There is, thus, a case for classifying the SP as an 'ordinary' social-democratic party in more recent years (Voerman and Lucardie 2007).[2]

Sporadic populist anti-establishment rhetoric could, nevertheless, still be found in the discourse of SP politicians and in the party's manifestos (Lucardie and Voerman 2012: 64–69). The financial and economic crisis at the end of the 2000s actually appeared to serve as a temporary catalyst for the SP's use of populist rhetoric. The SP, for example, held the 'political and economic elites' responsible for the crisis at the time of the 2010 parliamentary election (SP 2010: 5). A content analysis by Matthijs Rooduijn (2014b), however, showed that, after a surge in 2010, the degree of populist statements in SP programmes declined again in 2012. All in all, the contemporary SP is a party which may portray itself as an 'ordinary people's party', but also one for which populism has become more of an episodic rhetorical element, rather than an ideological core attribute. Although the SP will not be considered as a genuine populist party after the 1990s, the party's electoral credibility and the motivations of its voters will briefly be discussed later in the chapter. The main focus will be on the two populist parties that were most successful electorally: the LPF – even though its success did not last long – and Geert Wilders' PVV.

The rise and fall of the List Pim Fortuyn

Pim Fortuyn's rise came to symbolise the demise of the two 'Purple' coalition governments that had formed in 1994 and 1998. These coalitions consisted of the 'red' Labour Party (*Partij van de Arbeid*, PvdA), the 'blue' Liberal Party (*Volkspartij voor Vrijheid en Democratie*, VVD) and the smaller progressive liberal Democrats 66 (*Democraten 66*, D66). During this period, the Christian Democrats, since 1980 united in the Christian Democratic Appeal (*Christen Democratisch Appel*, CDA), were excluded from government for the first time since 1918.

After various failed attempts to build a political career, Pim Fortuyn, a provocative columnist and former sociology professor, became leader of the newly founded party 'Liveable Netherlands' (*Leefbaar Nederland*, LN) in November 2001. The party declared 'old politics' bankrupt and aimed to democratise the political order. In its manifesto for the parliamentary election of May 2002, LN claimed that politicians were busier with safeguarding their own positions than with realising their ideals (LN 2002: 2). The very short programme lacked much detail, but the party was clear about its desire to cut bureaucracy and to promote more decision-making at the local level (Lucardie and Voerman 2012: 81–82). The party's popularity increased steadily after Fortuyn became its leader. In February 2002, however, Fortuyn was expelled from the party following his controversial statements in a newspaper interview. The LN leader, most notably, called Islam a 'backward culture'. With only a few months to go to the parliamentary election in May, Fortuyn founded his own party: List Pim Fortuyn. The LPF could immediately count on substantial levels of support in the opinion polls, thereby eclipsing Fortuyn's old party LN.

There seems to be a broad consensus in the scholarly literature about describing Pim Fortuyn and his party as populist. This was also confirmed by the results from the expert survey conducted for this study; all eight scholars identified the LPF as a populist party (see Appendix E). Following Cas Mudde (2002b), Fortuyn could be classified as a populist, as he consistently criticised ' "the elite" for corrupting power and ignoring the "real problems" of "the people" '. Before entering the political stage, Fortuyn had in previous publications already criticised the 'political caste' for having lost touch with society (Lucardie and Voerman 2012: 106–108). In his book (and unofficial manifesto) 'The shambles of eight years Purple' from 2002, Fortuyn stated that '[t]he Netherlands should become a real lively democracy of and for the ordinary people, and depart from the elite party democracy we are currently acquainted with' (Fortuyn 2002: 186). The LPF's official election manifesto similarly argued that 'Purple' had left the Netherlands with a rigid and self-satisfied political culture of appointed executives lacking creative or learning capacities (LPF 2002: 1). According to Fortuyn, power had to be returned to the 'people in the country' (Lucardie 2008: 159). The number of managers and bureaucrats had to be reduced and responsibility would have to be returned to the 'real' experts: the nurses, teachers and police officers. The notion that the LPF was populist was actually shared by former LPF immigration minister Hilbrand Nawijn, who considered populism to be a positive rather than a pejorative term: 'one gets involved in politics for the people' (Interview, Zoetermeer, 8 September 2008).[3]

Apart from the party's populist features, the LPF's more substantive political programme was rather eclectic (Lucardie 2008). Fortuyn promoted a free-market economy, supported strict law and order measures, and stressed the need to cut red tape in the healthcare and education sectors. At the same time, his position on moral issues such as drugs and same-sex marriage was very liberal – in fact, Fortuyn was very open about his own homosexuality and promiscuous life style. Yet it was in his stance on immigration and cultural integration of minorities that Fortuyn attracted most controversy. According to the LPF manifesto, overcrowding in the Netherlands was causing growing societal tensions (LPF 2002: 5). It was, therefore, deemed necessary to resist immigration of more, often unemployed and unskilled, foreigners. The programme also spoke of problems caused by the social–cultural backwardness of large groups in society and related problems, such as criminality and discrimination against women – especially in fundamentalist Islamic circles.

Fortuyn sought to protect the Dutch way of life against foreign cultural influences that clashed with Dutch liberal Enlightenment values (Akkerman 2005). His ideology was at odds with the idea of a diverse multicultural society in which liberal principles were put at risk. People from other cultures were required to integrate into Dutch society and, in the words of Hilbrand Nawijn, the 'cuddle culture' (*knuffelcultuur*) as regards non-native people was to be dismissed (Interview, Zoetermeer, 8 September 2008). Fortuyn's programme thus provided an interesting mix of liberalism and illiberalism. At the same time, his project could also be perceived as 'conservative', in the sense that it emphasised the need to protect Dutch culture and identity, not in the last place from a process of 'Islamisation' (see Lucardie and Voerman 2012).

Fortuyn would not witness the results of the 2002 parliamentary election; on May 6 he was murdered by an environmental activist. The campaign was officially cancelled, but the election went on, and the remaining LPF members decided to participate. On 15 May the LPF won 17 per cent of the vote and 26 of the 150 seats in the Dutch parliament (see Table 4.1). This was an unprecedented result for a new party, the former 'record' for a newcomer being eight seats for DS '70 in 1971. The Purple coalition partners suffered an enormous defeat. After the election, the LPF joined a coalition government with the Christian Democrats and the Liberals, which would prove to be the shortest incumbent government in Dutch history. After 87 days the LPF's coalition partners brought it down after a period of severe LPF infighting, and a new parliamentary election was scheduled for January 2003. Under the leadership of Mat Herben, the LPF received 5.7 per cent of the vote and thus lost most of its previous support. At first sight, the results of the 2003 election

Table 4.1　Dutch parliamentary election results 1998–2012, in % of the vote

	1998	2002	2003	2006	2010	2012
Labour (PvdA)	29.0	15.1	27.3	21.2	19.6	24.9
Liberals (VVD)	24.7	15.4	17.9	14.6	20.5	26.6
Christian Democrats (CDA)	18.4	27.9	28.6	26.5	13.6	8.5
Democrats 66 (D66)	9.0	5.1	4.1	2.0	7.0	8.0
GreenLeft (GL)	7.3	7.0	5.1	4.6	6.7	2.3
Socialist Party (SP)	3.5	5.9	6.3	16.6	9.8	9.7
Christian Union (CU)	3.2	2.5	2.1	4.0	3.2	3.1
List Pim Fortuyn (LPF)		17.0	5.7	0.2		
Liveable NL (LN)		1.6	0.4			
Freedom Party (PVV)				5.9	15.5	10.1
Others	4.9	2.5	2.5	4.4	4.1	6.8

Note: The percentage for the CU in 1998 is the combined percentage of the parties that eventually merged into the CU. Data: Nordsieck (2013).

seemed to indicate a return to 'old' politics; in particular the PvdA recovered quite well from its electoral knockback in 2002, and no new parties entered parliament.

The rise of Geert Wilders

The subsequent parliamentary election of 2006 marked the entrance of another, more durable, populist party; the PVV of Geert Wilders received 5.9 per cent of the vote. Previously, as an MP for the Liberal Party, Wilders had become increasingly critical of Islam, and he eventually broke with his party in September 2004 after a conflict over the issue of Turkish EU membership – Wilders was very much against Turkish accession (Lucardie and Voerman 2012: 153–154). The politician refused to give up his seat in parliament and formed his own one-man fraction 'Group Wilders'. In February 2006 Wilders founded his Freedom Party (literally: 'Party for Freedom', PVV).

Wilders appealed to the 'ordinary people' even more explicitly than Fortuyn, and shared the latter's hostility towards the political elite. The PVV can, therefore, clearly be classified as a populist party. In his 'declaration of independence', written after his departure from the Liberals, Wilders (2005: 1) spoke of a 'range of interlinked crises flowing from the incompetence of the political elite in Brussels and The Hague'.[4] Wilders (2005: 2) further declared that he did not want the Netherlands 'to be hijacked by an elite of cowardly and frightened people (from whichever party) any longer', and that he intended 'to return this country to its citizens'. Following Wilders (2005: 16), 'politicians should no longer be deaf to the problems troubling ordinary people in every-day life'. With this declaration Wilders set the tone for later statements and PVV party documents, which were all characterised by a frequent use of typical populist rhetoric.

Wilders' positions on substantive issues were initially similar to Fortuyn's. In his 'declaration of independence' Wilders spoke negatively about the size of the public sector, overly generous subsidies and welfare entitlements, and smothering bureaucracy. Compared with Fortuyn, however, Wilders adhered to a more outspoken neo-conservative ideology, and became a more radical critic of Islam in particular (Vossen 2011).[5] In 2008 Wilders brought out the controversial short anti-Islam film 'Fitna', and by the time of the 2010 parliamentary election the PVV had become more strongly nationalistic, and its manifesto more outspokenly hostile to Islam (Lucardie and Voerman 2012: 174). The document nevertheless stressed that the PVV was not a single-issue party; 'Islamisation' was supposedly linked to a range of other social issues: '[e]conomically it is a disaster, it damages the quality of our education, it increases insecurity on the streets, causes an exodus out of our cities, drives out Jews and gay people, and flushes the century-long emancipation of women down the toilet' (PVV 2010: 6).

Even though Wilders, like Fortuyn, presented himself as a defender of personal liberty and women and gay rights, these issues were mainly discussed as part of Wilders' anti-Islam discourse. In its manifestos, the PVV actually remained silent about moral–cultural issues such as euthanasia and abortion. The documents, furthermore, contained clear elements of cultural conservatism (see Vossen 2011); Wilders repeatedly blamed the progressive (left-wing) elites for undermining traditional norms and values and for their lack of patriotism. The 2010 PVV manifesto, for instance, argued that the 'culture of the sixties' had to be abandoned, and that children at school had to be taught a 'canon of Dutch history' with a particular emphasis on the heroic elements of the Dutch past (PVV 2010: 33).

Although Wilders predominantly agitated against the 'left-wing' elites and their expensive 'left-wing hobbies' (such as development aid), the term 'left' was primarily given a cultural interpretation. The social–economic programme of the PVV in 2010 was actually eclectic and included various left-wing measures. Wilders had always been against raising the pension age, but previously favoured a small state and a flexible labour market (Wilders 2005; PVV 2006). In 2010, however, the PVV called for the preservation of the welfare state and opposed easing the rules for laying off employees, amending unemployment benefits and a 'marketisation' of the healthcare sector. With regard to certain policy domains, Wilders had thus shifted significantly to the socio-economic left. At the same time, the PVV still favoured typical *laissez faire* policies such as tax cuts and deregulation.

Wilders' party had won no less than 17 per cent of the vote in the European Parliament (EP) election of 2009, and the parliamentary election results of June 2010 confirmed that Geert Wilders had built up a considerable support base. With 15.5 per cent of the vote, the PVV came close to the result of the LPF in 2002, and became the third largest party in parliament. Wilders eventually signed an agreement to support the minority coalition between the Liberals and the Christian Democrats, in exchange for the implementation of some of the PVV's key policies (including stricter immigration rules). This minority cabinet – an unusual phenomenon in Dutch parliamentary history – was installed in October 2010. It would not last longer than April 2012, when Wilders refused to sign up to new austerity measures – drafted in response to the economic crisis – and withdrew his support.

Immediately after the government's breakup, which came at the height of the Eurozone crisis, Wilders vowed that 'Europe' would be the central theme of the campaign for the new election (which would be held on 12 September 2012). The PVV, indeed, paid attention to the EU issue as never before (see Van Kessel and Hollander 2012). The manifesto, tellingly titled '*Their* Brussels, *our* Netherlands', spoke derogatively of 'the blind inhabitants of the ivory towers in Brussels', 'unelected multi-culti Eurocrats' and the 'holy Great-European project' (PVV 2012: 11–12). National-level politicians, in turn, were blamed for their submissive compliance with the 'dictates from Brussels', for surrendering sovereignty to 'Europe', and for wasting taxpayers' money on supporting corrupt countries such as Greece and Romania at a time of economic hardship at home. Although the PVV had always been Eurosceptic, Wilders' anti-EU rhetoric clearly intensified, and he now went so far as to support a Dutch withdrawal from the EU.

Despite another forceful campaign, the PVV suffered a substantial loss in the parliamentary election of September 2012. The PVV received 10.1 per cent of the vote, but still remained the third largest party in parliament (at par with the SP). The PVV returned to its previous role as full-fledged opposition party. After having campaigned with an equally strong Euroreject message, the PVV received 13.2 per cent of the vote in the EP election of 22 May 2014, and also finished third.

The remainder of this chapter focuses on explaining the lasting electoral appeal of the PVV, as well as the electoral performance of the LPF and less successful populist parties. It will do so by considering three previously introduced factors in particular: the electoral system, the responsiveness of established parties, and the supply of credible populist parties.

Explaining the electoral performance of Dutch populist parties

Electoral system

The first condition in the explanatory model presented in Chapter 1 relates to the electoral system used in parliamentary elections. The Dutch electoral system has, in theory, always been very open to new political parties due to its extreme proportionality. It lacks artificial thresholds, and there is effectively only one electoral district (i.e. the Netherlands as a whole). As a consequence, parties are required to win a mere 0.67 per cent of the vote for a seat in the Dutch parliament. The electoral system, which has remained largely unchanged since 1918, was originally geared at securing proportional representation for each of the social groups that made up Dutch society (see Andeweg and Irwin 2009). The major Dutch parties and the most significant religious and social groups, or 'pillars', were closely aligned, and the electorate largely voted along traditional cleavage lines of religion and social class (Lijphart 1975). Thus, religious voters typically voted for one of the Christian democratic parties, while secular working-class voters opted for the Labour Party. The Liberal Party, finally, represented – albeit more loosely – the secular middle class. Due to this 'pillarised' structure of Dutch society, the Dutch party system was remarkably stable for a long time, in spite of the low institutional hurdles for new parties.

The dividing lines between the pillars gradually evaporated, partly due to the secularisation of society since the 1960s. People's sociological background still predicted voting behaviour reasonably well in the following decades (Andeweg and Irwin 2009: 112). By the turn of the 21st century, however, the explanatory power of social background had become very low; the Dutch electorate had become less constrained and more volatile in terms of its voting behaviour. Recent aggregate electoral volatility figures are among the highest in Western Europe (see Mair 2008).

Even though it would be inaccurate to claim that the Dutch electorate has become entirely footloose (see Van der Meer et al. 2012), the increased 'availability' of the Dutch electorate had serious consequences for the fortunes of small and newly formed parties. These previously used to remain marginal in terms of size and influence, if they managed to enter the Dutch parliament at all (Krouwel and Lucardie 2008; Van Kessel and Krouwel 2011). Now that the Dutch electorate had become much less loyal to established parties, the proportional electoral system genuinely worked in favour of new outsider parties. Institutional rules alone, however, cannot account for the (varying) levels of support for the Dutch populist parties. The next step, therefore, is to consider the role of the established mainstream parties.

Responsiveness of the established parties

For the QCA, presented in the previous chapter, the perceived responsiveness of the established parties was operationalised by considering levels of trust and satisfaction with regard to political institutions and democracy. As became clear from the data, public opinion in the Netherlands did not cause much reason for concern in this regard. Other studies have also demonstrated the high political trust levels in the Netherlands. On the basis of various survey data, Bovens and Wille (2011) found that towards the end of the 20th century two-thirds of the Dutch people thought that public authorities were performing well, and that 80 per cent were satisfied with the government and the way democracy was functioning. These were, in the words of the authors, figures of almost North Korean or Cuban proportions, and the Netherlands could be seen as a solid 'high-trust' country.

From 2002 onwards, however, trust in public authorities and government declined sharply. In 2004, about one-third of the respondents were satisfied with the functioning of public authorities, while just under half were satisfied with the performance of the government (Bovens and Wille 2011: 26). This decline in satisfaction more or less coincided with the rise of Pim Fortuyn in 2002, which could imply that the LPF benefited from a mood of discontent. In the following years, however, trust levels increased, almost reaching the levels recorded in the 1990s (Bovens and Wille 2011: 29). This trend seems at odds with the more recent popularity of Geert Wilders' PVV, which has so vigorously attacked established political institutions. Consistent with the lessons drawn from the QCA in the previous chapter, the survey findings indicate that general levels of satisfaction and trust in political institutions are not necessarily related to the electoral performance of populist parties.

Notwithstanding the high trust levels, some scholars already saw the potential for populist parties in the Netherlands before the rise of Fortuyn. Rudy Andeweg (2001: 123), for instance, argued that the Dutch consensus democracy was vulnerable to criticism from populist right actors, as consensus democracies were deemed 'strong on inclusiveness and weak on accountability'. Jacques Thomassen (2000) also asserted that established parties were prone to be challenged, in view of the convergence of the mainstream parties around the political centre (see also Pennings and Keman 2003).

Besides ideological convergence in general, the rise of Pim Fortuyn has often been related to political competition over more specific social issues, and the established parties' unresponsiveness with regard to the issues of immigration and multiculturalism in particular. Even if the Christian Democrats (CDA) and Liberals (VVD) took relatively restrictive positions with regard to these issues prior to the parliamentary election of 2002 (Van Heerden et al. 2013), none of the three traditionally dominant parties made an attempt to place the issues high on the political agenda. In the 1990s, VVD leader Bolkestein had been the most vocal mainstream politician voicing concern about a lack of social integration among ethnic minority groups (Prins 2002). After Hans Dijkstal replaced Bolkestein as VVD leader in 1998, however, the party became rather silent about the issue of multiculturalism. As a result, none of the established parties prioritised immigration and integration in their political programme in 2002.

This would not automatically have rendered the established parties unresponsive if these themes had been of little interest to voters. As Pellikaan et al. (2007) argued, however, the established parties failed to recognise that there were considerable concerns among the Dutch population about problems associated with immigration and the multicultural character of society. Fortuyn introduced a new 'cultural' line of political conflict which 'had been ignored by the political elite, but was highly salient to the electorate' (Pellikaan et al. 2007: 294). On the basis of Dutch Parliamentary Election Studies, Aarts and Thomassen (2008: 217) also found that issues related to minorities and refugees had become more important for many voters in the 1990s, while the issue of unemployment lost its salience. The LPF's victory in 2002 should thus not be interpreted as a 'shift to the right' of the Dutch electorate; Fortuyn tapped into already existing attitudes of many voters (see also Van Holsteyn et al. 2003). It can, then, be argued that the LPF was more responsive than any of the established parties to voters with clear reservations about immigration and multculturalism.

Other studies have, furthermore, indicated that LPF voters were also largely motivated by the party's substantive appeal, and by Fortuyn's stance on immigration and cultural integration in particular (Van der Brug 2003; Van Holsteyn and Irwin 2003). General economic issues such as unemployment, on the other hand, hardly played a role – which was unsurprising given the healthy state of the Dutch economy. In addition, Bélanger and Aarts (2006) showed that attitudes of discontent contributed to the electoral victory of the LPF (see Van der Brug 2003 for an alternative account). This suggests that support for populist parties denotes a typical mix between dissatisfaction with the established parties (regarding certain policy areas) and agreement with the policies of the populist party (see also Schumacher and Rooduijn 2013).

After Fortuyn's breakthrough, all three mainstream parties were, to different degrees, found to adopt more critical attitudes towards immigration and a more 'monoculturalist' position (Oosterwaal and Torenvlied 2010; Van Heerden et al. 2013). Apparently, however, their ideological reorientation did not hamper Geert Wilders' electoral successes in the years since 2006. The PVV's development as a key political actor in the Netherlands indicates that none of the mainstream parties succeeded in (re)gaining ownership of issues related to immigration and multiculturalism (Lucardie and Voerman 2012: 166). Clearly, the PVV was also the party that placed most emphasis on these matters and that took the most radical anti-immigration and monoculturalist positions. The mainstream parties needed to tread more carefully in this regard, in order not to lose the more moderate segment of their electorate (see Van Kersbergen and Krouwel 2008; Bale et al. 2012).

The electoral victory of the PVV in 2010, however, came after a campaign in which socio-economic issues had become more prominent again (van Kessel 2010). Even though these were not the signature issues of Wilders' party, the PVV ostensibly filled a gap that was left open by the established parties by adopting more left-wing socio-economic policies and sticking to its nativist principles. Van der Brug and Van Spanje (2009) showed that in Western Europe there are a substantial number of people who are left-leaning on socio-economic policies and right-leaning on questions related to immigration, but no parties representing both policy positions. Even if the Dutch mainstream parties have shifted away from unmistakable pro-multiculturalism positions, this has also been shown to be the case in the Netherlands (Van der Brug et al. 2011).

In order to assess whether the amendments in the socio-economic profile of the PVV have indeed contributed to its success, I considered data from the Dutch Parliamentary Election Study revealing the voting motivations of PVV voters (see Table 4.2). The answers to the open-ended question asking for the respondents' voting motivations were coded into several non-exclusive categories. A majority of PVV voters in 2006, 2010 and 2012 indicated that they voted for the party because they agreed

Table 4.2 Motivations of PVV voters (spontaneous response to open-ended question), in % of PVV-voting respondents

	2006 (n = 110)	2010 (n = 231)	2012 (n = 95)
Ideology	52.7	68.0	76.8
Social Policies	*1.8*	*16.9*	*9.5*
Immigration/Culture	*23.6*	*29.0*	*31.6*
Law and Order	*2.7*	*10.8*	*2.1*
European Integration	*0.0*	*0.4*	*16.8*
Protest and Change	16.4	21.2	8.4
Party Leader	25.5	16.9	17.9
Strategic/Negative Choice	4.5	6.5	2.1
Voting Advice Application	10.0	9.5	9.5
Vague/Other	13.6	2.6	6.3

Note: Own coding and calculations on the basis of DPES 2006 (CBS et al. 2007), 2010 (SKON et al. 2012) and 2012 (SKON et al. 2013). The categories are non-exclusive; a respondent's answer could relate to more than one issue category, and values therefore do not add up to 100 per cent. The categories in italics are subcategories of the overarching 'Ideology' category.

with its political programme or broader ideology – without necessarily mentioning specific policies. When respondents indicated they agreed with a particular policy or issue position, most PVV supporters across the three election years mentioned the party's position on immigration or the preservation of Dutch culture. Besides the programmatic features of the party, a substantial amount of respondents mentioned party leader Wilders among their motives – although more did so in 2006 than in 2010 and 2012. Many PVV voters also declared that they voted out of protest against the existing parties, or expressed a clear desire for 'change'.[6]

It is interesting to observe that, compared with the election year of 2006, clearly more PVV voters in 2010 mentioned the party's social policies (almost 17 per cent, compared with less than 2 per cent in 2006). These were not least policies related to care for the elderly and the preservation of the retirement age. This indicates that the adoption of welfare protectionist policies might indeed have paid off for Wilders, even though cultural issues remained the most important category.

In 2012, the theme of European integration was mentioned explicitly and spontaneously by 16.8 per cent of the PVV-voting respondents, whereas this issue was hardly salient for PVV voters in the previous elections. Wilders' Euroreject discourse in 2012 apparently struck a chord with some voters. It can also safely be claimed that the PVV was the only party who was responsive to voters who favoured an end to Dutch EU membership; none of the other parties in parliament supported a Dutch withdrawal. At the same time, however, immigration and culture remained more salient themes for PVV voters. It is questionable, therefore, whether Wilders' campaign strategy, which focused so explicitly on the theme of European integration, has been truly rewarding. Furthermore, among the population at large, support for a Dutch exit from the European Union has remained limited. Standard Eurobarometer data from Autumn 2012 indicated that three-quarters of the Dutch disagreed with the statement that the Netherlands could better face the future outside the EU, as opposed to one-fifth who were more favourably inclined towards a 'Nexit' (European Commission 2012: T86). Even though a considerable number of Dutch people may have a fairly or very negative image of the EU (30 per cent, according to the same Eurobarometer survey), the share of voters likely to be convinced by a full-fledged Euroreject message has thus remained fairly modest.

In the end, it is possible to conclude that, of the four 'populist themes' outlined in the first chapter, culture and ethnicity played the most important role in the Dutch case. To understand the electoral performance of the LPF as well as the PVV, one must consider the political competition over the issues of immigration and multiculturalism. In more recent years, these issues still remained more important for PVV voters than issues related to economic hardship and European integration. That is not to say, however, that Wilders cannot continue to mould the themes of Euroscepticism, cultural protectionism, immigration and welfare chauvinism into one coherent and electorally potent populist radical right message. In order to fully grasp the (variation in the) performances of the populist parties in the Netherlands, in any case, we should also consider the electoral credibility of these parties themselves.

Supply of credible populist parties

As discussed in previous chapters, a populist party is assumed to be electorally credible when it can rely on visible and persuasive leadership and is able to ward off an extremist image and to convincingly distance itself from the political establishment. In addition, organisational cohesion has been identified as a key attribute of electoral credibility; a party is prone to lose credibility when it fails to remain united and suffers from publicly visible squabbles. With regard to the leadership factor, the success of populist parties has often been related to the personal 'charisma' of the party leader. This is no different in the case of Pim Fortuyn (e.g. Ellemers 2004). However, this 'charisma hypothesis', based on the notion that a vote for a populist party is mainly based on the magnetism of the party leader alone, has rightly been criticised (Van der Brug 2003; Van der Brug and Mughan 2007). As has been discussed above, people voting for populist parties are largely motivated by substantive concerns. It can, nevertheless, be assumed that it is important for populist parties to have figureheads able to present their programme persuasively (see e.g. Carter 2005; Bos and Van der Brug 2010).

In the pre-Fortuyn era populist parties could not always rely on leaders with such qualities. One can think of the anti-immigrant CP and CD, led by Hans Janmaat, which achieved limited success in the 1980s and 1990s. Janmaat was hardly an appealing leader; although a confident speaker, he was 'not really eloquent and often too emotional to convince anyone but his own supporters' (Lucardie 1998: 116). Besides a lack of appealing leadership, the CP and CD were widely perceived as extreme right parties, for which there was little electoral potential in the Netherlands (Mudde and van Holsteyn 2000: 164–165). Both parties were, furthermore, marked by internal disputes – Janmaat was actually expelled from the CP in 1984 before founding the CD.

The radical left SP, in turn, lacked genuine nationwide visibility until the 1990s (Van der Steen 1995; Voerman and Lucardie 2007). After the disappointing 1989 parliamentary election, the party increased its campaign efforts and became known for its telling slogan 'Vote against, vote SP!' (*Stem tegen, stem SP!*). Having appealed to dissatisfied Labour voters, the SP entered parliament in 1994 with two seats. The party grew further in 1998, when it received 3.5 per cent of the vote and five seats. Party leader Jan Marijnissen developed into an eloquent debater, and a leader 'with an earthly appeal that transcended his party'. (March 2011: 130). In addition to its departure from its most radical left-wing policies, however, the SP's populist rhetoric waned in the following decade (De Lange and Rooduijn 2011; Lucardie and Voerman 2012). In 2002, for instance, the party's slogan had remarkably changed into 'Vote *for*, vote SP' (*Stem voor, stem SP!*). The party now presented itself as a more leftist alternative to Labour, rather than a genuine populist anti-establishment party. When the motivations of SP voters are considered – following the same procedure as outlined in the previous section – many SP voters in 2006, 2010 and 2012 explicitly mentioned the social policies of the party (30.1, 40.2 and 41.5 per cent, respectively), and far fewer declared that they cast a protest vote or desired 'change' (7.7, 2.7 and 2.7 per cent, respectively). Judging from these figures, it seems inaccurate to attribute the electoral successes of the SP to its remaining populist characteristics (cf. Akkerman et al. 2014).

The influence of leadership was shown most clearly in the election campaign in 2002, when the flamboyant Pim Fortuyn entered the political stage.[7] The support for LN in the polls only truly began to rise when Pim Fortuyn became party leader. After the forced departure of Fortuyn in February 2002, it became even clearer that Fortuyn's personal appeal truly mattered; most Liveable supporters followed him to his new party (Van Holsteyn and Irwin 2003: 56). Fortuyn dominated the campaign of 2002 and was also by far the most visible politician in the media; of the media coverage devoted to individual politicians, no less than 24 per cent went to Fortuyn – the percentage related to the second on the list being 7.3 (Kleinnijenhuis et al. 2003: 86). With his outspoken performance, he placed the established parties in a difficult position. One notable occasion when this happened was the TV debate following the municipal elections in March 2002, in which established parties were heavily beaten and Fortuyn's local party in Rotterdam triumphed. The broadcast showed the weary and grumpy-looking Labour and Liberal party leaders being unable, and seemingly unwilling, to respond to the gleeful rhetoric of Pim Fortuyn (Kleinnijenhuis et al. 2003: 10–11).

Irrespective of his dominance in the campaign, it is not the case that Fortuyn was loved by everyone. Van Holsteyn and Irwin (2003) even showed that Fortuyn was clearly perceived as the least sympathetic party leader, but also that a large number of the people who did evaluate Fortuyn favourably also cast a vote for him. Whereas Fortuyn and his ideas were, thus, controversial, he was seen as the right candidate by a substantial part of the electorate. Koopmans and Muis (2009), furthermore, found that the public visibility of Fortuyn, combined with the support from other actors in the public sphere, proved to be beneficial to Fortuyn's support in the opinion polls. Lacking a genuine party organisation to back him, the telegenic Fortuyn essentially built support on the basis of his own appearance and personal political programme (Lucardie and Voerman 2012: 119).

Once represented in parliament and government, however, Fortuyn's party failed to leave a good impression. It proved difficult, if not impossible, to replace Fortuyn with an equally appealing new party leader. The organisational disunity of the party after Fortuyn's assassination further undermined the LPF's credibility (De Lange and Art 2011). Directly after Fortuyn was murdered, the internal turmoil began, and the struggles continued after the LPF became part of the governing coalition. It was, without doubt, the continuous infighting between LPF cabinet members (most notably the ministers Heinsbroek and Bomhoff), MPs and party officials that caused the breakdown of the government and the more general demise of the LPF (Lucardie and Voerman 2012: 126). Without Pim Fortuyn, the party organisation of the LPF proved very unstable. Former LPF leader Mat Herben later stated that '[n]ot one organisation is able to function without (accepted) leadership, loyalty and discipline. After Pim Fortuyn had gone there was a lack of all three within the LPF' (Herben 2005: 25). In a personal interview, Herben furthermore identified the 'internal struggles and disunity' as the main reasons underlying the decline of the LPF (Interview, The Hague, 10 September 2008). Former LPF immigration minister Hilbrand Nawijn shared this analysis about the (electoral) demise of the party: 'the LPF consisted of a wide variety of people who, all of a sudden, desired to enter politics. [...] No unity whatsoever' (Interview, Zoetermeer, 8 September 2008).

The results of the 2003 parliamentary election seemed to indicate a return to 'old' politics. Yet the fact that the LPF, despite the enormous organisational chaos, still received 5.7 per cent of the vote showed that some voters were reluctant to return to the mainstream parties. In 2003, however, there was no credible populist contender to turn to. LN was torn by leadership struggles, and it was, strikingly, the inexperienced and unknown younger half-sister of LN campaign leader Kay van de Linde who eventually became the party leader. The person who missed out on LN leadership, the well-known 'motivation trainer' Emile Ratelband, competed with his own list, but was too much of a clownesque figure to be taken seriously.[8] Neither LN nor Ratelband received enough votes for representation in parliament. With her new party, former LPF MP Winny de Jong also stood in the election, but she lacked media attention, and was associated too much with the LPF skirmishes to secure seats.

In 2006 the situation was different. Several populist candidates with a certain political track record competed. Hilbrand Nawijn formed the Party for the Netherlands (PVN), while Marco Pastors, former alderman for Fortuyn's local party in Rotterdam, and Joost Eerdmans, who had been a prominent LPF MP, founded One NL (*EénNL*). Finally, List 5 Fortuyn emerged out of the original LPF, but its leader Olaf Stuger was by far the least known party leader of the newly formed populist parties. In the end, it was Geert Wilders' PVV that collected most of the 'populist votes' and entered parliament.

Wilders' vote share in 2006 was still modest, but the politician was able to increase his visibility in the years after the election with strong anti-establishment and anti-Islam statements. Even though Wilders was more radical than Fortuyn in this respect, he has avoided to become seen as an extremist pariah. Similarly to Fortuyn, Wilders framed his anti-Islam rhetoric in terms of defending liberal values, and in this way managed to 'dissociate himself from mere narrow-minded xenophobia and resentment' (Vossen 2011: 187). That is not to say that Wilders has been an uncontroversial politician, or that media attention through provocative statements automatically increased his popularity (see Van der Pas et al. 2013). The PVV leader, in fact, had to stand trial for inciting hatred against Muslims – but was cleared of all charges in June 2011. Yet the PVV was clearly not stigmatised to the same extent as, say, Janmaat's parties had been before.

Besides the PVV, another right-wing populist party participated in the 2010 parliamentary election: Proud of the Netherlands (*Trots op Nederland*, TON), headed by Rita Verdonk. Previously, 'Iron Rita' had been a popular immigration minister for the liberal VVD. After previously having lost this party's leadership election, Verdonk received more preferential votes than party leader Mark Rutte in the parliamentary election of 2006. In the period that followed, Verdonk would continuously challenge Rutte's leadership, which eventually led to her being ousted from the VVD fraction in September 2007. A month later, Verdonk launched her new movement TON, which could immediately count on a substantial amount of support in the opinion polls. TON explicitly appealed to 'the large majority of Dutch people' who no longer felt represented by the political elite (Vossen 2010; Lucardie and Voerman 2012: 143). Occupying a single seat in parliament, however, Verdonk struggled to retain media attention in the following years, and during the 2010 campaign she hardly played a visible role. Unlike Wilders, Verdonk was not invited to the televised debates that featured the presumed main contenders of the election. In organisational terms, TON also failed to leave a good impression; during 2008 Verdonk lost two of her closest trustees: Kay van de Linde, after his negative remarks about the party leaked out, and Ed Sinke, after a vicious conflict about party funds.

Having learned from the mistakes of the LPF, on the other hand, Geert Wilders managed to keep the ranks of his party closed for a long time (De Lange and Art 2011). Wilders exercised ultimate control over his party, which is illustrated by his choice to keep the PVV a party without (other) members. Up until the parliamentary election of September 2010, publicly visible intra-party conflicts were largely absent. As early as November 2010, however, the Dutch media reported widely about the questionable reputation of several PVV MPs, and Wilders was forced to admit having made errors in the selection of his candidates (Lucardie and Voerman 2012: 179).[9] Two years later, a handful of MPs split from the party in the months before the September 2012 parliamentary election. One prominent example was Hero Brinkman, who left in March 2012 after his repeated pleas to increase intra-party democracy proved fruitless. Brinkman also voiced his disagreement with some of the xenophobic positions taken by the party. On 3 July, furthermore, the presentation of the PVV manifesto was hijacked by PVV MPs Hernandez and Kortenoeven, who announced their departure from the party and similarly expressed their discontent with Wilders' authoritarian leadership. A few days later, Jhim van Bemmel left the parliamentary group – after not having been selected for the party's candidate list – and he also voiced his dissatisfaction with the iron party discipline.[10]

Developments such as these, as well as several incidents at local and provincial levels, appeared damaging for the electoral credibility of the PVV, particularly as they occurred relatively close to the parliamentary election. Compared with the chaos within the LPF, however, the internal problems of the PVV remained reasonably limited, and Wilders tried vigorously to portray the PVV dissidents as backstabbing traitors. The PVV also had little to fear from Hero Brinkman's fruitless attempt to enter parliament with his short-lived Democratic Political Turning Point (*Democratisch Politiek Keerpunt*, DPK), which came into being after a merger with Verdonk's TON.

Internal struggles may, nevertheless, have contributed to the significant loss of the PVV in the 2012 election, arguably more so than the PVV's support for the governing minority coalition. Even though the acceptance of the support role could have been interpreted as a betrayal of the party's populist values, the PVV continued to blame the government – in which it was not officially taking part – for taking unpopular measures. Wilders, for instance, attacked the government for contributing to Greece's bailout in 2011, a theme which would also play a large role in the subsequent election campaign. In this way, Wilders was largely able to maintain its profile as anti-establishment party.

Despite the PVV's loss in the 2012 parliamentary election, in any case, the party has not become a spent force. Opinion poll results after the election have underlined the enduring popularity of the PVV, which largely boiled down to the personal appeal of Wilders himself. The loyalty of many voters to Wilders became evident once more at the May 2014 European Parliament election, when the PVV was plagued by another series of defections, triggered by a controversial statement by Wilders himself.[11] Although the EP election results of May 2014 may have been disappointing for the PVV, the party still finished third, at a short distance from the two parties in front.

Conclusion

Dutch populist parties have only fairly recently been able to make a large electoral impact. Excluding the radical left SP, whose populist anti-establishment discourse has declined considerably since the late 1990s, these have been parties that became primarily known for their cultural protectionism and hostility towards immigration. The two most prominent examples have been the LPF and the PVV, both of which presented themselves as defenders of liberal values and warned against the cultural threats of Islam in particular. The PVV later added welfare protectionist elements to its programme and mainly focused on the malign consequences of European integration in the election campaign of 2012. In addition, the leaders of both the LPF and PVV added to their substantive policy proposals a harsh criticism of the ('leftist') political establishment and its cultural relativism.

The parties broke through at a time when voters had become increasingly 'available' due to the demise of the Dutch pillarised cleavage structure. This meant that the new populist parties were truly able to profit from the highly proportional Dutch electoral system. To fully understand the electoral performance of populist parties, however, the agency of the populist as well as the established parties must be considered. At the time of Fortuyn's breakthrough in 2002, political mainstream parties were, with some justification, perceived to be unresponsive to the demands and concerns of a substantial part of the electorate. The most important issues at stake were immigration and cultural integration of minorities, the issues central to the appeal of Fortuyn and, later, Wilders.

In order to explain the variation in the electoral performance of individual populist parties, the chapter has shown that the credibility of these parties themselves was crucial. Pim Fortuyn could win over many dissatisfied voters after having attracted ample media attention with his eloquent anti-establishment criticism. Fortuyn was murdered prior to the parliamentary election of 2002 and, although his party won a landslide victory, proved to be irreplaceable as party leader. The demise of the LPF was further hastened by continuous infighting. Whereas most other populist contenders lacked electoral appeal, Geert Wilders captured most of the 'populist vote' in the post-Fortuyn era. Under Wilders' firm leadership, the PVV initially did not suffer from evident intra-party disputes, and the PVV leader continuously reached the centre of attention with provocative statements. Even though Wilders' strict enforcement of party discipline stimulated dissatisfaction among PVV MPs, leading to several defections and expulsions, the party did not suffer from the organisational chaos that had previously marked the LPF. Despite losses in the 2012 parliamentary election and 2014 European Parliament election, the PVV remained a key player in Dutch politics.

If the four themes introduced in Chapter 1 are considered, issues related to ethnicity and culture were most relevant to explain the electoral performance of right-wing populists in the Netherlands. At the aggregate level, political trust has remained high, and political corruption has hardly been an issue in election campaigns. After the dawn of the economic crisis, economic hardship and European integration may have become more salient themes – also for PVV voters. Even though these themes have also been central to the discourse of the PVV in more recent years, regularly in connection with the issue of immigration, the party of Geert Wilders still seemed to mobilise support primarily on the basis of cultural issues (see Mudde 2007; Ivarsflaten 2008; Oesch 2008; Spies 2013).

An important implication from the Dutch case is that high levels of public trust in political institutions in general do not necessarily hamper the electoral success of populist parties. The case shows that established parties' responsiveness with regard to *specific issues* can be equally relevant in explaining the electoral performance of populist parties. Pim Fortuyn broke through after gaining the ownership of certain salient societal issues neglected by mainstream parties, and attracting voters who agreed with his policies (e.g. Van der Brug 2003). It is also clear that Dutch populist parties drew support from a particular dissatisfied segment of the electorate (e.g. Bélanger and Aarts 2006; Schumacher and Rooduijn 2013). It is important to note that 'protest voting' and 'policy voting' do not necessarily rule each other out; the dissatisfaction of the 'populist voters' may well stem from concerns related to real societal developments and substantive policies (see Eatwell 2003).

The Dutch case also suggests that mainstream parties do not automatically win back the support they lost to the populist parties if they become more responsive. Established parties in the Netherlands have revised their positions on immigration and cultural integration, but this has not automatically brought Geert Wilders' rise to a halt. This implies that, if a populist party manages to retain its credibility after seizing the ownership of a salient issue, it can ward off competition from its mainstream rivals (cf. Meguid 2008). By 'keeping one foot in and one foot out' of government as a support partner between 2010 and 2012, furthermore, the PVV seems to have been able to retain a credible anti-establishment appeal, similarly to other successful European populist parties in government (see Albertazzi and McDonnell 2005; Akkerman and De Lange 2012; Zaslove 2012).

Whether or not the PVV remains a serious contender to the established parties depends, first of all, on the personal future of Wilders. It is hard to think of a suitable successor to take over the reins of the PVV, not least because it has been such a highly personalised party. Developments in issue salience also play a role; Wilders has thus far appeared to make conscious ideological moves in response to societal developments such as the financial and economic crisis. Whether a discourse built around Eurorejection turns out to be a fruitful and durable electoral strategy, however, remains to be seen.

The chapter has, in any case, confirmed how important the agency of populist parties is in order to explain their electoral performance. This relates to their electoral appeal and cohesiveness, as well as their exploitation of social developments and ideological niches left vacant by established parties (Rydgren 2005). The next chapter focuses on Poland, a post-communist country where rather different issues have played an important role in the discourse of populist parties. I will investigate whether, despite the contextual differences, the same general logic applies as far as populist parties' success and failure is concerned.

5
Populist Parties in Poland

The previous chapter dealt with populist parties in a long-established Western European democracy. This chapter, which is structured in a similar way, moves beyond this part of the continent, and provides an analysis of populist parties in Poland. Similarly to the Netherlands, early 21st-century Poland has witnessed the rise and fall of populist parties, and in Poland populist parties have also taken part in a coalition government. The country thus lends itself equally well to the purpose of comparing successful and unsuccessful electoral performances of populist parties. As became clear in Chapter 2, post-communist Central and Eastern European countries often pose a challenge when the aim is to determine which parties are populist, and which are not. This is also the case in Poland. I will nevertheless argue that, in the period from 2001 onwards, two parties emerged that can be identified as populist parties: Self Defence (*Samoobrona Rzeczpospolitej Polskiej*, SO) and, since 2005, Law and Justice (*Prawo i Sprawiedliwość*, PiS). For the latter party, nevertheless, populism seemingly remained a relatively loose supplement to its national-conservative core ideology. The League of Polish Families (*Liga Polskich Rodzin*, LPR), often considered to be populist as well, is not classified as a genuine populist party in this book.

As will be discussed, the Polish populist parties were not much hindered by the electoral system and benefited from widespread discontent with the dominant Polish mainstream parties. A disregard for many voters' socio-economic concerns and involvement in corruption scandals seriously undermined the appeal and trustworthiness of the Polish political elites. SO, the party that most clearly appealed to the Polish 'transition losers', was one of the parties able to benefit from this. After the adoption of a more explicit populist discourse, however, PiS became the most credible party voicing populist anti-establishment rhetoric. The party could rely on a strong anti-corruption image and present itself as the chief agent of conservative and 'solidaristic' Poland, and it largely 'devoured' the support of its junior coalition partners in 2006 and 2007: SO and the LPR.

The following section first provides a brief overview of the developments in the Polish party system after the transition to democracy. These developments need be understood in order to identify the populist parties that have emerged since the turn of the 21st century. The subsequent section turns to the electoral performance of the populist parties identified in Poland. The concluding section summarises the findings and draws implications from the Polish case.

Identifying the populist parties in Poland

1989–2001: A fluid party political landscape

Towards the end of the communist period a mass opposition force was able to develop, embodied by the trade union federation Solidarity (*Solidarność*). In 1989 the 'Round-Table negotiations' between Solidarity and the communist government led to semi-open elections. Solidarity's overwhelming victory in these elections marked the beginning of the end for the communist party (Polish United Workers' Party, PZPR). Its position was severely weakened and the election results led to a 'negotiated retreat' of the PZPR from the political scene (Millard 1999: 9). The following decade in democratic Poland was characterised by the instability of the party system. Various parties emerged from the Solidarity movement, and the first truly free parliamentary election in 1991 resulted in an extremely fragmented Lower House (*Sejm*). No fewer than 29 parties or electoral committees occupied the 460 seats (Sanford 1999: 36). It proved to be a tumultuous period: three short-lived governments followed each other rapidly; a lack of party discipline contributed to frequent clashes between parliament and government; cabinets were internally divided; and their relationship with President Lech Wałęsa, the former chairman of Solidarity, was often difficult.

In 1993 a new parliamentary election was held under a new, less proportional, electoral system. This proved detrimental to the divided 'post-Solidarity camp', as the many, relatively small, parties with a Solidarity history failed to cross the threshold. Strikingly, no fewer than 34.5 per cent of the votes were 'wasted' (Sanford 1999: 41). At the same time, the pragmatic and much better-organised social democrats of the Democratic Left Alliance (*Sojusz Lewicy Demokratycznej*, SLD), which emerged out of the PZPR, benefited from the electoral system, and eventually formed a coalition government with the Polish Peasant Party (*Polskie Stronnictwo*

Ludowe, PSL). The social democrat Aleksander Kwaśniewski was elected as president in 1995, which meant that both executive branches were now dominated by former communist politicians.

The post-Solidarity camp finally managed to unite in a new alliance in June 1996: Solidarity Electoral Action (*Akcja Wyborcza Solidarność*, AWS). The unification of the centre-right proved successful, as AWS won the parliamentary election of 1997 with 33.8 per cent of the vote (see Table 5.1). The post-Solidarity alliance formed a coalition government with the liberals of the Freedom Union (*Unia Wolności*, UW), headed by AWS Prime Minister Jerzy Buzek. The governing coalition would become very unpopular and was, furthermore, internally divided over the reforms and the liberal economic policies pursued by UW Finance Minister Balcerowicz. In 2000 the coalition broke down, after which Buzek headed a minority government.

Less than a year later, several groupings began to split from AWS. In January 2001 the Civic Platform (*Platforma Obywatelska*, PO) was founded, which consisted of liberal-conservative AWS members and leading figures from the Freedom Union, including Donald Tusk. The most notable other grouping that split from Solidarity Electoral Action was Law and Justice (PiS). PiS was headed by Jarosław Kaczyński and supported by his twin brother Lech, at that time the politically independent justice minister. The programme of PiS mainly focused on law and order issues and combating corruption in public office. Some other former AWS members and a range of individual groupings formed the Catholic nationalist League of Polish families (LPR). The remainder of AWS rebranded itself as Solidarity Electoral Action of the Right (AWSP).

In the Polish parliamentary election of September 2001 the unpopularity of the Buzek government was translated into an electoral punishment for the AWS, or what was left of it (see Table 5.1). The AWSP failed to cross the threshold, but the two new centre-right parties, PO and PiS, received 12.7 and 9.5 per cent of the vote, respectively. The largest victors in 2001, however, were the social democrats of the Democratic Left Alliance. In an alliance with the smaller Labour Union (*Unia Pracy*, UP), the SLD won no less than 41.0 per cent of the vote. The social democrats formed a coalition government with the Peasant Party, and Leszek Miller became prime minister.

After the parliamentary election of 2001, the Polish party political landscape would become much more stable than before. It is also from this election onwards that the electoral performance of populist parties will be considered, even though various (short-lived) parties voicing populist rhetoric had already emerged in the 1990s. One example is Stanisław

Table 5.1 Polish parliamentary election results 1997–2011, in % of the vote

	1997	2001	2005	2007	2011
Solid. Electoral Action (AWS)	33.8	5.6			
Democratic Left Alliance (SLD)	27.1	41.0	11.3	13.2	8.2
Freedom Union (UW)	13.4	3.1	2.5		
Polish Peasant Party (PSL)	7.3	9.0	7.0	8.9	8.4
Civic Platform (PO)		12.7	24.1	41.5	39.2
Law and Justice (PiS)		9.5	27.0	32.1	29.9
Self Defence (SO)	0.1	10.2	11.4	1.5	0.1
League of Polish Families (LPR)		7.9	8.0	1.3	
Palikot's Movement (RP)					10.0
Others	18.3	1.0	8.7	1.5	4.3

Notes: In 2001 the SLD – now a unified party rather than a party federation – formed an electoral alliance with the Labour Union (UP). In 2005 the Freedom Union (UW) figure stands for the vote share of the Democrats which emerged out of the UW. The percentage for the SLD in 2007 reflects the vote share of the centre-left Left and Democrats alliance, and that of SO in 2011 the vote share of Our Home Poland–Self Defence. Data: Nordsieck (2013).

Tymiński's Party X, which won a few seats in the 1991 parliamentary election (see Wysocka 2010). In order to provide a meaningful comparison between long-established European democracies and the Polish case, however, only the populist parties that emerged after the apparent stabilisation of the Polish party system are studied here. In the 1990s the party political situation was so fluid and the lifespan of parties so short that it was hard to speak of a truly developed party system in the first place. During this period it is, therefore, also difficult to distinguish between a political establishment and 'new' parties challenging it.

By the end of the decade, however, two camps had developed that could reasonably be perceived to make up the political establishment in democratic Poland: the 'communist successor' camp and the 'post-Solidarity' camp. As discussed, while the former communists managed to organise quite successfully in the Democratic Left Alliance (SLD), the post-Solidarity camp was much more disjointed. Several governments in the 1990s were nevertheless formed that were dominated by parties and politicians from this latter camp. It was also after the parliamentary election of 2001 that two radical anti-establishment parties entered parliament that did not affiliate themselves with either the post-communist or the post-Solidarity heritage (Stanley 2010: 86): SO and the LPR.

Enter Self Defence and the League of Polish Families

While the SLD's return to power in 2001 came as no great surprise, the entrance of two radical parties into the Polish parliament was less expected. The more successful of the two, SO, received 10.2 per cent of the vote. Rather than a political party in the conventional sense, SO was a social movement born out of a farmers' trade union in the early 1990s, built around its indisputable leader Andrzej Lepper. As a political organisation, SO can clearly be classified as a populist party, in view of its anti-establishment character and its appeal to a heartland of ordinary Polish people. Lepper himself was not afraid to label SO as populist if, as he stated, 'populism means an uncompromising struggle against a corrupt establishment in defence of ordinary people and national interests' (quoted in Jasiewicz 2008: 14). In his rhetoric Lepper clearly portrayed an antagonistic relationship between the elite and the common people. According to Lepper, 'the authorities in Poland can be called "them". They rule, they make laws, they give, they take, they permit – or not – others to live' (quoted in Stanley 2008: 103). SO claimed to be 'the only one in Poland, which speaks in the name of all people' with the aim to 'defend pure and unemployed people, honest and enterprising, but disadvantaged by the economic system' (quoted in Kucharczyk and Wysocka 2008: 77). In its pre-parliamentary period the organisation was notorious for the demonstrations and roadblocks it organised, and SO did not lose much of its disruptive anti-establishment character once represented in parliament (Jasiewicz 2008; Stanley 2010: 195–196).

SO's more substantial political programme was ambiguous (Millard 2009: 105; Pankowski 2010: 136, 140), even though it was clearly characterised by a left-wing and protectionist socio-economic discourse. A party document written by the former party spokesman Mateusz Piskorski explained that 'Self Defense has strongly expressed the voice of people and all social classes, which – due to the reforms of the 90-ies – have been standing on the edge of poverty and hopelessness' (Piskorski 2004). The party appealed to the 'losers' of the transition from communism to a free-market economy, and denounced the 'successive "liberal elites" who had destroyed Poland and their "theft" of national assets in the privatisation process' (Millard 2006: 1016). SO also presented itself as a 'patriotic' party, aiming to protect the national economy, and the agricultural sector in particular (Wysocka 2010: 158). Even so, SO's self-definition, even with regard to socio-economic issues, has been changeable over time. The party, for instance, shifted from seeking a 'third way' between capitalism and socialism to describing itself as an anti-liberal party, while using the label 'socio-liberal' after the parliamentary election of 2005 (Kucharczyk and Wysocka 2008: 78).

The second radical party that entered the *Sejm* in 2001 was the Catholic nationalist LPR, which received 7.9 per cent of the vote. In the scholarly literature, the League is, like SO, regularly described as a populist party (e.g. Jasiewicz 2008; Kucharczyk and Wysocka 2008; De Lange and Guerra 2009; Pankowski 2010). Indeed, the LPR expressed harsh criticism of the Round-Table settlement from 1989 and the political parties that had emerged from it (Wysocka 2010: 195). In a personal interview, former presidential candidate and LPR MEP Maciej Giertych argued that the Round-Table settlement allowed communists to remain represented in public office (Interview, Brussels, 9 September 2008). Giertych considered the so-called right-wing parties to be 'also post-communist, but of an earlier vintage', and stated that the League's aim was to 'get rid of all the socialist thinking'. The LPR portrayed itself as defender of national traditions and called for the preservation of Catholic values in Polish society (Wysocka 2010: 195). Its nationalism dovetailed with a Euroreject attitude; EU membership was considered to threaten both Polish national identity and sovereignty (Jasiewicz 2008; De Lange and Guerra 2009). In socio-economic terms, the party was protectionist and critical of full-fledged capitalism. Although state involvement in the economy was not explicitly encouraged, the state was supposed to protect the national market and key industries from foreign competition (Wysocka 2010: 195).

While the League had a clear conception of a Polish Catholic 'heartland' and undoubtedly criticised the political establishment, support for popular sovereignty could not truly be observed in its discourse. The League's conservative position on issues such as abortion and same-sex marriage was inspired by an adherence to Catholic values, more so than an urge to follow the 'popular will'. Following Maciej Giertych, the League wished to 'see the state functioning according to the ethical principles as defined by the Catholic Church' (Interview, Brussels 9 September 2008). In the discourse of the LPR, furthermore, 'the people' were not portrayed as essentially virtuous. According to Giertych, the people were actually 'aware of the fact they are not very good Catholics', as their own actions were often in conflict with Church values. These values, rather than the people's 'common sense', were thus taken as the foundation for the party's ideology. Taking this into account, the LPR is not considered as a genuine case of populism.[1]

The 'transformation' of Law and Justice

Four years after having assumed office in 2001, the Miller government had become the most unpopular administration in post-communist Poland (Szczerbiak 2007: 207). This showed in the September 2005 general election results: the governing Democratic Left Alliance only received 11.3 per cent of the vote, a loss of almost 30 percentage points. The big winners were the two centre-right parties, PiS and PO, which received 27.0 and 24.1 per cent of the vote, respectively. The vote shares of SO and the LPR were roughly the same as in 2001. For the first time in post-communist Poland, the *Sejm* was composed of the same parties as in the previous parliamentary period, despite the large shift in votes between the elections of 2001 and 2005.

Before the election, PO had broadened its appeal beyond the relatively small group of liberal voters by re-profiling itself as more socially conservative and articulating a 'stronger national-patriotic discourse' (Szczerbiak 2007: 206). During the final stages of the campaign, PiS, on the other hand, 're-framed the election as a choice between the Civic Platform's vision of a "liberal" Poland, which they argued would benefit the better off and "winners" primarily, and their more egalitarian concept of a "social" or "solidaristic" Poland' (Szczerbiak 2007: 211).[2] Radoslaw Markowski (2008: 820) even spoke of a 'spectacular change' of PiS from a 'fairly typical conservative party' into a 'radical nationalist, and visibly populist-socialist one'.

Although it may be more accurate to speak of a shift in emphasis instead of a 'spectacular change' (Millard 2009: 135–136), PiS certainly sharpened its discourse. Besides its more pronounced 'solidaristic' image, PiS continued to express anti-establishment rhetoric, a great deal of which was centred on the concept of *układ*. Millard (2009: 147) defined this as the

> putative shady network of business oligarchs, politicians, and the security services that formed the webs of corruption, cronyism, intrigue, and informal relations between 'liberals' and 'ex-communists' that had effectively ruled Poland after 1989.

As such, PiS linked corruption, which was the major campaign theme in 2005, with the issues of decommunisation and lustration (the removal from public office of former communists), which were salient themes in the 1990s (Millard 2006). The party also referred to a Polish 'Fourth Republic' in its 2005 manifesto title, expressing the need to (symbolically) bring an end to the Third Polish Republic (established in 1991) and to start a new era of clean and moral government.

Kucharczyk and Wysocka (2008: 79), furthermore, argued that the party changed from an elitist into a populist party, and began 'to speak in the name of "the people"' more explicitly. In the 2006 local elections campaign, for instance, PiS employed the slogan 'Close to the People'

(*Bliżej ludzi*), and promised 'a closer engagement in things common to everyday people'; declared 'a construction of a citizens' society'; and spoke of bringing law and order, 'because this is in the interests of ordinary Polish citizens' – thereby stressing that PiS was the 'party of ordinary Polish citizens' (quoted in Kucharczyk and Wysocka 2008: 79). Ben Stanley (2010: 185) similarly argued that PiS's populist credentials 'would be sharpened substantially' in these years. The more pronounced use of populist rhetoric 'identified PiS as representative of an ordinary, authentic, legitimate "people" against an illegitimate and usurping elite' (Stanley 2010: 235). Millard (2009: 135) also observed that in the campaign of 2005 'PiS hammered home its new central theme: for well over a decade liberal reforms had wreaked havoc on the fortunes of ordinary folk'. All in all, apart from its already prevalent anti-establishment discourse, marked by the aim of fighting corruption and pushing for further decommunisation and lustration, PiS strengthened its rhetorical appeal to the 'ordinary people' and, thus, became a more unmistakable populist party.

Populist parties in power and the aftermath

The presidential election of 2005 was held one month after the parliamentary election, which meant that both election campaigns were effectively intertwined. While PO candidate Donald Tusk won most votes in the first ballot, he was beaten in the second, decisive, round by PiS candidate Lech Kaczyński. Both elections were thus effectively won by PiS, and PO would remain in opposition after coalition negotiations with PiS broke down. Although before the parliamentary election it was widely expected that the two centre-right parties would form a coalition, the relationship between the parties had deteriorated after the fierce campaign battles (Szczerbiak 2007; Stanley 2013).

PiS instead formed a minority government headed by Prime Minister Kazimierz Marcinkiewicz, which relied on the support of SO and the LPR. In May 2006 the three parties signed a coalition agreement and the two radical parties officially became part of government. Two months later, Prime Minister Marcinkiewicz was replaced by Jarosław Kaczyński, even though the latter had previously declared himself unavailable for the prime ministership in order not to hamper his brother's presidential ambitions. After Jarosław's U-turn, the Kaczyński twins thus headed both branches of the Polish executive. SO leader Lepper became minister of agriculture and deputy prime minister. He shared the latter post with the League's leader Roman Giertych – Maciej Giertych's son – who also became education minister.

The government of Jarosław Kaczyński proved to be unstable, as the two junior coalition parties quarrelled repeatedly with PiS (Szczerbiak 2008). SO was even temporarily expelled from the coalition in September 2006, after Lepper expressed ever more outspoken criticism of PiS. Lepper's party took part in the government again, however, after coalition negotiations between PiS and the Peasant Party broke down. The coalition would eventually tumble in the summer of 2007, shortly after Minister Lepper had been accused of taking bribes, and subsequently dismissed. Prime Minister Kaczyński called for new elections and, as a result, an end came to 'two years of ceaseless turmoil, culminating in an orgy of political lunacy for much of 2007' (Millard 2009: 143).

In the election of September 2007 PO received 41.5 per cent of the vote and ended well ahead of PiS. The latter party received 32.1 per cent of the vote, which was more than the 27.0 per cent in the previous election, but the party failed to mop up all the votes of the former LPR and SO supporters (Markowski 2008). The latter two parties disappeared from the *Sejm* after receiving only 1.3 and 1.5 per cent of the vote, respectively. Subsequent attempts of SO and the LPR in nationwide elections failed, and on 5 August 2011 Andrzej Lepper was found dead after having committed suicide. The social democrats, now in a new alliance named 'Left and Democrats', failed to leave a great impression in the 2007 election, with a vote share of 13.2 per cent. After the election, PO formed a coalition government with PSL, led by Prime Minister Donald Tusk.

The government's cohabitation with President Lech Kaczyński was far from congenial, and PiS 'positioned itself as a party of total opposition, determined to use the president's veto power to block government actions' (Tworzecki 2012: 618). This situation would endure until 10 April 2010, when a plane crash killed 96 people, including President Kaczyński and other members of the Polish (political) elite. The plane was on its way to a ceremony in Smolensk, Russia, to commemorate the Polish officers killed by the Soviet secret police in 1940.[3] Jarosław Kaczyński subsequently lost the early presidential elections in July against PO-allied candidate Bronisław Komorowski. While Kaczyński had shown his milder side in the presidential election campaign, he would return to his confrontational style after the lost election (Tworzecki 2012: 618; Stanley 2013: 191; Szczerbiak 2013: 485). Besides a continuation of PiS's cultural conservative course, the Smolensk tragedy became a central element in Kaczyński's rhetoric, whereby the PiS leader held the government responsible for the errors leading up to the crash. As this aggressive rhetoric appeared rather ineffective electorally, PiS concentrated more on bread-and-butter issues such as unemployment and healthcare in the campaign for the October 2011 parliamentary election (Szczerbiak 2013). The fluctuations in the discourse and attitude of PiS over the years give reasons to suspect that the party's populism has been less of a core ideological element of the party than it was for Lepper and his SO.

Meanwhile, a new party had formed which appealed to the anti-clerical electorate: the Palikot Movement (*Ruch Palikota*, RP), named after its founder and leader, the flamboyant former PO MP Janusz Palikot. While the party had an anti-establishment character, it did not portray 'the people' as a homogeneous entity or sketch a dichotomy between the people and the elite. The RP combined economic liberalism with a liberal position on issues such as same-sex marriage, drugs and abortion, and surprisingly won 10 per cent of the vote in the parliamentary election of 2011. PO, taking credit for the relatively good economic situation, gathered 39.2 per cent of the vote in the election, and again became the largest party by a considerable margin. PiS's vote share was 29.9 per cent, and the Democratic Left Alliance received a mere 8.2 per cent of the vote. The PO–PSL coalition remained in office.

The following section of this chapter focuses on explaining the electoral performance of the populist parties in Poland: SO and, since 2005, PiS. The chapter again focuses on the three main conditions central in this book: the electoral system, the responsiveness of established parties and the credibility of populist parties. The performance of the borderline case LPR will be analysed as well, to determine whether or not the electoral performance of this, essentially non-populist, party rested on a different logic. I will concentrate mainly on the years between 2001 and 2007; this is the most relevant period for this study, as it covers the years in which populist parties broke though, entered government, and also competed for votes with one another.

Explaining the Electoral Performance of the Polish Populist Parties

Electoral system

Due to various electoral reforms, the proportionality of the Polish electoral system has varied considerably over the years. As mentioned, no fewer than 29 parties or electoral committees gained representation in the *Sejm* after the first genuinely free parliamentary election in 1991. The entrance of all these parties was facilitated by the almost pure PR electoral system, characterised by the absence of entry thresholds and fairly large electoral districts (Markowski 2006). The following parliamentary election of 1993 was held under a much less proportional system.

Among other features, the new electoral law introduced thresholds of 5 per cent for parties and 8 per cent for electoral coalitions, and a lower district magnitude. The fragmented post-Solidarity camp in particular suffered from these new rules.

The parliamentary election of 1997 was held under the same institutional conditions, but, when the AWS-led coalition was heading towards defeat in the 2001 general election, a new electoral system was introduced which would be less beneficial to larger parties, and thus to AWS's main rival, the Democratic Left Alliance (Millard 2003). The d'Hondt electoral formula was replaced by the Sainte Laguë formula (which favours medium-sized rather than large parties), the district magnitude was increased, and the second tier national list removed. The new electoral system of 2001 thus denoted a move back to more proportionality, although it was still much less proportional than the system of 1991. The system applied in 2005 only saw the reintroduction of the d'Hondt electoral formula, and no changes were made for subsequent Lower House elections.

The disproportionality between votes and seats in the Polish parliamentary elections between 2001 and 2011 has been relatively high compared with countries with a 'purer' PR system – the Netherlands being the most obvious case in point (see Appendix C, Table A.2). Compared with the majoritarian and plurality systems of France and the UK, however, the Polish electoral system has in theory been much less hostile to smaller newcomers. Although, for instance, the 5 and 8 per cent thresholds could be seen as sizeable hurdles, they are not exceptionally high in comparison with other countries with PR systems.

To appreciate the effects of the electoral system, one should also consider the Polish electoral context, which has been marked by low levels of party affiliation and turnout, and high levels of electoral volatility (see e.g. Szczerbiak 2002a; 2008; 2013; Markowski 2006). In addition to the absence of strong partisan alignments, the more general distrust of political parties implied that Polish voters were potentially highly 'available' to new challengers. As we will see in the next section, the availability of the Polish electorate was only increased due to the ideological positioning and behaviour of the dominant mainstream parties. Seen in this light, the challenge for (credible) new parties posed by the electoral system should not be overestimated.

Responsiveness of the established parties

As discussed, it was hard to speak of a political 'establishment' in Poland in the early years after the transition to democracy. By the turn of the 21st century, however, it was possible to distinguish two dominant political camps: the communist successor camp, represented by the Democratic Left Alliance, and the post-Solidarity camp, which was much more disjointed prior to the establishment of Solidarity Electoral Action in 1996. Taken together, these camps made up the political establishment which the radical anti-establishment parties opposed. The following analysis suggests that it was the unresponsiveness of the political establishment with regard to socio-economic issues, as well as the lack of integrity of the mainstream parties, that lay at the roots of the electoral success of populist parties.

Socio-economic conditions

With regard to socio-economic policies, the tone was set by Finance Minister Balcerowicz in the first government after the semi-free election in 1989. Balcerowicz was a fervent advocate of free-market capitalism and fiscal austerity, and his controversial 'big bang' or 'shock' policies were meant to secure a swift retreat from the state's role in the economy (Millard 1999: 144–145). Although Balcerowicz was replaced after the parliamentary election of 1991, the subsequent governments – including those led by the Democratic Left Alliance – maintained a commitment to the free-market economy and the privatisation of public assets. The consensus among the dominant political actors also extended to matters of foreign policy, leading Frances Millard (1999: 100) to observe that the ideological spectrum of Polish politics in the 1990s was rather narrow: '[a]ll the parliamentary parties professed commitment to continuing economic reform, including further privatization. All stressed the need for reform of state health, education and welfare provision. All favoured accession to NATO and the European Union'.

What did divide the Polish centre-left and centre-right parties more clearly was, first of all, their attitudes towards the communist past. The post-Solidarity centre-right parties were much more committed to decommunisation and lustration than the former communists of the centre-left (Szczerbiak 2002b). Second, the parties took different positions with regard to moral and cultural issues, and the role of the Church in public life in particular. The centre-left adopted a more liberal and secular position with regard to these themes than the post-Solidarity parties (Castle and Taras 2002: 113–115).

Irrespective of these differences, the political elite's consensus in other policy areas raises the question of whether dominant parties were genuinely responsive to the concerns among the Polish electorate. As regards foreign policy, there was not much disparity between the political

mainstream and most of the voters. The wider Polish public generally approved of the internationalist orientation of the political elite,
although foreign policy issues were far from electorally salient (Millard
1999: 20). EU membership would also never become a salient issue in
election campaigns, or in terms of general public interest (Szczerbiak
and Bil 2009). Support levels for EU accession had always been relatively
high, and the Eurosceptic sentiments that did exist, for instance among
farmers, largely faded after the benefits of EU membership materialised
(De Lange and Guerra 2009; FitzGibbon and Guerra 2010). It is, therefore,
unlikely that an anti-EU party, such as the LPR, would have been able to
gain large successes in national elections on the basis of this issue.[4]

The story as regards socio-economic issues is different. In the 1990s
most voters based their party choice mainly on their position with regard
to moral–cultural and religious issues (Jasiewicz 2003; 2008). Socioeconomic issues, such as unemployment, privatisation and social security, were considered important by many Polish voters (Markowski 2006;
Millard 2009: 62), but only became truly salient when economic growth
slowed and unemployment rose by the end of the 1990s. According to
data from the 2001 Polish National Election Study, 57.4 per cent of the
voters considered unemployment to be the most important issue facing
Poland (McManus-Czubinska et al. 2004). A survey from the Polish Public
Opinion Research Centre (*Centrum Badania Opinii Społecznej*, CBOS) in
the summer of 2001 further indicated that Poles were highly dissatisfied with the economic circumstances: 71 per cent of the respondents
considered the economic situation 'bad' (CBOS 2001a: 4). An October
2001 CBOS report furthermore showed how support for privatisation
had declined sharply towards the end of the 1990s, and that – not least
due to the economic conditions – the centre-right Buzek government
had 'lower social support and evoked more criticism than any of the
previous governments' (CBOS 2001b: 2; see also Stanley 2013: 179).

In this light, it is understandable that SO – a party that from the outset
preached solidarity with the poor and opposed privatisation policies –
managed to do well in the 2001 parliamentary election. Although rural
areas remained the main electoral strongholds for SO, party leader Lepper
was also able to appeal to (unemployed) 'transition losers' in more urban
areas (Szczerbiak 2002a: 57; Millard 2009: 113; Wysocka 2010: 157). The
Democratic Left Alliance, meanwhile, still did not pursue unequivocally
left-wing economic policies. This was, for instance, exemplified by the
austerity measures the party presented prior to the 2001 election. This
further increased the opportunity for Lepper to capture dissatisfied left-
wing voters.

Since the LPR had recurrently portrayed the process of privatisation as an 'anti-national act' (Kucharczyk and Wysocka 2008: 74), it may well have benefited from public opposition to these policies as well. The League's stance against privatisation did not truly stem from a left-wing position on economic issues, however, and was framed more in terms of fears of foreign investments and supranational interests harming Polish cultural and economic independence (Stanley 2013: 182). To explain the League's breakthrough, it is more important to consider its ability to appeal to a core of conservative religious right-wing voters who became available after the disintegration of the Solidarity Electoral Action alliance (Szczerbiak 2002a: 62). Compared with the rest of the Polish electorate, the League's supporters were more anti-internationalist, culturally conservative and favourable to a role of the Church in public life (CBOS 2001c: 19–20). In the end, the electorate of the League seemed to be driven more by its agreement with the party's Catholic nationalist message than by dissatisfaction with the economic policies of the incumbent government (Szczerbiak 2002a: 61).

Corruption and probity in public life

Besides dissatisfaction with the government's socio-economic policies, explanations for the electoral success of the radical parties in 2001 can be sought in the more general reputation of the political elite. Back in the 1990s, the Democratic Left Alliance–Peasant Party coalition that formed after the election of 1993 was already accused of practices of clientelism, as party supporters were given key positions in various local administrations and economic institutions (Millard 1999: 23; Castle and Taras 2002: 128). Consequently, in the run up to the 1997 election the newly formed Solidarity Electoral Action made pledges to 'clean up' government. Once in power, however, the AWS was also unable to disassociate itself from an image of clientelism and corruption (Szczerbiak 2004: 71). In 2001, for instance, corruption allegations forced two ministers in the Buzek government to resign (Millard 2006: 1011).

Such incidents contributed to an increasing salience of corruption as a political issue. Whereas in 1991 one-third of the Poles believed that corruption in public life was a 'very big' problem, ten years later this figure had risen to two-thirds, with a sharp increase in the year before the 2001 parliamentary election (CBOS 2001a: 5–6). According to 2001 Polish National Election Study data, 84.6 per cent of the voters thought that corruption was very or quite widespread among politicians (McManus-Czubinska et al. 2004). Unsurprisingly, anti-establishment rhetoric was commonly used in the 2001 election campaign, and the moderate PO also aimed to tap into the electorate's dissatisfaction with the political elite (Szczerbiak 2002a; Millard 2009: 100). Yet corruption was an important theme for PiS and the two radical newcomers, SO and the LPR, in particular.

In terms of dubious political practices, the following period under the Democratic Left Alliance–Peasant Party coalition did not prove to be a break with the past. The Miller government soon ran into problems: the economy was in a bad shape; unemployment was on the rise; the government's reform policies appeared ineffective; and the coalition was plagued by internal struggles (Szczerbiak 2007: 204–205). The SLD, moreover, became tainted by a series of proven or alleged corruption scandals (Markowski 2006: 818; Stanley 2013: 182). The most prominent example was the 'Rywin affair', a corruption scandal centred on the amendment of a media ownership law, in which various social democratic politicians, including Prime Minister Miller, were alleged to be involved. The Miller administration would turn out to be the most unpopular government of post-1989 Polish politics (Szczerbiak 2007: 207). In a CBOS survey of May 2003, 18 per cent of the respondents stated that they saw 'widespread corruption and scandals' as the most important failure of the government (CBOS 2003a: 2–3). Only unemployment and the lack of progress in fighting it were perceived as greater failures (by 34 per cent of the respondents).

The scandals did little to improve the public perception of political actors. In a CBOS survey of June 2003, a great majority of respondents thought that politicians were dishonest (77 per cent), unreliable (78 per cent), and merely cared for their own interests (87 per cent) (CBOS 2003b: 4). A mere 6 per cent of the respondents answered that politicians were the sort of people who 'wanted to do something for others' – compared with a percentage of 22 per cent in 1993 – and no less than 52 per cent of the respondents thought that politicians first and foremost wanted to have a lot of money. Consequently, the environment for populist parties seemed very favourable; following Millard (2006: 1012–1013), '[c]orruption fed perceptions of a divide between the corrupt political elite on the one hand and ordinary people on the other'. A September 2005 CBOS pre-election poll furthermore indicated that voters primarily desired their preferred party to adhere to the principles of 'honesty, reliability, social sensitivity and understanding of the problems of ordinary people' (CBOS 2005: 2).

As could be expected, the issues of probity in public life and corruption again played a major role in the 2005 electoral campaign (Millard 2006; Szczerbiak 2007). PiS, SO and the LPR were not the only parties to focus strongly on these issues; PO also promised a radical break with the past, and declared that public life needed to be cleansed (Wysocka 2010: 268–269). However, the PO's main rival, PiS, could lay a greater claim to the ownership of those issues, as fighting corruption had been at the core of its programme from the outset (Szczerbiak 2007: 212; Stanley 2010: 214).

The economy was another dominant campaign theme in 2005, as the handling of unemployment was perceived as one of the government's largest failures. Whereas the liberal PO could be seen as the main representative of the 'modernisation winners', SO portrayed itself most clearly as the defender of the economically anxious 'transition losers' (Millard 2009: 113). Yet, as previously discussed, in 2005 PiS also presented itself as a party favouring a more egalitarian 'solidaristic Poland', taking care of the Poles who had become victims of the rigorous liberalisation policies (Markowski 2006: 821). It was this strategy that proved particularly effective in order to beat PO in the 2005 election, as PiS was able to 'capitalize on most Poles' broad sympathy to state intervention in the economy and economic redistribution' (Szczerbiak 2007: 211).

The vote shares of SO and the LPR stagnated in 2005. In view of the prevailing anti-establishment mood, the results were somewhat disappointing for the two parties. In order to understand fully why SO and the LPR did not perform better in this election, the electoral credibility of PiS and the two radical parties must be considered.

Supply of credible populist parties

As previously outlined, the electoral credibility of a populist party is considered to be dependent on the party's appeal – assessed by considering its leadership's visibility and persuasiveness, and its ability to dissociate itself from political extremism as well as from the political establishment – and organisational cohesion. With regard to SO, the leadership factor has been of crucial importance, as the party was essentially a personal vehicle of Andrzej Lepper. Throughout the 1990s the party still lacked media attention, and only fielded candidates for parliamentary elections in a limited number of constituencies (Millard 2009: 102–103). In 1999 SO was involved in more high-profile protests related to a pork meat crisis. The events attracted considerable media attention, and many citizens were favourable towards the protesters (Wysocka 2010: 139–140). Lepper, meanwhile, began to develop 'a martyr's reputation for his challenges on behalf of the "little folk" against the police and the bureaucracy' (Millard 2009: 103).

The campaign of SO for the 2001 parliamentary election was run in a more professional way than before. Lepper, with the help of a media consultant, presented himself as a more serious candidate (Szczerbiak 2002a: 58).[5] In the words of Millard (2003: 78), the SO leader 'made an efficient transition from streetwise thug to persuasive spokesman for the poor and alienated'. As such, the party broadened its appeal beyond the most radical protest-voters, and could benefit from the general anti-establishment mood that had emerged at the time of the election. Following Aleks Szczerbiak (2002a: 58), 'Lepper was able to develop a distinctive and attractive electoral appeal as a "man of the people" who was articulate and determined enough to take on the Warsaw elites'. Moreover, since politicians from both the post-Solidarity and communist successor camps had been represented in governments before, the party could credibly claim to constitute a real alternative (Stanley 2013: 181).

After SO had been elected into the *Sejm*, the party became known for its disruptive behaviour within parliament. SO MPs, for instance, brought in their own loudspeakers in order to outshout their opponents (Jasiewicz 2008: 14), an act which only reinforced the party's anti-establishment status. It was ostensibly more problematic for the party that internal conflicts arose. Various MPs, who did not accept Lepper's autocratic style of leadership, came into conflict with their party leader (Wysocka 2010: 151). By August 2003, nearly half of the deputies had been expelled or had defected from the party. Several SO politicians also suffered reputational damage. Lepper himself had in the past already been accused of several criminal offences, including 'planned assassination, assaults, lies, extortion, tax evasion, public order offences, and bribe taking' (Millard 2003: 83). Other SO politicians also attracted controversy; several MPs were, for instance, accused of falsifying documents and having contacts in the criminal milieu (Wysocka 2010: 152–153).

Strikingly, however, neither the organisational problems nor the controversies surrounding SO politicians seemed to have a negative impact on the popularity of the party (Szczerbiak 2007: 206–207). The party was still able to profit from the immense unpopularity of the centre-left Miller government, which could be seen to eclipse the controversies surrounding SO (Wysocka 2010: 153). In view of its higher standing in previous opinion polls, the parliamentary election result of 2005 (11.4 per cent of the vote) was somewhat disappointing for Lepper's party.

In 2001 the newly founded LPR relied much less on a high-profile leader (Marek Kotlinowski). Instead, the electoral breakthrough of the

League is often attributed to the backing of the fundamentalist Catholic radio station *Radio Maryja* (Szczerbiak 2002a; Millard 2009: 109; Stanley 2013: 180–181). This radio station, spearheaded by the controversial Father Tadeusz Rydzyk, could count on a loyal share of conservative listeners.[6] Rydzyk had previously supported Solidarity Electoral Action, but shifted his allegiance to the League after AWS's disintegration. Upon entering parliament, the LPR saw various breakaways from the parliamentary fraction (Wysocka 2010: 182). Nevertheless, the new leader, Roman Giertych, was able to raise the profile of the party in the Polish media (Szczerbiak 2007: 206; Millard 2009: 126). Prior to the 2005 election, however, the LPR faced a major setback when *Radio Maryja* shifted its support to PiS. The party was eventually unable to expand its share of the vote.

The modified discourse of PiS in 2005 can be seen as one of the main reasons behind the stagnating support for SO and the LPR. The Kaczyński brothers were able to present themselves as political outsiders and 'launched a campaign as if they had been absent from the Polish politics of the past decade and a half' (Markowski 2006: 821). In reality, both brothers had been close to the centre of power in the years after the transition to democracy.[7] The Kaczyńskis, however, successfully denied that PiS was an elitist party (Millard 2009: 122), and particularly thrived on Lech's popularity and crime-fighting image. PiS was especially effective with its promise to tackle corruption and bring 'clean' government (Szczerbiak 2007: 212). Since the party had previously entered the *Sejm* on an anti-corruption ticket, it 'had the better claim to issue ownership in this field' (Stanley 2010: 214).

What is more, the support of Father Rydzyk's *Radio Maryja* prior to the election of 2005 improved PiS's appeal to the religious right electorate, at the electoral cost of the LPR. While PiS had not placed much emphasis on the teachings of the Church in its 2001 campaign (Szczerbiak 2002a: 58–59; Millard 2009: 104), this theme became more important in the party's rhetoric in 2005 (Markowski 2006: 827; Millard 2009: 140). In terms of foreign policy, in addition, PiS adopted a more 'hawkish' stance and became more explicitly Eurosceptic (Wysocka 2010: 282). The party had thus moved into the territory of the LPR, but also aimed to win over SO voters by emphasising its 'solidaristic' character. Former spokesperson for SO, Mateusz Piskorski, did indeed see the programmatic development of PiS as one of the main reasons behind the somewhat disappointing election results of SO in 2005: 'if you look at the programmes of the parties [...] you will very easily find many similarities between the programme of Self Defence with regard to social issues, and the programme of PiS from 2005' (Interview, Warsaw, 22 September 2008).

Both SO and the LPR lost parliamentary representation after having taken part in the PiS-dominated coalition government between May 2006 and August 2007. This episode was hardly a success for the LPR and SO. League leader Roman Giertych was criticised for the chaotic way in which his education ministry was ran, and SO became entangled in practices of sleaze and corruption (Stanley 2010: 249; 255–256). In December 2006, for instance, SO functionaries were accused of offering women jobs in return for sexual activities. The League was accused of patronage as well, and the Polish media reported widely about the incompetence of both junior coalition partners (Millard 2009: 146). Former SO spokesperson Piskorski admitted that 'if we would find a kind of method to estimate the degree of programme realisation [...] it would be very small in the case of Self Defence, after two years of coalition. Very small' (Interview, Warsaw, 22 September 2008). Both parties, moreover, continued to suffer from defections. For the two radical parties, it thus proved very difficult to remain credible after taking part in a (generally disliked) government (see CBOS 2006a).

PiS, however, remained popular among a significant section of the electorate; the party refrained from taking radical austerity measures, unemployment was falling and the government received credit for its anti-corruption measures (Szczerbiak 2008: 418; Stanley 2013: 187).[8] This was far from irrelevant; people saw reducing unemployment and fighting corruption as important tasks for the government (CBOS 2006b: 4). PiS could claim credit for these achievements, while the junior coalition partners failed to play a visible role in the 2007 election campaign and to differentiate themselves from their governing partner in a positive way. What is more, PiS had, in the words of Stanley (2013: 186), 'outstripped their coalition partners for populist rhetoric'. The party had thus largely absorbed 'the *raison d'être* of its smaller coalition parties' (Stanley 2010: 18), and the LPR and SO ended up as '"appetisers" for PiS to swallow' (Markowski 2008: 1064).

As discussed, PiS would nevertheless end up in opposition after the 2007 election – and once again after the election of 2011. This placed PiS in a position where it could retain its anti-establishment rhetoric and present itself as the representative of economically hard-pressed and culturally conservative voters (Tworzecki 2012: 619). At the same time, Jarosław Kaczyńsky remained 'a charismatic figure who generated an extremely loyal following on the Polish right' (Szczerbiak 2013: 497). Kaczyńsky's confrontational style nevertheless alienated many other voters, and, following Szczerbiak (2013), the ability of PO to generate fears about PiS's potential return to power was one of the key reasons behind PO's victory in 2011. PiS, furthermore, failed to remain united. After Kaczyńsky's loss in the 2010 presidential election, several more moderate party members were expelled or broke away, and formed the new party 'Poland is the Most Important' (*Polska jest Najważniejsza*, PJN), which failed to win any seats in 2011. After the parliamentary election, open criticism of Kaczyńsky's leadership led to the expulsion of several more PiS deputies, indicating that PiS's party organisation was beginning to show serious cracks (Stanley 2013: 194). The party nevertheless ended second in the 2014 European Parliament election with 31.8 per cent of the vote, not far behind PO. At the time of writing, the party still constitutes the main opposition force in Polish politics.

Conclusion

In the first decade after communism, Polish party politics was marked by a considerable degree of chaos. After 2000, the party system stabilised, and by this time it was possible to identify a political establishment consisting of two camps: the post-Solidarity camp and the communist successor camp. In the parliamentary election campaign of 2001, the members of this establishment were criticised by two radical anti-establishment parties: Andrej Lepper's Self Defence (SO) and the League of Polish Families (LPR). As I have argued, only the former can be considered a genuine populist party. The LPR is a more ambiguous case, as it based its ideology primarily on the values of the Catholic Church, instead of the 'common sense' of the ordinary people. Law and Justice (PiS), the newly formed party of the Kaczyński brothers, which also entered parliament in 2001, is another borderline case. It is questionable whether populism has been a core attribute of the party's ideology, or a more episodic rhetorical device. In agreement with various observers, this party is here considered to be a populist party from 2005 onwards, when it adopted a more explicit populist discourse.

SO and PiS, as well as the LPR, arguably shared a national-conservative message. For the latter two parties, traditional (Catholic) values played a central role in defining the shared identity of the Poles. For SO, socio-economic themes were more essential. The party primarily appealed to 'transition losers' who had supposedly been exploited by the liberal elites. In addition, the three parties shared a criticism of the post-communist political elites, and aimed to capitalise on the widespread public dissatisfaction with Polish politicians – although they were not the only political actors to do so.

Concerning their electoral performance, the populist parties in Poland did not face an insurmountable hurdle as far as the electoral system was concerned, certainly taking into consideration the availability of the mostly unaligned Polish electorate. The agency of the mainstream political parties further contributed to a conducive environment for populist parties. While many Poles were favourable towards economic state intervention and wary of free-market-oriented policies, none of the mainstream parties occupied a clear left-wing socio-economic position when economic conditions deteriorated towards the end of the 1990s. This left open an electoral niche for SO in particular. In addition, parties from both the post-Solidarity and communist successor camps earned a bad reputation due to their practices of cronyism and corruption, and became vulnerable to populist criticism. Economic hardship and corruption were, thus, important themes on the basis of which Polish opposition parties – genuinely populist or not – could mobilise support. Unlike the Dutch case, issues related to immigration or multiculturalism did not play a role in ethnically homogeneous Poland, which was also still primarily a country of emigration. European integration, meanwhile, remained an issue of relatively low salience, and worries about the effects of EU membership largely faded after Poland's EU accession (Szczerbiak and Bil 2009; FitzGibbon and Guerra 2010).

In the end, the agency of the Polish radical parties themselves has been key to explaining their individual performances. In 2001 Lepper presented himself and his SO as a less outlandish alternative to the mainstream parties, and became a credible spokesperson for the economically weak (Szczerbiak 2002a; Millard 2003). Backed by *Radio Maryja*, the LPR primarily appealed to religious right-wing voters, who became available after the demise of Solidarity Electoral Action. PiS, however, later attracted many (potential) SO and LPR voters by employing a more explicit populist discourse and by presenting itself as the more trustworthy proponent of a conservative and 'solidaristic' Poland (e.g. Stanley 2013). PiS was better organised than SO and the League, which were both plagued by defections and scandals, and was able to claim credit for the perceived successes of the governing coalition between the three parties. While SO and the LPR disappeared from parliament in 2007, PiS remained a key player in the polarised political landscape.

Three important observations can be made on the basis of the Polish case. First, in a context of widespread disillusion with politics, it is not always possible to distinguish clearly between populist and non-populist parties, or between the motives of their electorates. In Poland, as in several other post-communist countries, corruption and related issues have played an important role in the general political debate (see Chapter 2). The LPR – here considered to be an essentially non-populist party – also campaigned with a message of 'political purification'. What is more, also the moderate centre-right PO played into the public dissatisfaction with the Polish political elite. This implies that, if corruption, or the more general reputation of established parties, is one of the key issues at stake, the relevance of distinguishing between populist and non-populist actors may not be that great. That said, differences in voter motivations indicate that there might still be empirical relevance in setting populist parties apart from the others. More than other voters, supporters of SO – arguably the purest populist party in the Polish context – found it important that politicians 'understood the problems of ordinary people' (CBOS 2005). LPR voters, on the other hand, were motivated largely by the party's nationalism and religious conservatism, themes with regard to which mainstream parties could not genuinely be considered unresponsive (e.g. Millard 2010: 69). Even so, the concept of populism seems to have less 'discriminating power' in post-communist countries such as Poland than in many long-established Western European democracies.

Second, the Polish case shows that it is possible for populist parties to survive, even when they suffer from organisational disunity and personal scandals. SO faced numerous splits and scandals after it entered parliament in 2001, but Lepper's party nevertheless retained its vote share in the subsequent parliamentary election. This could mean that, if public dissatisfaction with the political establishment has reached sufficiently high levels, populist parties can afford a certain amount of negative exposure. The Polish case also suggests, however, that voters become less forgiving if scandals continue once the party is in government. As discussed, SO, as well as the LPR, disappeared from parliament after they took part in a short-lived government.

The third observation is that it is possible for a mainstream party to appeal to voters of radical populist parties if it seizes the ownership of the issues central to their appeal. PiS managed to win over many (potential) SO and LPR voters after it resorted to a more explicit populist discourse and moved into their ideological grounds. PiS's success in doing so is likely to be related to the aforementioned credibility of the two radical parties, which was seriously tainted during their period in office. Voters may be inclined to prefer the radical original over the mainstream copy, as has been evident in the Dutch case, but this is likely to change when the original discredits itself too much.

The competition over issue ownership will also be an important theme in the next chapter, which focuses on populist parties in the United Kingdom, and their electoral failure in general elections up until 2010.

6
Populist Parties in the United Kingdom

Whereas the previous two chapters dealt with countries in which some populist parties could rely on considerable levels of support in parliamentary elections, this chapter provides a study of a country where, at least up until 2010, populist parties have failed to make a great impact at the national level: the United Kingdom.[1] By means of this case study I aim to discover whether the conditions underlying the electoral success of populist parties are also essential in explaining their failure. The main focus will be on two parties that can (in their present form) be considered populist parties: the British National Party (BNP) and the UK Independence Party (UKIP).

As I will argue, the Single Member Plurality (SMP) electoral system has thrown up a serious hurdle for new or small (populist) parties in British general elections. Yet the agency of established and populist parties also needs to be taken into account. The Conservative Party in particular has been responsive to voters concerned about the issues central to the British populist parties: immigration and European integration – even though the latter issue has been of limited electoral salience. To understand why British populist parties failed to seize the ownership of these issues, we also must consider their own characteristics. The BNP and UKIP have (long) failed to present themselves as credible alternatives to the established parties. Despite its attempts to forge a more acceptable image, the, formerly neo-fascist, BNP remained stigmatised and was still characterised by a militant xenophobic discourse. UKIP, at least up until the general election of 2010, long lacked visible and persuasive leadership. Both parties have, furthermore, faced numerous internal conflicts and defections. UKIP has embarked on a more successful course in more recent years, and became the largest party at the European Parliament (EP) election of

May 2014. To what extent this is a sign of improved prospects for first-order general elections remains to be seen. The chapter begins with identifying the populist parties in the UK. As will be argued, this is not a straightforward exercise, due to the presence of regionalist parties and the adversarial character of British party competition. In the subsequent section I discuss the electoral performance of the BNP and UKIP. The final section concludes and draws the implications from the British case study.

Identifying the populist parties in the United Kingdom

Academic accounts on radical politics in Britain have in the past often focused on fascism or the extreme right (e.g. Cronin 1996; Eatwell and Goodwin 2010; Goodwin 2011), instead of populism (see Fella 2008 for an exception). The latter term has, nevertheless, regularly been used to refer to individual politicians. Two Conservative politicians in particular have been associated with populism: Enoch Powell and Margaret Thatcher (Fry 1998). In the case of Powell this often relates to the politician's controversial 'Rivers of Blood' speech from 1968, in which he expressed his concern about immigration and racial violence. Thatcher's alleged populism is regularly associated with her appeal to the common 'middle England' people, her concerns about the decline of Britain, and her crusade against socialism – Thatcher's main enemy 'from within' (Fella 2008: 188). Whether these elements should all be associated with 'populism' in the first place is questionable, but not immediately relevant to this chapter, which is concerned with party-based populism in contemporary Britain.

Two parties have dominated British politics in the past decades: the centre-right Conservatives (the 'Tories') and the centre-left Labour Party. Until the general election of May 2010, governments in post-Second World War Britain had always been formed by one of these two parties. The Tories and Labour did become increasingly challenged, most notably by the Liberal Democrats, which in recent decades secured their position as the third largest party in Britain. Opposition also came from regionalist parties – notably the Scottish National Party (SNP) and the Welsh *Plaid Cymru* (PC) – that entered the British lower house (House of Commons) in the 1970s (see also Webb 2005).

Both of these latter parties have regularly portrayed Labour and the Conservatives as being part of the same 'Westminster elite'. According to the 2010 general election manifesto of the Welsh nationalists, for instance, 'Labour has slavishly followed Tory policies for 13 years and

[Conservative Party leader] Cameron has modelled himself and his politics on [former Labour prime minister] Tony Blair' (Plaid Cymru 2010: 4). The Scottish Nationalists, in turn, stated that '[t]he London parties are part of the same metropolitan political machine – a machine that leaves the ordinary men and women of our country on the outside' (SNP 2010: 7). While the latter passage can certainly be seen as a populist statement, the regionalist parties will not be discussed in the remainder of the chapter, since I focus on populist parties that had – at least potentially – a countrywide appeal. It is, furthermore, questionable whether the SNP and PC should be treated as genuine populist parties, since their personality has, so to speak, been split between the national and the regional level. At the national level, they may have operated in the guise of anti-establishment parties, but the main regionalist parties in Scotland and Wales – and Northern Ireland for that matter[2] – have entered the devolved governments at the regional level. At the sub-national level, therefore, these parties have very much been part of the political establishment. In the elections of May 2011, the SNP even won an outright majority of the seats in the Scottish parliament.

Another regionalist and separatist party from Scotland, the radical left Scottish Socialist Party (SSP), is a more evident case of populism (March 2011: 133–139). Prior to the 2005 general election, the party proclaimed that it had 'a well-earned reputation as the party that stands up for ordinary people, whether it be offering solidarity to striking workers, campaigning against the injustice of the Council Tax or taking to the streets in opposition to Blair's illegal war on Iraq' (SSP 2005: 2). The SSP also targeted the political establishment in Scotland itself, and rejected 'the gravy trains of both Westminster and Holyrood' (SSP 2005: 12).[3] In view of its regionalist appeal, however, the party inherently played a marginal role in general elections; it fielded candidates in only ten constituencies in 2010. Its credibility has, furthermore, been undermined by scandals and a party split (March 2011: 137–139).

Another radical left-wing party, Respect, can also be classified as a populist party. In 2005 the party won a Lower House seat on the basis of an anti-Iraq war platform (which it would lose again in 2010). The party argued that Britain's 'huge' wealth 'remains largely in the hands of a tiny elite', and that the major parties all subscribed to the same free-market economic principles (Respect 2005: 18). Unlike most populist parties in Western Europe, Respect actually conveyed a pro-multiculturalist message and argued that Britain 'is under threat by those who would rather ordinary people turn against one another than come together to confront the real culprits – big business and the mainstream politicians who do its bidding' (Respect 2005: 13). Yet, since Respect, like the SSP, has only played a very marginal role in national-level British politics – the party only fielded 11 candidates in 2010 – it will be excluded from the analysis. Suffice it to say that its image as a 'narrow and sectarian coalition' and a party split in 2007 did not lend the party much electoral credibility (March 2011: 134).

The use of populist anti-establishment rhetoric has not been limited to regionalist and smaller fringe parties – the Green Party, which entered the House of Commons in 2010, being another example. The Liberal Democrats, the junior partner of the Conservatives in the coalition government formed in 2010, also emphasised the unresponsiveness of the two main parties in their 2010 manifesto: '[w]e've had 65 years of Labour and the Conservatives: the same parties taking turns and making the same mistakes, letting you down' (Liberal Democrats 2010: 4). The party promised to 'do things differently, because we believe that power should be in the hands of people, not politicians' (Liberal Democrats 2010: 87). Previously, the (New) Labour Party under Tony Blair has also been associated with populism (Mair 2002; Mudde 2004). In its 2010 general election manifesto, furthermore, also the Conservative Party claimed that 'our political system has betrayed the people' (Conservative Party 2010: iii).

Populism may thus constitute a more general feature of contemporary British party politics. The common use of (populist) anti-establishment rhetoric is likely to be related to the majoritarian and adversarial character of British democracy. For parties of opposition, the 'establishment' to blame has been easy to identify: the Labour-Conservative hegemony. When in opposition, furthermore, Labour and the Tories themselves could criticise freely the single-party governments formed by their main opponent. It would, nevertheless, be incorrect to claim that most British political parties are populist parties. The three largest parties, at least, have not consistently portrayed themselves as the representatives of a homogeneous body of 'ordinary people', or expressed unreserved support for popular sovereignty.

A content analysis of party manifestos performed by Rooduijn et al. (2014) confirmed that not all British parties expressed populist rhetoric to the same degree. Even though the British mainstream parties scored relatively high on the 'populism scale' compared with their counterparts in other European countries, they clearly trailed two more usual suspects: the BNP and UKIP.[4] The results of the expert survey conducted for this case study provided further substantiation for classifying only these two parties as populist parties. Both the BNP and UKIP were considered to be populist parties by ten out of the 15 respondents. Respect was mentioned four times, whereas none of the respondents included Labour, the Conservatives or the Liberal Democrats. Consequently, the remainder of this chapter will focus on the ideology and electoral performance of the BNP and UKIP.

The British National Party

The BNP was founded in 1982 by the extreme right hardliner John Tyndall, who had been ousted from the neo-fascist National Front (NF) two years earlier (see e.g. Copsey 1996; Eatwell 1996). Under the leadership of Tyndall, the BNP 'clung rigidly to the core pillars of biological racism, radical xenophobia and anti-democratic appeals' (Goodwin 2011: 37). In the first decade of its existence the party was occupied more with participating in 'rights for whites' marches than with fighting elections. The only electoral achievement of the BNP was to win a local borough council seat in East London in 1993, which the party lost again a year later. By this time, the party had begun to follow a new strategy, which involved 'sinking local community roots through "public-spirited" activity' (Copsey 1996: 130). The BNP sought to gain political legitimacy and to shrug off its extremist neo-Nazi image by focusing on the grievances of local white residents (Copsey 2008; Goodwin 2011).

Real programmatic reforms were pushed through when Nick Griffin replaced John Tyndall after a leadership battle in 1999 – despite the fact that Griffin had previously not been known as a real 'moderniser' (Copsey 2008: 74–75). The party took inspiration from the more successful radical right-wing parties on mainland Europe, most notably the *Front National* in France (Goodwin 2011), and now explicitly rejected a political and economic system of fascist totalitarianism. The party also dropped its commitment to compulsory repatriation of immigrants, and adopted a 'differentialist' line on race (Eatwell 2004). Accordingly, the BNP stepped away from a notion of racial superiority, but instead claimed that mixing people from different ethnic backgrounds threatened cultural identity and social cohesion. The party warned against the cultural threat of Islam in particular, especially after the terrorist attacks on 11 September 2001 (Copsey 2008). The BNP also continued to pursue its 'community-based' strategy and to develop a more acceptable agenda of social conservatism (Goodwin 2008; Rhodes 2009; Ford and Goodwin 2010). It moved away from a narrow focus on immigration and focused increasingly on commonplace local issues 'such as crime, antisocial behaviour, rubbish collection and pressures on social housing' (Goodwin 2008: 356). The party further favoured a British withdrawal from the European Union, as the EU was perceived as an 'aspiring super state' that would 'bring about the eventual liquidation of Britain as a nation and a people' (BNP 2005: 5). The extent to which the BNP truly changed can be debated. According to Nigel Copsey (2007: 61), ideological renewal under Griffin constituted 'a recalibration of fascism rather than a fundamental break in ideological continuity'. As the BNP's commitment to liberal democracy remained doubtful, its modernisation could, according to Copsey (2008: 164–165), better be perceived as nothing more than an opportune 'change of clothing'. BNP insiders might, indeed, still have been driven by fascist and racist convictions (Goodwin 2010: 179).

However, based on the way the party has presented itself to the outside world, the 'modern' BNP can be treated as a populist party. In recent years, the BNP explicitly aimed to present itself as a democratic party (Ford and Goodwin 2010: 5). The manifesto for the 2005 general election was actually titled 'Rebuilding British Democracy' and warned against excessive central state control, in relation to which the party referred to the 'excesses and horrors of totalitarianism on mainland Europe throughout the 20th century' (BNP 2005: 9). In the party's 2010 general election manifesto ('Democracy, Freedom, Culture and Identity') Griffin explained that '[t]he word "democracy" appears in the title of our manifesto for good reason. It represents our desire to preserve this great institution' (BNP 2010a: 12).

The party, furthermore, combined a strong anti-establishment rhetoric with an explicit appeal to 'ordinary British folk' (BNP 2005: 53; see also Fella 2008). The party manifesto of 2005, for instance, expressed clear populist discourse:

> It is the 'average' man and woman who suffers from the failings of our politicians to grasp the issue and restore genuine democracy [...] The British National Party exists to put an end to this injustice. We will return power to the men and women of Britain, the taxpayers, pensioners, mums and dads and workers (BNP 2005: 3).

On the BNP's website, Nick Griffin made further populist statements: '[w]hile we struggle to pay the bills and live in fear of losing our jobs, the crooked politicians are fiddling their expenses and stealing taxpayers' money' (BNP 2010b). The BNP, according to Griffin, was 'a patriotic, democratic alternative to the old parties that have wrecked our great country' (BNP 2010b).

The more 'moderate' and populist course of the BNP resulted in limited electoral success at the local level, predominantly among dissatisfied white working-class voters, who felt 'threatened by immigration and ethnic change' (Ford and Goodwin 2010: 3). In 2002 the party won three local council seats, and this number steadily rose to 55 in May 2009 (Tetteh 2009: 5) – to fall again afterwards. In European Parliament (EP) elections, the BNP also made a modest impact: in 2009 the BNP received 6.2 per cent of the vote and two seats, Griffin taking up one of them. However, the BNP never managed to win a seat in the House of Commons. In the general election of June 2001, the 33 BNP candidates received a mere 3.9 per cent of the vote on average in the contested constituencies. In 2005 the party fielded 119 candidates and received an average of 4.3 per cent of the vote in the constituencies where it stood (translating into 0.7 per cent of the total national vote). The Barking (London) candidate recorded the best result for the party with 16.9 per cent of the vote. In 2010 the party again extended its number of candidates significantly, and the 339 BNP candidates now received about 564,000 votes, or 1.9 per cent of the total vote. Even though the BNP vote thus increased throughout the years, the party failed to come even close to winning in key battlegrounds. In 2010 party leader Griffin came no further than winning 14.8 per cent of the vote in Barking.

The UK Independence Party

UKIP was founded in 1993 by historian Alan Sked, as the successor of the Anti-Federalist League (established in 1991). From the outset, the main aim of UKIP has been to end British European Union membership. UKIP criticised 'Brussels' for being undemocratic, ineffective and corrupt, and argued that European integration was detrimental to British sovereignty. In a personal interview, former leader Sked argued that Britons 'didn't want to be run by a Committee of unelected bureaucrats' (Interview, London, 10 July 2010). The 'interim manifesto' of 1994 was also clear in its denunciation of 'Brussels': '[t]he European Union represents government by decree, and the bureaucratic waste over which it presides feeds immeasurable graft and corruption. Its symbol is the gravy train. It constitutes institutionalised fraud' (UKIP 1994: 2).

At the same time, UKIP accused the British political establishment of mischievously pushing ahead with EU membership: 'the electorate has been lied to [...] and MPs have been blackmailed and manhandled into the government lobby' (UKIP 1994: 9). UKIP's anti-establishment criticism has clearly not waned over the years, as became clear from a personal interview with UKIP MEP Godfrey Bloom: 'there aren't any policy differences between the Labour Party and the Conservative Party, on anything. So it doesn't matter whether it's fiscal policy, social policy, welfare reform, the NHS, EU, it doesn't matter. You couldn't put a ciga-rette paper between the two parties' (Interview, Brussels, 9 September 2008). The Liberal Democrats were also on the receiving end of Bloom's criticism: 'the Liberal Party in England is supposed to be the nice people. [...] They're not very bright, but they're nice. And they lie and cheat just like everybody else.'

Although UKIP did not refer to the 'ordinary' people very explicitly in its 1994 interim manifesto, it did demand sovereignty for 'the people of the United Kingdom' (UKIP 1994: 3), and described these people's virtuous character:

> The UKIP looks at a country badly led for 40 years, deeply depressed in a mood of hopelessness in which cancers breed, trapped in a feeling of being helpless to prevent national decline. But we believe in the only national resource that ultimately matters, the innate character and abilities of the British people (UKIP 1994: 11).

UKIP remained committed to its populist and anti-EU message after Sked was ousted from the party in 1997, and after various subsequent leader-ship changes. Thus, in its 2005 general election manifesto, titled 'We want our country back', the party claimed: '[o]nly outside the EU will it be possible to begin rebuilding a Britain which is run for British people, not for career politicians and bureaucrats' (UKIP 2005: 1). In the 2010 manifesto ('Empowering the People'), the party voiced similar rhetoric: 'the British system of government is in serious disarray. Bureaucracy overrules democracy at every level, from Brussels to Whitehall to the town hall. UKIP will give meaningful power back to the British people' (UKIP 2010: 13).

In addition to its anti-EU and populist discourse, UKIP began to place more emphasis on the issue of immigration over the years. The 1994 interim manifesto still explicitly stressed its acceptance of 'multi-racialism' and rejection of racist views (UKIP 1994: 9). While UKIP continued to distance itself from racism, the party did take a more restrictive position on the issue of immigration in the 2000s (Gardner 2006: 176). In 2010, under the leadership of Lord Pearson of Rannoch, UKIP's manifesto urged an end to 'mass, uncontrolled immigration', and the party called for 'an immediate five-year freeze on immigration for permanent settlement' (UKIP 2010: 5). UKIP also proposed to make it easier to deport 'dangerous Imams' and to end 'the active promotion of the doctrine of multiculturalism by local and national government and all publicly funded bodies' (UKIP 2010: 6). Pearson, furthermore, invited

Dutch Freedom Party leader Geert Wilders to show the anti-Islam film 'Fitna' in the House of Lords in February 2009. With its greater emphasis on issues related to immigration and Islam, UKIP moved closer to the BNP's territory. The 2010 manifestos of both UKIP and the BNP picked up on the allegation that the Labour government had deliberately stimulated immigration in order to 'water down the British identity and buy votes' (UKIP 2010: 5; see BNP 2010a: 19). Both parties also intended to employ stricter immigration rules in order to counter environmental problems; these measures were meant to curb overpopulation (BNP 2010a: 24) or building demands (UKIP 2010: 11). On the whole, however, the immigration-related statements of the BNP were more numerous and radical, while UKIP (2010: 13) stressed its commitment to civic nationalism and rejection of 'the "blood and soil" ethnic nationalism of extremist parties'.[5]

There have also been differences with regard to other policy areas. Concerning law and order issues, the BNP was, again, more radical than UKIP. Whereas UKIP promoted a robust zero tolerance approach in 2010, the BNP favoured reintroducing capital punishment for grave offences. On economic issues UKIP has traditionally favoured the free market, promoting free trade and tax cuts, cutting bureaucracy and reforming the welfare system. The BNP, on the other hand, has taken a more protectionist and welfare chauvinist position. The party, for instance, blamed the established parties for surrendering the British economy to a 'rootless, amorphous globalist philosophy' (BNP 2010a: 69).

UKIP outperformed the BNP in terms of electoral success. Prior to 2013, the party won a modest number of local council seats, but became particularly successful in EP elections. In 1999, with the PR system in effect, the party received 7 per cent of the vote and three EP seats. In 2004 the party improved its result, with a vote share of 16 per cent and 12 seats, becoming the third largest party in this election. The EP election of 1999 was a greater success for UKIP; the party finished second behind the Conservatives with 16.5 per cent of the vote, enough for 13 seats in the EP. UKIP caused an even larger shock by beating both Labour and the Tories in the EP election of 22 May 2014, and ending first with 27.5 per cent of the nationwide vote.

In general elections, however, UKIP has thus far been much less successful. In 1997, for instance, the party was overshadowed by the Referendum Party, a project of Eurosceptic millionaire James Goldsmith. In 2001 UKIP fielded over 400 candidates and received 1.5 per cent of the nationwide vote. Four years later, with almost 500 candidates, the party increased its overall vote share to 2.3 per cent. None of the candidates came close to winning a seat. In 2010 UKIP again failed to obtain seats in the House of Commons, although it increased its vote share to 3.1 per cent: over 900,000 people voted for UKIP. In UKIP's main target constituency, Buckingham, candidate Farage – after having survived a crash in his small campaign aeroplane – obtained 17.4 per cent of the vote and finished third. In North Cornwall, North Devon and Torridge, and West Devon the party also finished third. This indicated that UKIP has mainly relied on support in traditional Tory and Liberal Democrat strongholds. The BNP, in contrast, has been strongest in more industrial urban areas, particularly in Northern England, traditionally dominated by the Labour Party (Copsey 2008: 193; Ford and Goodwin 2010; Whitaker and Lynch 2011; Ford et al. 2012). Neither of the two parties has performed very well in Scotland and Wales. Here the BNP and UKIP faced competition from the regionalist parties campaigning on the basis of a more appealing mix between 'Celtic nationalism' and anti-Westminster rhetoric (Ford et al. 2012).

Compared with the populist parties in the Netherlands, Poland and various other European countries, the electoral performance of the BNP and UKIP in parliamentary elections has been quite poor. Neither party came close to winning a single seat in the House of Commons, even though, as will be discussed later, prospects for UKIP seem to have improved after the election of 2010. The remainder of this chapter turns to the explanations for the meagre electoral performance of the British populist parties, focusing on the electoral system, the responsiveness of established parties, and the supply of credible populist parties.

Explaining the electoral performance of the British populist parties

Electoral system

As is typical of Western European countries, levels of partisan identification have gradually declined in the United Kingdom (see e.g. Crewe et al. 1977; Webb 2000). Throughout the past decades, more and more voters have begun to opt for parties other than Labour or the Conservatives, the two parties on either side of the traditional post-World War II socio-economic divide. Until 1970 the two dominant parties jointly received about 90 per cent of the vote in general elections, and the political system in Britain could justifiably be described as a two-party system. After 1970 the combined vote share of the Tories and Labour in consecutive elections decreased to about 75 per cent, and this figure fell to roughly 65 per cent in the elections of 2005 and 2010 (see Table 6.1). The declining

Table 6.1   UK general election results 1997–2010, in % of the vote and seats

	1997		2001		2005		2010	
	Vote	*Seats*	Vote	*Seats*	Vote	*Seats*	Vote	*Seats*
Labour	43.2	*63.6*	40.7	*62.7*	35.2	*55.2*	29.0	*39.7*
Conservatives	30.6	*25.0*	31.7	*25.2*	32.3	*30.5*	36.1	*47.2*
LibDems	16.7	*7.0*	18.3	*7.9*	22.0	*9.6*	23.0	*8.8*
UKIP	0.3	*0*	1.5	*0*	2.2	*0*	3.1	*0*
BNP	0.1	*0*	0.2	*0*	0.7	*0*	1.9	*0*
Others	9.1	*4.4*	7.6	*4.2*	7.6	*4.7*	6.9	*4.3*

Note: Own calculations on the basis of data from Nordsieck (2013).

clout of the two dominant parties was also visible in the elections (since 1999) for the devolved assemblies in Wales and, especially, Scotland. In these elections, in which mixed-member PR electoral systems have been applied, regional parties secured a large share of the vote (see Dunleavy 2005; Lynch 2007).[6]

In terms of the seat distribution in the House of Commons, however, the Tories and Labour have remained dominant. The parties still occupied more than 85 per cent of the seats after the elections of 2005 and 2010, even though neither party won an outright majority in parliament after the latter election. The Liberal Democrats, on the other hand, were allocated fewer than 9 per cent of the seats after the 2010 general election, while their vote share was 23 per cent. It had been worse for them: in 1983 the Social Democratic Party–Liberal Party Alliance only took up 3.5 per cent of the seats with a vote share of 25.4 per cent.

This disproportionality between votes and seats is due to the Single Member Plurality (SMP) or 'first past the post' electoral system that has been applied in UK general elections.[7] The UK is divided into constituencies – 650 in 2010 – and each of those constituencies elects one representative to the House of Commons. A candidate needs a simple plurality of the vote in order to become a member of parliament, while the votes for the other, less successful, candidates are effectively 'wasted'. This leads to a considerable disproportionality between the votes cast for a party, and the seats it receives in parliament.

For smaller or new parties, which lack abundant resources and/or sufficient credible candidates, standing in a large number of constituencies can be difficult. Parties with a specific regional concentration of support, such as the Welsh and Scottish nationalists, have a larger chance of winning seats, although their success is inherently limited due to their regionalist appeal. As Maurice Duverger (1959) suggested, the SMP electoral system is likely to produce a two-party system. This is not only due to the 'mechanics' of the plurality system, but also because of the psychological effects it generates. As voters know the system hampers the success of smaller parties, their incentive to vote for these parties decreases. At the same time, political entrepreneurs may be less inclined to establish a new political party, with an eye on the institutional hurdle which an SMP system throws up. The electoral system, then, not only affects how votes are translated into seats, but is likely to have an impact on the initial vote shares as well.

Data from the British Election Study of 2010 do, indeed, show that a significant share of the electorate did not vote for their genuinely preferred candidate (Clarke et al. 2010). Of all respondents, 8.1 per cent stated that they voted for another party because their preferred party stood no chance of winning in their constituency. Another 8.9 per cent indicated that they voted tactically. Most of these two groups of respondents declared that the candidate they actually preferred was a member of one of the three largest parties. Only 15 and 6.4 per cent stated that they would have preferred to vote for a UKIP or a BNP candidate, respectively. These findings suggest that, if everyone had voted according to their first preference, the overall impact on the vote shares of UKIP and the BNP would have been limited.

Assessing the psychological impact of the electoral system still largely remains a matter of speculation. It is, nevertheless, clear that both the BNP and UKIP suffered from the electoral system's mechanical effects. Under the PR system applied in the Netherlands, both parties would have won seats in the 2010 general election. Being represented in parliament, in turn, could have increased the parties' exposure and opportunities for further development. Furthermore, the EP election results of UKIP, in particular, show that British populist parties can perform well under more proportional electoral rules, even though one cannot genuinely compare the 'second-order' EP elections with national elections (see Reif and Schmitt 1980).

Although it is safe to conclude that the electoral system in general elections has certainly not helped the British populist parties, it would be too simple to attribute their failure to the SMP system alone. The Liberal Democrats have shown that it is possible to build up a considerable support base despite being disadvantaged by the electoral system. Other small parties, such as the Greens and Respect, have also been able to win at least one seat by focusing their efforts more effectively on certain target areas (Ford and Goodwin 2014: 237–241). In order to

provide a more comprehensive explanation for the electoral performance of the BNP and UKIP, the chapter turns to the agency of both established and populist parties.

Responsiveness of the established parties

Two issues have been central to the appeal of populist parties in Britain:
immigration and European integration. As will be argued here, the
failure of populist parties to attract significant levels of support on the
basis of these issues is partly due to the responsiveness of the established
parties, and the fact that European integration has never been a salient
issue in general election campaigns.

Immigration

Although the failure of anti-immigration parties in Britain has regularly
been attributed to the tolerant British political culture, this explanation
might be a little too simplistic (see Cronin 1996; Lewis 1987). John and
Margetts (2009) pointed at the growing resentment against immigration
among the British population. On the basis of opinion poll research,
they showed that since the end of the 1990s an increasing number of
British people have perceived immigration as the most important societal issue (see also Ford 2010; Goodwin 2011). Data from Ipsos MORI
(2012a) also revealed this trend. Whereas around 5 per cent of the
respondents considered race relations or immigration the 'most important issue facing Britain today' throughout 1998 and 1999, the figure
rose to over 25 per cent from 2003 onwards. The average yearly figure
even climbed to 38.2 per cent in 2007, and was 31.1 and 29.6 per cent
in the election years of 2005 and 2010, respectively. Another series of
Ipsos MORI polls also showed that the issues of asylum or immigration
had become electorally salient: in 2001 around a quarter of the respondents answered that these issues were very important to them in deciding
which party to vote for (Ipsos MORI 2010). This percentage surged to
over 35 per cent in the following years, and to about 50 per cent in 2006
and 2007.

These 'salience figures' do not automatically reveal the existing attitudes among Britons towards immigration-related issues. Data from
YouGov, however, showed that in March 2010 78 per cent of the
respondents – and 92 per cent of the Conservative supporters – found
levels of immigration too high (YouGov 2010a). A majority (69 per cent),
moreover, disapproved of the way the Labour government had handled
immigration since 1997. These figures implied a wariness among the
British population about the relatively liberal immigration policies of

the Labour government, the rise in asylum applications, and the accession of new Central and Eastern European countries to the EU in 2004 and 2007 (Goodwin 2011: 56). Attitudes towards Islam, another issue central to the BNP in particular, also tended to be negative. In a May 2010 YouGov poll, 19 per cent of the respondents 'tended to agree' or 'strongly agreed' with the statement that Muslims had a positive impact on British society, whereas 41 per cent 'tended to disagree' or 'strongly disagreed' (YouGov 2010b; see Goodwin 2011, Chapter 3, for more opinion data on related issues).

These indicators suggest that there was potential for parties with critical attitudes towards immigration and multiculturalism, such as the BNP and UKIP. Yet, despite the fact that the issue had caused internal divisions in the past (Eatwell 2000), immigration-sceptic rhetoric was also voiced by Labour and Conservative politicians. The soon-to-be Labour Prime Minister Gordon Brown, for instance, attracted controversy in 2007 with his promise to provide 'British jobs for British workers', and throughout the 2000s other Labour politicians also made critical comments about immigration and multiculturalism (Goodwin 2011: 57). It was, nevertheless, the Conservative Party that voiced anti-immigration rhetoric most clearly throughout the past decades.

In 1978, for instance, Conservative leader Thatcher controversially expressed sympathy for people who felt 'swamped' by people from a different culture, and the subsequent Conservative governments would tighten immigration and citizenship laws (Goodwin 2011: 42). Indeed, Martin Durham (1996: 82) argued that, due to its restrictive position on immigration, 'Thatcherism was to play a crucial role in the failure of the National Front', the BNP's predecessor. Under John Major's leadership (1990–1997) the Conservatives played down the issue of immigration (Eatwell 2010: 220), but, since the theme was hardly salient throughout the 1990s, this did not provide the BNP with a real opportunity (Goodwin 2011: 42).

When the issue's salience rose after the turn of the century, the Conservatives toughened their stance again in the election campaigns of 2001 and 2005 (Copsey 2008: 117–119; Eatwell 2010: 219; Goodwin 2011: 57). Even though David Cameron afterwards aimed to steer the party away from traditional conservatism – for instance, by focusing more on environmental issues and taking a more liberal line on same-sex relationships – the Tory manifesto of 2010 still proposed to set an annual limit to immigration and to limit access 'only to those who will bring the most value to the British economy' (Conservative Party 2010: 21).

What is more, YouGov data suggested that the Conservatives were also successful in retaining the ownership of immigration-related issues (see also Hayton 2010: 32). A poll prior to the general election of 2005 showed that 39 per cent of the respondents considered the Conservatives to be the best party to handle problems related to immigration and asylum, compared with 16 per cent who opted for Labour and 12 per cent who chose the LibDems (YouGov 2005). A poll carried out shortly before the general election of 2010 yielded similar results, and indicated that only 9 per cent of the respondents opted for other, unspecified, parties (YouGov 2010c).

In comparison with the other parties, the Conservatives have thus been the party with the best public image where issues of immigration and asylum were concerned. That said, on the basis of similar opinion data, Matthew Goodwin (2011: 65) noted that there have been a considerable number of people who thought that none of the parties had good policies on these issues. This suggests that the BNP and UKIP have failed to win over culturally conservative voters who were not particularly attracted to the Conservative Party. The failure of the two populist parties to do this was, in turn, likely to be related to their own electoral credibility, to which this chapter will turn later.

European integration

While 'Europe' has been the central issue for UKIP, the BNP has also been known for its Euroreject attitude. Both parties fitted Chris Gifford's description of British right-wing Euroscepticism in re-imagining 'Europe' as 'the "other" of British political identity and interests' and considering the EU as 'a threat to Britain's exceptional social and political development' (Gifford 2006: 858). The positions of the two parties were compatible with the attitudes of many British voters. A series of Ipsos MORI (2012b) surveys between March 2001 and November 2012 showed that between 39 and 49 per cent of the respondents would opt for leaving the European Union if a referendum on EU membership were to be held. As the Eurobarometer data for the QCA in Chapter 3 indicated, the British have been far more inclined to perceive EU membership as a 'bad thing' than the citizens of most other member states (see Appendix C, Table A.2). On average, 27.8 per cent of Britons shared this opinion between 2000 and 2011, whereas the mean figure for the EU-28 was 14.1 per cent.

Even though a large share of the British electorate has evidently shown little enthusiasm for European integration, the problem for UKIP and the BNP has been that it remained hard to win elections on the basis of a Eurosceptic platform. 'Europe' has from the outset been an issue of low salience for British voters. Baker et al. (2008: 105) argued that 'for the majority of the post-war period a "permissive consensus" existed in which a compliant British electorate regarded Europe as a second-order issue and happily accepted the parties' presentation of European integration as an esoteric process best dealt with by technocratic and bureaucratic expertise'. British people's dislike of Europe was apparently exceeded by their apathy on the subject.

Baker et al. (2008: 107) nevertheless argued that public concern with Europe has increased since the late 1980s. Indeed, a series of Ipsos MORI (2010) polls published since the second half on the 1990s suggested that, until 2005, between approximately a fifth and a quarter of Britons found 'Europe' very important in deciding which party to vote for. In September 2006, however, the percentage dropped to 13 per cent, and a year later to 11 per cent. The same surveys suggested that, over the whole period, issues such as healthcare, education, law and order, pensions, unemployment and immigration were much more salient to British voters. In the 2006 State of the Nation poll, furthermore, only 3.2 per cent of the respondents answered that the European Union was the most important issue facing Britain (see ICM 2006; John and Margretts 2009: 499). A February 2010 YouGov poll also suggested that Europe was not a very salient issue: 10 per cent of the respondents (who could select three issues in total) indicated that 'Europe' was an important issue for them in deciding which party to support in the upcoming general election (YouGov 2010d). This compared with 56 per cent who selected 'the economy' and 43 per cent who chose 'immigration and asylum'.

Compared with other issues, European integration was thus a theme of relatively minor importance to British voters. The mainstream parties, meanwhile, had little reason to politicise and prioritise 'Europe', as it was above all an issue accentuating internal divisions (Baker et al. 2008; Lynch and Whitaker 2013). In general terms, Labour, from the outset the more Eurosceptic party, became more pro-European by the end of the 1980s (see Webb 2008), as the party began to recognise the value of European integration in the promotion of social policies. Euroscepticism within the Conservative Party, on the other hand, grew when political integration accelerated. This was illustrated, for instance, by the 'Bruges speech' of Margaret Thatcher in 1988, in which the Tory leader voiced concern about the federalist direction in which the European Community was heading. Euroscepticism arguably became 'the defining characteristic of the Conservative Party's identity and enshrined in its policies' (Baker et al. 2008: 97).

Under the leaderships of William Hague, Ian Duncan Smith and Michael Howard, the Conservative Party indeed adopted an increasingly Eurosceptic position (Gifford 2006), even though the latter two leaders 'turned down the volume' on Europe in order to avoid unnecessary attention to the party's internal divisions (Bale 2006; Baker et al. 2008: 109; Lynch and Whitaker 2013). By 2005, as research by Paul Webb (2008) has shown, internal divisions within the parliamentary party had significantly decreased: most Tory MPs were clearly Eurosceptic by this time.

Under Cameron's leadership (which started in 2005), the course of the party did not change. This was illustrated by the Conservatives' decision to pull out of the European People Party-European Democrats (EPP-ED) group after the 2009 EP election, to form a new group (the European Conservatives and Reformists, ECR) together with Eurosceptic parties from mainland Europe. During the 2010 general election campaign, furthermore, Cameron promised to take on the alleged pro-European 'Lib-Lab' consensus and expressed unmistakable Eurosceptic language: '[w]hat the British people want is Britain in Europe but not run by Europe. They do not want a state called Europe' (quoted in Bale 2010: 8). After the election, the Conservatives retained their course on Europe while in office. In January 2013, seemingly under pressure from Eurosceptic Tory MPs and the rising popularity of UKIP, Cameron pledged to renegotiate the terms of Britain's EU membership and to organise an in–out referendum if the Conservatives were to be victorious in the 2015 general election (see *Economist* 2013).

Despite the Tories' critical stance on European integration, UKIP has been well placed to attract anti-EU voters in EP elections, in which the issue of 'Europe' plays a more central role. EP elections are, furthermore, characterised by their 'second-order' character, which provides opportunities for smaller (anti-establishment) parties (Reif and Schmitt 1980). The late UKIP MEP Graham Booth actually considered this to be one of the main reasons behind his party's success in 2004: 'people were prepared to give us a chance because they had nothing much to lose' (Interview, Brussels, 9 September 2008). In the June 2009 EP election, furthermore, both the British populist parties ostensibly benefited from the high-profile news about the 'expenses scandal', which involved the misuse of allowances and claimed expenses by MPs from all three major parties (see Pattie and Johnston 2012). Indeed, besides their Eurosceptic (and anti-immigration) profile, UKIP voters in the EP election of 2009 were also characterised by dissatisfaction with, and lack of trust in, the political system (Whitaker and Lynch 2011; Ford et al. 2012). In addition to attitudes of racism and xenophobia, anti-establishment sentiments were also prevalent among BNP voters (Cutts et al. 2011; see also Ford and Goodwin 2010). Unlike UKIP, the BNP did not attract voters who were motivated by their opposition to European integration, indicating that UKIP was clearly the owner of this issue at the time of the EP election (cf. Cutts and Goodwin 2014).

Be that as it may, in 'first-order' general elections UKIP's Eurorejection could not be considered a real vote-winner. Ford et al. (2012) actually showed that many of the UKIP voters who were driven by their opposition to the EU in the 2009 EP election were 'strategic defectors' likely to return to the Conservative Party in general elections. The smaller core of loyal UKIP supporters – who resembled BNP voters more closely in terms of social background and attitudes – were actually attracted more by UKIP's anti-immigration and anti-establishment message. Another study by Ford and Goodwin (2014: 195–196) also indicated that UKIP needed to tap into additional concerns besides Euroscepticism alone – namely, resentment of the political elite and opposition to mass immigration – in order to mobilise its potential voters. Since the Conservatives also could not truly be blamed for being unresponsive to Eurosceptic voters, the theme of European integration in isolation provided limited electoral opportunities for the two populist parties in general elections.

That said, even though the direct consequences of the expenses scandal for the general election results of 2010 were found to be muted, Britons' more general opinions about politicians remained poor (Pattie and Johnston 2012). According to Ipsos MORI (2011) survey data, for instance, between May 2009 and December 2010 about two-thirds of the British believed that the present system of governing in Britain needed quite a lot or a great deal of improvement. In order to explain why the populist parties were unable to benefit from more general dissatisfaction with the political elite, or to seize the ownership of the salient issue of immigration, we also need to consider the electoral credibility of the BNP and UKIP.

Supply of credible populist parties

To recapitulate, a populist party is assumed to be electorally credible when it can rely on visible and persuasive leadership, is able to ward off an extremist image and manages to convincingly distance itself from the political mainstream (i.e. the three factors related to its electoral appeal). Organisational cohesion is also assumed to be an important condition for the preservation of electoral credibility. Although neither the BNP nor UKIP has had problems in distancing itself convincingly from the political establishment, both parties lacked persuasive leadership for most of the time and failed to preserve organisational unity. The BNP, moreover, has found it hard to build an image as an ideologically 'acceptable' political party.

Previously, the lack of success of the NF, the BNP's predecessor, could to a large extent be related to its association with extremism, violence and Nazism (Eatwell 2000). The BNP's more recent 'local community' strategy, which was meant 'to cultivate an image of electoral credibility and legitimacy in local arenas', was an improvement in this regard (Goodwin 2008: 350). The BNP also managed to run its campaigns in a more professional manner. The party, for instance, employed full-time officials, improved its canvassing organisation, and paid more attention to its website (Eatwell 2004: 70).

However, the party still found it difficult to get rid of its extremist stigma (Goodwin 2011). Notwithstanding Griffin's attempts to portray the BNP as a non-racist party, the BNP leader was haunted by his own past. Griffin has, for instance, been caught on tape questioning the occurrence of the Holocaust, and published a series of anti-Semitic articles during the 1990s (Goodwin 2010: 173). What is more, even though the BNP has worded its references to ethnicity more carefully throughout the years, the 2010 general election manifesto still includes statements with a fascist taint. The party, for instance, argued that 'British people may take pride from knowing that the blood of an immense column of nation-building, civilisation-creating heroes and heroines runs through their veins', and that being British ran far deeper than possessing a passport: 'it is to belong to a special chain of unique people who have the natural law right to remain a majority in their ancestral homeland' (BNP 2010a: 23).

While it is clear that many Britons have been concerned about immigration in recent years, it is questionable whether they also approved of the BNP's convictions on race and ethnicity. Judging from British Social Attitudes data, for instance, only a relatively small group of British people (15 per cent) perceived being white as one of the key features of national identity (Ford 2010: 150). A YouGov poll from May–June 2009, moreover, indicated that most people had a negative attitude towards the BNP (YouGov 2009a): 72 per cent of respondents felt negative about the party, compared with an equivalent figure of 38 per cent for UKIP, of whom 62 per cent felt very negative. Only 11 per cent felt fairly or very positive. British Election Study data from 2010 also illustrated the general dislike of the BNP (Clarke et al. 2010). On a scale from 0 (strongly dislike) to 10 (strongly like), a clear majority (58.2 per cent) of the respondents gave the lowest possible score. Nearly three-quarters gave a score between 0 and 2, while a mere 4.4 per cent gave a score between 8 and 10.

While most people thus clearly disliked the BNP with a passion, it can still be argued that there was a small, yet not inconsiderable, group of voters who were less unsympathetic towards the party. The BNP was, moreover, able to reach out to more than eight million people when Griffin appeared on the TV show *Question Time* in October 2009 (Goodwin 2011: 37). The BNP leader faced a hostile audience and panel, but in a YouGov poll held after the broadcast 22 per cent of the respondents answered that they might consider voting for the party (YouGov 2009b). However, most of these people answered, rather lukewarmly, 'yes, possibly' (15 per cent of the total sample), 3 per cent answered 'yes, probably', and 4 per cent 'yes, definitely'. On the other hand, 66 per cent of the respondents answered that they would 'under no circumstances' consider voting for the BNP.

It thus seemed difficult for the BNP to appeal to a considerable number of more 'mainstream' voters. The BNP's leadership and party organisation has, furthermore, not been particularly conducive to a breakthrough. Eatwell (2010: 222) described Griffin's limited personal-image skills and lack of ' "centripetal" charismatic appeal' (see also Goodwin 2011: 77). Like its predecessors, moreover, the BNP has been seriously plagued by internal dissent. This was shown, for instance, when dozens of senior members rebelled against party leader Griffin in December 2007, setting up a 'Real BNP' faction. In the run-up to the 2010 election there were signs of disunity within the party as well (Cutts and Goodwin 2014). Notably, the BNP candidate for Stoke-on-Trent, one of the main target constituencies, decided to stand as an independent candidate. After the disappointing election result, further (grass-root) discontent surfaced, and in the following year the party was plagued by organisational, as well as financial, problems (*Guardian* 2011).

In terms of party organisation, UKIP did not fare much better. Founder Alan Sked resigned in 1997 under pressure from fellow party members, and the subsequent leader, Michael Holmes, underwent the same fate in 2000 (see Daniel 2005; Gardner 2006). Under the subsequent leadership of Jeffrey Titford, the party sailed into calmer waters,[8] and in 2002 former Conservative MP Roger Knapman became UKIP's leader after the party's first non-conflictual leadership change. However, when Robert Kilroy-Silk, former Labour MP and BBC chat show host, joined the party in 2004 the calm would quickly vanish.[9] Soon after the controversial Kilroy was elected in the 2004 EP election, he began to criticise

Knapman's leadership and openly expressed his ambitions to replace him as party leader. UKIP was heavily divided about this affair, but its members in the end chose Knapman's side (Daniel 2005; Gardner 2006). Kilroy resigned from the party in January 2005 and went on to form his own party, *Veritas*, which he left half a year later. Besides leadership conflicts, various members have been expelled from UKIP, including the MEPs Ashley Mote and Tom Wise (due to fraudulent behaviour). After the European election of 2009, UKIP could not preserve unity in its fraction either. Nikki Sinclaire was expelled from the party after she refused to sit in meetings with UKIP's foreign allies in the Europe of Freedom and Democracy (EFD) group.

It should be noted that, due to the party's limited media exposure in the years before the 2010 general election, few British people may have been aware of all of UKIP's internal troubles. Party disputes are probably more damaging to a party's credibility if they receive widespread attention. That said, it is safe to say that internal party disputes did not contribute to the electoral credibility of UKIP – or the BNP for that matter.

Besides organisational malaise, UKIP's previous failure to present itself as a credible alternative to the mainstream parties was related to the ambiguity of UKIP's appeal. In the words of Simon Usherwood (2008: 260), 'the party's core ideological identity is placed around a negative definition; there is no clear agreement on why the party is opposed to the EU, less as to what should be the response to this opposition, and less still as to any other policy preferences'. Even though UKIP adopted more outspoken positions on, most notably, immigration, the party's profile with regard to matters not directly related to European integration remained either rather unclear, or quite similar to the Conservatives (see also Hayton 2010).

In terms of visibility and leadership, the party has also long failed to impress. Following Stefano Fella (2008: 196), for most of the time UKIP has lacked an 'instantly recognizable and charismatic leader with considerable media skills'. Or, in the words of former MEP Graham Booth: 'Our problem is: we are all unknowns, nobody knows who the hell we are' (Interview, Brussels, 9 September 2008). Kilroy-Silk, the most high-profile and visible UKIP figure in the past, proved to be a very divisive figure, and thus hardly an electoral asset in the long run (Abedi and Lundberg 2009). In the run up to the September 2010 election, UKIP's leader was Lord Pearson of Rannoch, a former Conservative peer in the House of Lords. His elitist profile appeared somewhat at odds with the anti-establishment character of UKIP, and Pearson failed to leave a great impression in the campaign. He was, for instance, unable to recollect points from his party's manifesto in an interview with the BBC television programme *The Campaign Show*. After resigning his leadership, the politically rather unexperienced Pearson himself declared: 'I have learnt that I am not much good at party politics, which I do not enjoy' (*Guardian* 2010).

Hence, poor leadership and organisational struggles – as far as these were noticed by the general public – did little good for UKIP's performance in general elections. The electoral appeal of the party increased, however, after Nigel Farage was elected as party leader following the 2010 general election. Having previously led UKIP between September 2006 and November 2009, Farage had become known for his controversial speeches as an MEP, in which he frequently mocked European Commission members and European Council President Herman van Rompuy. With its 'blokeish, telegenic leader' (*Economist* 2014), and the Conservatives in government, UKIP was in a better position to present itself as the main Eurosceptic and socially conservative opposition force (see Lynch and Whitaker 2013). Even though the Conservatives, seemingly under pressure from UKIP, continued their firm line on immigration and European integration, both David Cameron's leadership and the coalition with the socially liberal LibDems were unpopular among socially conservative Tory supporters.

In the local elections of May 2013, UKIP showed its potential by winning 25 per cent of the vote in the wards where it stood (BBC 2013), and the EP election of May 2014 confirmed that UKIP had become an important electoral force. By presenting itself as the 'more polite' alternative to the BNP, UKIP succeeded in extending its appeal to a broader spectrum of culturally conservative and working-class voters, who were dissatisfied with the Conservatives as well as Labour (Ford et al. 2012; Ford and Goodwin 2014). Whether the party will truly be able to win a substantial number of seats in general elections, however, remains to be seen. By concentrating resources in regional strongholds and using local council seats as a springboard to national politics, as the Liberal Democrats have done before, UKIP may at least succeed in finally returning MPs to Westminster (*Economist* 2014; Ford and Goodwin 2014).

Up until the general election of 2010, however, populist parties in the UK failed to present themselves as credible alternatives to the dominant parties, despite operating in a context where the issue of immigration had become highly salient and public dissatisfaction with established parties widespread. Both the BNP and UKIP have been plagued by leadership struggles and controversies surrounding party figures. In the case of the BNP, in addition, the failure to get rid of its extremist stigma has been another important reason for the party's lack of credibility. For UKIP, the main problems were its ambiguous ideological profile and a lack of visible and appealing leadership.

Conclusion

Two political parties in the UK have been identified as the most prominent genuine cases of populism, operating on a countrywide basis: the British National Party (BNP) and the UK Independence Party (UKIP). Both parties have appealed to a heartland of ordinary British people, threatened by European integration – which has been alleged to jeopardise British sovereignty and identity – as well as immigration and the rise of Islam. While 'Europe' has been the signature issue of UKIP from the outset, issues related to immigration have always been at the core of the BNP's programme.

Despite (varying degrees of) success at the local and European levels, neither of the two parties made an impact in elections for the House of Commons up until 2010. In general elections, the BNP and UKIP faced an electoral system that was ostensibly unfavourable to their success. Lacking a strong regional base of support, the Single Member Plurality (SMP) system made it difficult for the two parties to enter parliament. European Parliament (EP) elections, held under a system of Proportional Representation since 1999, proved more conducive to populist party success. In view of the second-order character of EP elections, however, their results are not necessarily good indicators for the popularity of populist parties at the national level. It remains difficult to assess to what extent the electoral system has influenced the willingness of people to vote for UKIP and the BNP. In any case, taking into consideration that the Liberal Democrats did build up a substantial support base despite suffering the effects of SMP, the electoral system should be seen as only part of the explanation.

Reasons for the limited support for populist parties should also be sought in the responsiveness of the established parties with regard to the BNP's and UKIP's core issues: immigration and European integration. The Conservatives, in particular, have taken a Eurosceptic position and a restrictive stance towards immigration in recent decades. European integration has not been a theme on the basis of which many British voters have based their decision, yet in view of the considerable electoral salience of immigration, the Tories' ownership of this latter issue is likely to have hampered the populist parties' success. Even so, a more general mood of dissatisfaction with the established political parties materialised towards the end of the 2000s (see e.g. Pattie and Johnston 2012). Even though the theme of corruption did not play such a central role in the election campaigns as it did in Poland, the British populist parties seemingly had a chance to capitalise on this mood in 2010. To explain the failure of the BNP and UKIP to do so – or to seize the Conservatives' ownership of the immigration issue – we must also consider the electoral credibility of the populist parties themselves.

Both UKIP and the BNP have experienced many internal conflicts, reducing their trustworthiness as competent political actors. This would probably have been even more harmful to the parties if they had broken through at the national level and, consequently, been under closer public scrutiny. Irrespective of the party's attempts to forge a respectable image, the BNP's lack of electoral success also related to its extremist image. Besides the problem that 'Europe' has not been a very salient issue in general elections, UKIP, in turn, lacked genuinely visible and persuasive leadership up until the general election of 2010. Since then, however, party leader Nigel Farage has undoubtedly raised the profile of the party.

An observation from the British case is that, as in Poland, many essentially non-populist opposition parties have used populist anti-establishment rhetoric as well. In the British case this is likely to relate to the majoritarian character of British democracy. Most opposition parties never shared government responsibility and could, therefore, easily define themselves against the Labour–Conservative hegemony. In addition, nationalist sentiments played an important role in the anti-establishment appeal of the Scottish and Welsh nationalist parties. The regionalist parties have blamed the political establishment in Westminster for ignoring the interests and demands of the people within their own nation. The British case thus indicates that the distinction between populist and non-populist parties is not always easily made, even in countries that can be considered long-established democracies.

In terms of the electoral performance of the 'full' cases of populism, the British case study has shown that a disproportional electoral system and a responsive political establishment limit the opportunities for populist parties. That said, the fact that the populist parties have, up until 2010, been unable to seize the ownership of a salient issue, such as immigration, or to capitalise on a more general anti-establishment mood has largely been due to their own lack of credibility. The British case, thus, again indicates that the credibility of populist parties themselves is of crucial importance to their electoral performance, irrespective of the broader institutional or political opportunity structures. Indeed, if UKIP manages to retain its newly found credibility and to translate this into an effective campaign for the next general election, the House of Commons may see the entrance of multiple populist MPs in the near future.

7

Conclusion: Populist Parties and Their Electoral Performance

In the previous chapters I investigated the manifestation of party-based populism across Europe by identifying populist parties in long-established and post-communist European democracies, and explaining these parties' electoral performance. Populism still requires clarification, both as a theoretical concept and as an empirical phenomenon. Particularly in the vernacular, the term is frequently used yet ill defined (Bale et al. 2011). It is evident that 'populism' is often used pejoratively, and that the concept is habitually related to political extremism and the ideology of the radical right. Several commentators and politicians have therefore treated populism as a phenomenon that needs to be opposed. In the academic sphere, the threats of populism to liberal democracy have also been acknowledged, but many scholars have also underlined the value of populism as a corrective for representative democracy (e.g. Canovan 1999; Mény and Surel 2002; Taggart 2002; Panizza 2005; Mudde and Rovira Kaltwasser 2012). Considering the confusion surrounding the concept, as well as the presumed significance of populism as a phenomenon, it is required to come to a closer and more accurate understanding of how and why populism occurs.

In order to shine light on the manifestation of populism in European politics – a sphere in which political parties have remained key actors – the first aim of this study was to clarify which cases could be considered as populist parties. This was done on the basis of a minimal definition inspired by the academic literature. Populist parties, according to this definition, 1) portray 'the people' as virtuous and essentially homogeneous; 2) advocate popular sovereignty, as opposed to elitist rule; and 3) define themselves against the political establishment, which is alleged to act against the interest of 'the people'. Second, the book sought to explain the electoral performance of the identified populist parties, and

169

to reveal the conditions underlying their success or failure. This final chapter first focuses on the results of this study with regard to these two central aims, before drawing implications and discussing avenues for further research.

Identifying populist parties

If one seeks to identify populist parties, it is hard to disregard the more usual suspects in Western Europe that have received ample attention in the academic literature. Cases such as the French *Front National*, the Belgian Flemish Interest, the Austrian Freedom Party, the Italian *Lega Nord*, and the Danish and Swiss People's Parties have often primarily been studied as parties of the radical right, but their populist character has also received attention (e.g. Mudde 2007; Albertazzi and McDonnell 2008a). It is widely accepted, though, that populism is not necessarily a feature of the radical right; cases of left-wing populism, such as the German *Linke*, have also been identified (e.g. March 2011).

While several parties can be identified that constitute relatively undisputed cases of populism, there are certain factors that complicate the construction of a definitive 'universe' of populist parties (see Van Kessel 2014). These factors became evident in the second chapter of this book, which discussed the populist parties and borderline cases across Europe. A first key issue is that populist rhetoric can be used to various degrees and that it is unclear when a political party should be classified as a 'full' instance of populism. The second, often related, difficulty is that populist rhetoric can be added and removed from the repertoire of political actors relatively easily, so that identification of a stable universe of populist parties is perhaps not even achievable.

As became clear from Chapter 2, both these issues have been particularly apparent in former communist countries with fluid party systems, where new political parties often voiced fierce (populist) anti-establishment rhetoric. The criticism of elites often evaporated if these parties took the opportunity to enter government themselves (see Deegan-Krause and Haughton 2009; Sikk 2009). In several post-communist countries in Central and Eastern Europe, such as Bulgaria, Romania, Slovakia and the Baltic States, it has thus been difficult to separate the populist from the non-populist parties. In these countries it was also hard to distinguish between genuine populist and more general anti-establishment rhetoric, especially in contexts where the issue of corruption was politically salient and the integrity of the political elite open to doubt (see

Učeň 2007; Sikk 2012). In those cases, all newly formed parties were likely to present themselves as clean representatives of the people, even though explicit calls for popular sovereignty were sometimes harder to detect (see Hanley and Sikk 2014).

The above observations imply that using the concept of populism as an instrument of classification can be problematic, especially in those contexts where the concept lacks real 'discriminating power' (Sartori 1970). We therefore need to be open to the idea that populism can manifest itself as a more loosely applied rhetoric, as well as an essential defining feature of certain politicians and parties (Van Kessel 2014). Yet, looking beyond borderline cases, it is fair to contend that several political parties have emerged in European party systems with populism at the very core of their appeal. Those parties cannot truly be described without taking their populist anti-establishment discourse into account. Chapter 2 of this book aimed to identify those 'populist parties'.

The three case study chapters (4, 5 and 6) provided a more in-depth assessment of populist parties in the Netherlands, Poland and the United Kingdom. These chapters also showed that identifying populist parties is not always a straightforward exercise. In the Netherlands, the radical left-wing Socialist Party can be seen as a borderline case of populism. The party was excluded from the analysis, since it moderated its populist anti-establishment rhetoric significantly after the turn of the 21st century (see De Lange and Rooduijn 2011; Lucardie and Voerman 2012; Rooduijn 2014b). In Poland, the League of Polish Families (LPR) and Law and Justice (PiS) were borderline cases. In the end, the LPR was not treated as a populist party, since it sought more ideological inspiration from Catholic values than from the *vox populi*. PiS, in turn, could be seen as a 'full' case of populism only since the parliamentary election campaign of 2005. Even then, however, populism seemed to remain a relatively loose supplement to its national-conservative core ideology. A more general complicating factor in the Polish case was the anti-establishment mood which prevailed during the 2001 and 2005 parliamentary elections. As in several other post-communist countries, the issue of corruption was a highly salient theme, providing an incentive for all parties of opposition to be highly critical of the post-communist Polish establishment. This does not mean that each of these parties could also be classified as a populist party, but it did increase the resemblance of populist and non-populist parties in terms of their electoral appeal.

In the UK, identifying populist parties has been challenging for different reasons. Even though I argued in Chapter 6 that the British National Party (BNP) and the UK Independence Party (UKIP) were the only genuine cases of populism at a nationwide level, I also observed that populist rhetoric has been voiced by other parties across the British ideological spectrum (see also Rooduijn et al. 2014). This is likely to be related to the majoritarian character of British democracy and the related antagonistic mode of party competition. Most notably, due to the traditional dominance of the Conservatives and Labour, it was easy for opposition parties to identify a political establishment that was to blame. Populist anti-Westminster rhetoric was further voiced by the regionalist parties in Scotland and Wales, even though these parties actually became very much part of the establishment in their regional assemblies and executives.

All in all, the case study chapters also demonstrated that applying the concept of populism too uncritically as a means to classify political parties is bound to lead to conceptual confusion. Both Chapter 2 and the three case studies have also shown that it is not correct to automatically relate populism to extremism or xenophobia, even if many populist parties in Europe can be placed in the populist radical right (PRR) category (Mudde 2007), or at least take a critical stance towards immigration and multiculturalism. This includes the Dutch List Pim Fortuyn (LPF) and Freedom Party (PVV), as well as the BNP and UKIP. All of these parties have, to different degrees, taken a restrictive position on immigration and voiced concern about the cultural influence of Islam. On the other hand, despite their 'patriotism', the Polish Self Defence (SO) and PiS lacked such appeals and did not focus on issues related to immigration or ethnic minorities, but, rather, on corruption and socio-economic concerns.

This shows that populist parties focus on issues that are relevant to their particular political context and adopt an ideological programme that is consistent with the supposed needs of 'the people' they appeal to. The diversity among populist parties is a reflection of populism's thin ideological, or chameleonic, character (Taggart 2000; Mudde 2004; Stanley 2008). This is not to say that the populist parties' choice of policies is entirely random, and the previous chapters have shown that many concentrated on issues related to the four themes identified in Chapter 1: culture and ethnicity; economic hardship; European integration; and corruption. These themes were considered especially compatible with the thin ideology of populism. Depending on the political context, they were also assumed to be relevant for the electoral performance of populist parties, the topic which I will discuss now.

The electoral performance of populist parties

In order to study the electoral performance of the populist parties in Europe, I started out from an explanatory model including three general conditions: the electoral system; the responsiveness of established parties; and the supply of credible populist parties. Regarding the third explanatory factor, the credibility of populist parties was deemed to rely on their electoral appeal and organisational cohesion (see e.g. Carter 2005; Mudde 2007). The electoral appeal of a populist party was assumed to relate to its leadership's visibility and persuasiveness, and its ability to dissociate itself from both the political establishment and political extremism. As far as organisational cohesion is concerned, populist parties were assumed to lose their credibility if they suffered from publicly visible conflicts and defections. In addition to the three general conditions, I also expected that the salience of the four themes (culture and ethnicity; economic hardship; European integration; and corruption) would have an effect on the potential for populist parties to mobilise support. If these themes were salient, and established parties perceived to be unwilling or unable to cope with related issues, populist parties were assumed to face a more favourable opportunity structure.

Results from the QCA

The fuzzy set Qualitative Comparative Analysis (fsQCA) presented in Chapter 3 evaluated the relationship between the three fundamental conditions, as well as the four more specific themes, and the electoral performance of populist parties in 31 countries. I assessed whether it was possible to distinguish different paths to populist success or failure, depending on the social, economic and political context in which the parties operated.

The analysis did not lead to very straightforward results in this regard. A theoretically plausible finding was that populist parties performed well in the latest parliamentary election in several post-communist or crisis-stricken Mediterranean countries, where a supply of credible populist parties was combined with high levels of perceived corruption and either economic hardship or high degrees of nativist sentiments and Euroscepticism (e.g. Greece, Hungary, Italy and Slovakia). Yet, rather counterintuitively, successful populist parties were also found in contexts where low levels of nativism were combined with a relatively Europhile population, or low levels of perceived corruption (e.g. Belgium, Denmark and Norway). At the same time, in some countries populist parties were unsuccessful despite a seemingly favourable opportunity structure: for instance, where high levels of perceived corruption were combined with high levels of nativism or economic hardship (e.g. Portugal and Slovenia). These results indicate that populist success or failure is not necessarily related to general economic conditions or dominant public attitudes towards issues central to the appeal of many populist parties. Indeed, as will be discussed below, populist parties can become successful if they manage to appeal to a certain niche of (dissatisfied) voters.

The QCA did show that the credibility of populist parties was of vital importance to their electoral performance. The results suggested that the supply of credible populist contenders is a necessary condition for the electoral success of populist parties. Conversely, the lack of credible populist parties has in most cases been crucial in explaining the electoral failure of such parties. Even though the results should be approached with some caution, since it has been difficult to operationalise precisely the credibility of populist parties in a relatively large number of cases, the findings suggest that the agency of populist parties should not be ignored in theories and studies on their electoral performance.

The electoral system and the responsiveness of the established parties – which was operationalised for the QCA by considering general levels of satisfaction with democracy and trust in political institutions – were not part of the 'solutions' for either populist success or failure. Irrespective of the presence or absence of other conditions, populist parties have performed well under proportional, but also under more disproportional, electoral systems. At the same time, populist parties have done well in low-trust countries such as Bulgaria, Poland and Romania, but also in countries such as Denmark, the Netherlands, Norway and Switzerland, where people have been relatively satisfied with the way democracy works, and where trust in parliament and political parties has been relatively high.

In order to explain the success of populist parties in these latter countries, it seemed necessary to assess the responsiveness of established parties more precisely, by considering more specifically the salience of individual issues and the way established parties were perceived to handle them. The three case studies thus considered the responsiveness of established parties in more detail, and also focused more closely on the competition between established and populist parties.

Results from the three case studies

The three case studies, which focused on populist parties in the Netherlands, Poland and the United Kingdom, showed that the populist parties aimed to compete with established parties on the basis of typical populist themes: culture and ethnicity (Netherlands and the UK), economic hardship and corruption (mainly Poland), and European integration (the UK and, later, the Netherlands). The case studies further indicated that the agency of both established and populist parties has been important in explaining the electoral performance and endurance of individual populist challengers. In the Netherlands and Poland, populist parties were successful in capitalising on the unresponsiveness, or lack of integrity, of the political establishment (see Chapters 4 and 5). At the time of the 2002 Dutch parliamentary election, none of the established parties placed immigration and issues related to multiculturalism high on their political agendas, whereas there were clear concerns with regard to these issues among the population (e.g. Pellikaan et al. 2007; Aarts and Thomassen 2008). In Poland's first post-communist decade, there was a general consensus among the political mainstream in favour of free-market capitalism and state deregulation. Yet, when economic conditions soured at the end of the 1990s, there was a growing popular resentment against neo-liberal policies (e.g. Szczerbiak 2002a). Moreover, the involvement of established parties in practices of cronyism and corruption seriously undermined the reputation of members of the Polish political elite (e.g. Szczerbiak 2007; Millard 2009).

Support for populist parties in the Netherlands and Poland – and the UK, for that matter – reflected dissatisfaction with the political establishment. In Poland this dissatisfaction was widespread, and the corruption of the established parties became a central political theme in electoral campaigns (CBOS 2005; Szczerbiak 2007). The Netherlands remained a 'high-trust' country overall, but populist parties were nevertheless able to attract the support of a certain dissatisfied segment of the electorate (Bélanger and Aarts 2006; Schumacher and Rooduijn 2013; cf. Van der Brug 2003). As discussed in Chapter 6, in elections for the European Parliament, British populist parties were also able to attract a considerable share of voters who were partly driven by dissatisfaction (Cutts et al. 2011; Whitaker and Lynch 2011; Ford et al. 2012).

This is not to say that the concrete policies of populist parties were irrelevant. Successful populist parties occupied a certain niche left vacant by the established parties, and attracted voters who, besides being disgruntled, simply agreed with the populist parties' proposals (see Van der Brug et al. 2000; 2005; Rydgren 2005). At the same time, reasons for the failure of British populist parties at the national level should partially be sought in the responsiveness of the Conservative Party with regard to the issues central to the populist challengers: immigration and European integration. In the past decades the 'Tories' have, generally speaking, adopted a Eurosceptic discourse and a restrictive position with regard to immigration (e.g. Webb 2008; Goodwin 2011; Lynch and Whitaker 2013). While European integration has been an issue of limited salience in general elections, many British voters were concerned about immigration, and the Conservatives were, on balance, seen as the party best able to handle the issue (see YouGov 2005; 2010c). This has decreased the electoral scope for both the BNP and UKIP. The reason why the British populist parties have been unable to seize the Conservatives' issue ownership, or to capitalise on the more general dissatisfaction with British political institutions, should, in turn, be sought in the lack of credibility of the populist parties themselves.

Up until the 2010 general election, the British populist parties had never been able to present themselves as credible alternatives to the political establishment. In recent years, the formerly neo-fascist BNP moderated its discourse on matters related to ethnicity, but it remained difficult for the party to shed its extremist stigma (Goodwin 2011). The BNP, furthermore, continued to suffer from internal conflicts and lacked genuinely persuasive leadership. Internal strife has plagued UKIP as well, and, up until 2010, UKIP failed to put forward visible and convincing leaders in general election campaigns (see Fella 2008; Usherwood 2009). The fortunes of UKIP may have turned since, as the party has been a much more effective opposition force with the Conservatives in government, and with Nigel Farage as an energetic and telegenic leader (see Lynch and Whitaker 2013; Ford and Goodwin 2014).

In the other two cases, the credibility of populist parties has also been important in explaining the success and failure of individual populist parties. In the Netherlands, many voters were convinced by the strong performance of Pim Fortuyn in the parliamentary election campaign of 2002 (Lucardie and Voerman 2012). After his assassination he proved irreplaceable as party leader, and the LPF's credibility further waned due to continuous internal strife (De Lange and Art 2011). Afterwards, Geert Wilders' PVV became the most important populist actor in Dutch politics. Wilders attracted a substantial number of voters with his harsh anti-Islam and anti-establishment rhetoric. Notwithstanding the manifestation of intra-party conflicts in the run up to the parliamentary election of 2012, Wilders was able to avoid organisational meltdown, and also

managed to dissociate himself from political extremism (Vossen 2011).
Even though many Dutch political parties have adopted more restrictive immigration and cultural integration policies, Wilders remained the actor with the clearest profile on these issues. Furthermore, by adding more welfare protectionist policies to its nativist programme in 2010, the PVV moved to a unique, and seemingly electorally potent, position in the Dutch political landscape (see Van der Brug et al. 2011). Whether the party's focus on Eurorejection as a core message in 2012 has been fruitful electorally is more doubtful.

In Poland, Andrzej Lepper's party Self Defence (SO) ran a more professional campaign at the time of the 2001 general election (Millard 2009). As a result, 'Lepper was able to develop a distinctive and attractive electoral appeal as a "man of the people" who was articulate and determined enough to take on the Warsaw elites' (Szczerbiak 2002a: 58). Even though the party suffered from a large number of defections after it entered parliament, it was able to sustain its electoral support in the following election of 2005. Once in office, however, more defections followed and the party's image was blemished by involvement in sleaze and corruption scandals. In 2007, SO and its coalition partner LPR, which faced similar problems, lost parliamentary representation. After it had adopted a more full-blown populist discourse, Law and Justice (PiS) had stolen the electoral thunder of the two radical parties, as it was able to remain well organised, to retain a credible anti-corruption image and to present itself as the most trustworthy agent of 'solidaristic' Poland (Markowski 2008; Stanley 2010; 2013).

The case studies have indicated that having persuasive and visible figureheads, as well as the related ability to seize the ownership of salient issues, are prerequisites for populist parties to break through. On the other hand, the case of the BNP has shown most clearly that an extremist image is likely to be damaging for a populist party's electoral appeal. In addition, especially for those populist parties that enter office, it can be testing to retain a credible anti-establishment message (Betz 2002; Heinisch 2003). The LPF in the Netherlands and SO in Poland clearly failed in office, although their electoral demise should also be seen in light of their organisational problems (see below). The Dutch PVV fared better after having supported a minority government between 2010 and 2012. Having officially remained outside office, the party was able to enact some of its desired policies and to criticise the government for less popular measures at the same time. The party lost in the subsequent election of 2012, but was far from a spent force. PiS in Poland, in turn, was even able to retain its populist appeal while taking full government responsibility. This was due to its ability to uphold a credible anti-corruption image; in office the party claimed to be cleansing the debased established system which its 'liberal' predecessors had left behind (see Stanley 2013).

Organisational stability is another important factor as far as the longevity of a populist party is concerned (Mudde 2007; 2010). The LPF and SO were both troubled by intra-party conflicts, tainting their image as responsible alternatives to the political establishment. For SO, however, organisational disunity in its first parliamentary period did not prove fatal, as the party was able to maintain its vote share in the subsequent election. After a short period in power, its supporters were less forgiving. This may indicate that organisational instability is more lethal for governing than for opposition parties, because voters scrutinise the former more stringently. If this assumption is correct, the failure of the British populist parties should perhaps primarily be sought in their lack of electoral appeal, rather than their infighting – which may not always have received widespread public attention in the first place.

Finally, the UK case has shown that the proportionality of the electoral system can also be a relevant, though not sufficient, condition for populist electoral success or failure. Even though it remains difficult to gauge precisely the psychological effects of electoral systems – notably, the extent to which the system influences voting behaviour – the mechanical effects of the Single Member Plurality system applied in UK general elections are evident; under a pure proportional electoral system both UKIP and the BNP would have entered the House of Commons. At the same time, the case of the Liberal Democrats – and the Front National in France for that matter – showed that it is not impossible for third parties that are disadvantaged by the electoral system to break through. Besides electoral rules, the responsiveness of established parties and the populist parties' credibility were also of vital importance to explain the performance of populist parties in the UK, as was the case in the Netherlands and Poland.

All in all, the study has indicated that the more successful populist parties were those which could build up (lasting) electoral credibility, allowing them to seize the ownership of electorally salient issues and to appeal to dissatisfied voters. Their electoral breakthrough has been facilitated where established parties could be blamed for their unresponsiveness or – as was the case in Poland – for their more general lack of integrity. Once a populist party has established itself, traditional mainstream parties may not automatically win back the support of voters if they become more responsive. This is clearly illustrated by the Dutch case, where established parties have become more sceptical of multi-culturalism and placed more emphasis on the need for migrants and minorities to adopt Dutch cultural norms (Van Heerden et al. 2013). This hardly resulted in the annihilation of Geert Wilders' PVV, however, and it thus seems wrong to assume that populist parties – or 'niche parties' in general – are in all cases merely 'by-products of competition between mainstream parties' (Meguid 2008: 22).

Hence, populist parties – at least the credible ones – need to be considered as serious contenders in the competition for the ownership of salient issues. Depending on the national context, populist parties often compete for the ownership of issues related to the four previously identified themes: culture and ethnicity; economic hardship; European integration; and corruption. These are not necessarily all vote-winning issues. In none of the three case studies, for instance, did European integration come out as an issue of major electoral salience in national elections. At the same time, as the results of the QCA have shown, populist party success is not guaranteed, even if these themes are seemingly salient in a given country. Non-populist parties are also able to seize the ownership of 'populist issues'. Examples include the essentially non-populist parties in post-communist countries that were successful on the basis of an anti-corruption platform. Populist parties are, thus, not necessarily the only 'agents of discontent'. This implies that populist parties should not be studied in isolation from their party political environment, and should also not be treated as completely different 'animals' in comparison with their electoral competitors. This will be discussed further in the following section, which draws the wider implications of this study's findings and identifies avenues for further research.

Implications

The findings of this study have several implications for the study of populism, populist parties, and party competition in general. A first implication of a conceptual nature relates to the study's aim to identify a circumscribed universe of populist parties in contemporary Europe. I outlined several challenges with regard to this, for instance, related to the observation that parties can voice populist rhetoric to different degrees over time. Observers should not be careless in describing certain cases as 'populist parties', as an uncritical application of the concept as a 'classifier' is bound to lead to conceptual confusion (see Sikk 2009; Van Kessel 2014). There is a risk that 'populism' is used to describe political parties that actually do not belong to the same class. Using the analogy of Giovanni Sartori (1991), describing too many parties as 'populist parties' resembles lumping together cats and dogs in one category, and ending up with the fairly useless concept of a cat-dog.

Identifying populist parties should be based on an accurate definition of populism, but also on substantive knowledge about the nature of the parties under consideration. Since my knowledge of many of the 31 countries in this study is limited, I relied heavily on secondary literature and the feedback of country experts to make judgements about which parties to include. In order to identify and study cases of populism cross-nationally, collaborative research projects that accumulate sufficient in-depth knowledge seem suitable. Several edited volumes on populism have already appeared, which started out from a common definition and aim, and which included a range of in-depth case studies (e.g. Albertazzi and McDonnell 2008a; Mudde and Rovira Kaltwasser 2012).

An alternative is to perform quantitative content analyses of party documents or other sources that reflect party discourse. Indeed, measuring populism in this way has become increasingly popular among populism scholars (see Jagers and Walgrave 2007; Hawkins 2009; Rooduijn et al. 2014; Pauwels 2014). Provided that measurement is based on sound indicators and valid sources, such a method also makes it possible to gauge the *extent* to which a party is populist, and to assess levels of populism in the wider party system. A challenge for these studies is to interpret meaningfully the differences in the degrees of populism between political actors. Without clear qualitative anchors, results may not automatically indicate which parties are populist and which are not. A certain level of in-depth knowledge is still required to identify 'full' cases of populism.

It is important to note that some scholars doubt the usefulness of using populism as a 'classifier' and distinguishing between populist and non-populist actors, especially since populism can be used as a more episodic rhetorical device (e.g. Deegan-Krause and Haughton 2009; Sikk 2009; Rooduijn et al. 2014). Indeed, particularly in the post-communist context, where populist discourse appears to be more widespread in party systems, singling out 'genuine' cases of populism has proven difficult. In some of the countries in Central and Eastern Europe it makes more sense to study populism as a more general phenomenon of post-communist politics. In other (Western European) countries, however, it is possible to identify the parties that stand out from the rest in terms of their populism, even if discussions about borderline cases will inevitably exist. The content analysis of Rooduijn et al. (2014) actually showed that there is a substantial difference between mainstream and several non-mainstream parties in Western Europe as far as the use of populist rhetoric is concerned. Even though it seems a bad idea to always stick to a rigid dichotomous approach (treating parties as either populist or not), this does not mean that the concept of populism has no value as a classifier (see Van Kessel 2014). Indeed, populism has been treated as a core element of party families such as the populist radical right and social populists (Mudde 2007; March 2011). For most parties, populism can be seen as only one component of a broader ideology – which is logical in view of the 'thinness' of the populist ideology. It can still be meaningful to move up the ladder of abstraction (Sartori 1970), and to study the broader category of populist parties. First of all, even though it is a thin core that binds populist parties of various kinds, this core may still be vital to these parties' behaviour and performance. For instance, it is typical for populist parties of all kinds to 'seek to enact the redemptive side of politics, and re-politicise those problems that intentionally or unintentionally are not being addressed by the establishment' (Rovira Kaltwasser 2014: 484). Second, as discussed in Chapter 1, populist parties on the radical left and radical right may have more in common than the terminology suggests: for instance, in view of their shared welfare chauvinism and wariness of globalisation and European integration. The financial and economic crisis in Europe may have created an incentive for populist parties on both sides of the presumed ideological divide to focus on issues related to these themes. Here lies scope for further research. At the time of writing, we can actually already observe considerable scholarly interest in comparing the populist left and right in terms of their ideological profile and electoral support (e.g. Mudde and Rovira Kaltwasser 2013; Akkerman et al. 2014).[1]

Concerning populist parties' electoral performance, the results of the study indicated that populist parties can only break through and sustain their success if they present themselves as credible alternatives to the political establishment. Populist parties are, to a certain extent, the masters of their own destiny, and can even survive in office if they retain a credible anti-establishment appeal (see Albertazzi and McDonnell 2005; Akkerman and De Lange 2012; Zaslove 2012). Studies on the electoral performance of populist parties should, therefore, not ignore these parties' own credibility. The importance of the agency of radical political outsiders has been acknowledged in earlier accounts (Betz 2002; Carter 2005; Rydgren 2005; Mudde 2007; 2010), yet especially 'larger-N' quantitative studies tend to ignore this factor too often.

This is understandable, for 'credibility' is difficult to operationalise and an assessment of credibility requires in-depth knowledge about individual cases. Again, collaboration between various country specialists might be a way to overcome this problem. On the basis of insights from previous accounts, this study has proposed a way to assess the credibility of populist parties, and will hopefully inspire researchers to consider the agency of populist parties, or other political outsiders, also in 'larger-N' projects.

Notwithstanding the importance of the populist parties' own credibility, their chances of success do improve when established parties fail to be responsive with regard to salient societal issues. This is consistent with the theoretical argument of scholars who have linked the rise of populism with the elite's disregard for important issues, or the more general 'redemptive' side of politics (e.g. Canovan 1999; Mény and Surel 2002; Taggart 2002; Rovira Kaltwasser 2014). This does not mean that all populist parties contribute to the quality of democracy. Indeed, the more extreme and xenophobic cases in particular may pose a threat to values at the heart of liberal democracy, such as respect for individual and minority rights (see Abts and Rummens 2007; Mudde and Rovira Kaltwasser 2012). But commentators and politicians alike should not dismiss the notion that populism fulfils an important function as 'bellwether' for the health of representative democracies (Taggart 2002: 63).

It is, at the same time, not accurate to perceive a typical vote for a populist party as an uninformed protest vote. People support populist parties not only out of discontent with the establishment, but also because they agree with their policies (see Van der Brug et al. 2000; 2005; Eatwell 2003). This, in turn, implies that the logic behind the performance of populist parties is not radically different in comparison with other parties. What is more, in the contemporary European political context, traditional parties and populist parties seemingly compete on an equal basis. Electorates across Western Europe have become much more 'available' due to the weakening ties between parties and voters (e.g. Dalton et al. 2000; Krouwel 2012; Van Biezen et al. 2012). After the fall of communism, voters in Central and Eastern European countries hardly built up strong partisan allegiances in the first place (e.g. Rose 1995; Casal Bértoa 2013). General theories about party competition, for instance related to the concept of issue ownership, are very much applicable to populist parties as well (see Budge and Farlie 1983; Petrocik 1996; Mudde 2010).

Yet it would go too far to claim that populist parties are identical to established parties in terms of the logic behind their electoral success and failure. Crucially, populist parties rely on the support of voters who tend to be exceptionally dissatisfied with the political establishment, which is evidently not the case for parties that have traditionally been part of the governing elite. As we have seen in this study, however, making a distinction between mainstream and populist parties still tends to be easier in Western European than in post-communist countries. The more widespread distrust of political parties and the greater salience of corruption as a political issue in many post-communist countries provided an incentive for all new political parties to voice anti-establishment rhetoric, and blurred the lines between populist and non-populist parties. (see e.g. Minkenberg 2002; Mudde 2002a; Pop-Eleches 2010; Pirro 2014a; Hanley and Sikk 2014). It remains to be seen whether this situation will persist or whether we will eventually be able to employ populism as a useful classifier in most post-communist cases, and observe a more general convergence between the party systems of 'East' and 'West' (see Casal Bértoa 2013). Future studies, in particular those with a pan-European focus, should shed light on this matter.

If it is assumed that populism fulfils an important function in serving as an indicator for the health of democracy, it is necessary to come to an even closer understanding of the use and impact of populist discourse, and the conditions underlying the rise and fall of populist parties. These parties are typical 'agents of discontent', but their substantive message should not be ignored, as discontent is normally related to concerns about important political issues.

Appendices

Appendix A: List of Consulted Country Experts

The following country experts have shared their knowledge of particular countries during the period of my investigation (mostly spring 2011 and/or winter 2013–2014). The case descriptions in Chapter 2 ultimately reflect my own assessment, for which I am solely responsible.

Austria:	Franz Fallend, Kurt Richard Luther, Wolfgang C. Müller
Belgium:	Koen Abts, Teun Pauwels, Marc Swyngedouw
Bulgaria:	Blagovesta Cholova, Kirsten Ghodsee, Georgi Karasimeonov, Lyubka Savkova, Markéta Smrčková
Croatia:	Miljenko Antić, Goran Čular, Andrija Henjak, Anđelko Milardović, Višeslav Raos, Marko Stojic
Cyprus:	Giorgos Charalambous
Czech Republic:	Vlastimil Havlík, Vit Hloušek, Petr Kaniok, Alexander Martynau
Denmark:	Ann-Christina Lauring Knudsen, Jens Rydgren, Lars Svåsand
Estonia:	Allan Sikk, Rein Taagepera, Henri Vogt
Finland:	David Arter, Tapio Raunio
France:	Florent Gougou, Sally Marthaler
Germany:	Daniel Hough, Jan Kette, Michael Koss
Greece:	Elias Dinas, Kostas Geminis, Takis Pappas, Susannah Verney, Lefteris Zenerian
Hungary:	Agnes Batory, Andras Inotai, Andrea Pirro, Nick Sitter, Gabor Toka
Iceland:	Hulda Þórisdóttir, Ólafur Harðarson, Gunnar Helgi Kristinsson
Ireland:	John FitzGibbon, Conor Little, Duncan McDonnell
Italy:	Daniele Albertazzi, Fabio Bordignon, Stefano Fella, Simona Guerra, Emanuelle Massetti, Duncan McDonnell, Carlo Ruzza
Latvia:	Daunis Auers, Ilze Balcere, Tatyana Bogushevitch, Aleksejs Dimitrovs, Allan Sikk

Lithuania:	Kjetil Duvold, Mindaugas Jurkynas, Algis Krupavicius, Ainė Ramonaitė, Allan Sikk
Luxembourg:	Patrick Dumont, Martine Huberty
Malta:	Roderick Pace
The Netherlands:	*Anonymous Expert Survey (see Appendix E)*
Norway:	Anniken Hagelund, Anders Ravik Jupskås, Anders Widfeldt
Poland:	*Anonymous Expert Survey (see Appendix E)*
Portugal:	Madalena Resende, Thomas Davis
Romania:	Sergiu Gherghina, Edward Maxfield, Paul Sum, Markéta Smrčková
Slovakia:	Kevin Deegan-Krause, Tim Haughton, Karen Henderson, Peter Spáč
Slovenia:	Alenka Krašovec, Drago Zajc
Spain:	Thomas Davis, Ariadna Ripoll Servent, Luis Ramiro
Sweden:	Nicholas Aylott, Jens Rydgren, Anders Widfeldt
Switzerland:	Daniele Albertazzi, Simon Bornschier
United Kingdom:	*Anonymous Expert Survey (see Appendix E)*

Appendix B: Country Expert Questionnaire

Populist parties and their credibility

The study seeks to identify populist parties that managed to enter national parliament in 31 European countries between 2000 and 2013. In one chapter I aim to provide a short description of populist parties (and borderline cases) in these 31 countries. In addition, I make a rudimentary assessment of the electoral credibility of populist parties in each of these countries.

Populist parties are defined as parties that

1. portray 'the people' as virtuous and essentially homogeneous;
2. advocate popular sovereignty, as opposed to elitist rule;
3. define themselves against the political establishment, which is alleged to act against the interest of 'the people'.

All three conditions need to be satisfied.

The credibility of the populist parties in election campaigns is assessed using two indicators:

1. *Electoral appeal*: visibility and persuasiveness of the populist leadership, the populist party's ability to ward off an extremist image and its ability to convincingly distance itself from the political establishment.
2. *Organisational cohesion*: absence of publicly visible conflicts and splits.

On the basis of these indicators, a judgement is made about whether a country has been characterised by a *substantial, reasonable, limited,* or *no* supply of credible populist parties during the period of study (2000–2013).

Questions

1. Is the description below accurate and complete?
2. Are there any other notable populist parties that I have not included?
3. Have there been any populist parties that did not manage to enter national parliament but were nevertheless electorally appealing and cohesive (i.e. parties that were credible yet unsuccessful)?

Thank you very much!

* * *

[Description of populist parties in country X and assessment of their credibility]

Appendix C: QCA Data

Table A.1 Election results of populist parties between 2000 and 2013

					Results				POPSUC
Case (elec. years)	Party	t1	t2	t3	t4	t5	t6	Mean
AUS (13; 08; 06; 02)	FPÖ	20.5	17.5	11.0	10.0			
	BZÖ	–	10.7	4.1				
	TS	5.7						
AUS Aggregate		26.2	28.2	15.1	10.0			19.9
BEL (10; 07; 03)	VB	7.7	12	11.6				
	FN	0.5	2.0	2.0				
	LDD	2.3	4.0					
BEL Aggregate		10.5	18.0	13.6				14
BUL (13; 09; 05; 01)	NDSV	7.3	9.4	–	42.7			
	ATAKA			8.1				
	GERB	30.5	39.7					
	RZS	1.7	4.1					
BUL Aggregate		39.5	53.2	8.1	42.7			35.9
CRO (11; 07; 03; 00)	HL-SR	5.2						
	HSP-AS	2.8						
CRO Aggregate		8	0	0	0			2
CYP (11; 06; 01)	–	0	0	0				0
CZR (13; 10; 06; 02)	VV		10.9					
	ANO	18.7						
	Úsvit	6.9						
CZR Aggregate		25.6	10.9	0	0			9.1
DEN (11; 07; 05; 01)	DF	12.3	13.9	13.3	12.0			12.9
EST (11; 07; 03)	–	0	0	0				0

Continued

Table A.1 Continued

		Results					POPSUC
FIN (11; 07; 03)	PS	19.0	4.1	1.6			8.2
FRA (12; 07; 02)	FN	13.6	4.3	11.3			9.7
GER (13; 09; 05; 02)	PDS/LIN	8.6	11.9	8.7	4.0		8.3
GRE	LAOS	1.6	2.9	5.6	3.8	2.2	
(12;12;09;07;04;00)	SYRIZA	26.9	16.8	4.6	5.0	3.3	
	ANEL	7.5	10.6				
GRE Aggregate		36	30.3	10.2	8.8	5.5	15.1
HUN (10; 06; 02)	FIDESZ	52.7	42.0	–			
	JOBBIK	16.7	2.2			0	
HUN Aggregate		69.4	44.2	0			37.9
ICE (13; 09; 07; 03)	BF	9.9	7.2				1.8
IRE (11; 07; 02)	SF	9.9	6.9	6.5			7.8
ITA (13; 08; 06; 01)	FI/PdL	21.6	37.4	23.7	29.4		
	LN	4.1	8.3	4.6	3.9		
	M5S	25.6					
ITA Aggregate		51.3	45.7	28.3	33.3		39.7
LAT (11; 10; 06; 02)	VL	7.3	7.7	1.5			2.3
LIT (12; 08; 04; 00)	TT	7.3	12.7	11.4			
	DP	–		28.4			
LIT Aggregate		7.3	12.7				
LUX (13; 09; 04)	ADR	6.6	8.1	39.8	0		15.0
MAL (13; 08; 03)	–	0	0	0			8.2
NET	LN					1.6	0
(12; 10; 06; 03; 02)	LPF				5.7	17	
	PVV	10.1	15.5	5.9			
NET Aggregate		10.1	15.5	5.9	5.7	18.6	
NOR (13; 09; 05; 01)	FrP	16.3	22.9	22.1	14.6		11.2
POL (11; 07; 05; 01)	SO	16.3	1.5	11.4	10.2		19.0

	PiS	29.9	32.1	27.0	–	
POL Aggregate		**29.9**	**33.6**	**38.4**	**10.2**	28.0
POR (11; 09; 05; 02)	–					0
ROM (12; 08; 04; 00)	PRM	1.5	3.2	13.0	19.5	
	PP-DD	14				
ROM Aggregate		**15.5**	**3.2**	**13.0**	**19.5**	12.8
SLK (12; 10; 06; 02)	HZDS	0.9	4.3	8.8	19.5	
	Smer	–	–	29.1	13.5	
	SNS	4.6	5.1	11.7	3.3	
	OLaNO	8.6				
SLK Aggregate		**14.1**	**9.4**	**49.6**	**36.3**	27.4
SLV (11; 08; 04; 00)	SNS	**1.8**	**5.4**	**6.3**	**4.4**	4.5
SPA (11; 08; 04; 00)	–					0
SWE (10; 06; 02)	SD	**5.7**	**2.9**	**1.4**		3.3
SWI (11; 07; 03)	SVP	26.6	28.9	26.6		
	LdTi	0.8	0.6	0.4		
	SD	0.4	0.5	1		
	MCG		0.1			
SWI Aggregate		**27.8**	**30.1**	**28.0**		28.6
UK (10; 05; 01)	–					0

Notes: The (aggregate) figures underlined are used to calculate the final raw POPSUC value. Only the electoral results of parties that have entered the national parliament at least once after elections between 2000 and 2013 have been recorded. For countries with populist parties that did not manage to cross the threshold, the combined vote share in a single election is never higher than 5 per cent (UKIP and BNP in the 2010 UK general election). Certain parties, such as the Austrian BZÖ, Hungarian FIDESZ and Polish PiS, are not considered to have been populist parties throughout their existence, and their electoral results have therefore not been included across the whole period of study (see Chapter 2).

Table A.2   Raw data for the PR, ECOHARD, EURSCEP and CORRUP conditions

Case	PR*	ECOHARD^	EURSCEP°	CORRUP~
AUS	15.09	4.3	22.3	2.1
BEL	13.63	7.7	9.7	2.8
BUL	10.31	11.7	7.8	6.1
CRO	8.94	12.9	29.6	6.0
CYP	15.83	5.4	19.4	3.9
CZR	11.09	7.1	12.9	5.5
DEN	16.53	5.3	16.2	0.6
EST	13.72	10.3	8.1	3.8
FIN	14.63	8.3	21.0	0.6
FRA	0	9.0	17.1	3.0
GER	13.22	8.4	12.7	2.2
GRE	9.18	11.6	12.5	5.8
HUN	9.4	7.9	16.9	4.9
ICE	14.19	4.5	–	1.0
IRE	10.68	7.5	7.0	2.6
ITA	8.5	8.2	12.6	5.3
LAT	13.33	12.2	16.9	5.7
LIT	8.81	11.8	10.7	5.2
LUX	13.47	4.1	7.3	1.5
MAL	16.06	6.9	17.1	4.1
NET	16.78	4.0	8.9	1.2
NOR	14.84	3.5	–	1.3
POL	11.75	13.8	7.6	5.5
POR	12.3	8.9	13.6	3.7
ROM	12.27	7.0	7.4	6.6
SLK	10.3	15.3	6.1	5.7
SLV	14.27	6.5	11.1	3.9
SPA	12.29	13.7	8.9	3.4
SWE	15.8	7.0	25.5	0.8
SWI	14.8	3.7	–	1.2
UK	1.2	6.0	27.8	1.8

Note: More specific raw data are available from the author on request.

* PR is calculated by means of the least squares (LSq) index, which measures disproportionality between the distributions of votes and of seats (see Gallagher 1991). The average value over the parliamentary elections between 2000 and 2013 is taken. For the PR condition, the scores have been inverted, allocating a zero to France, which recorded the highest average disproportionality. Data from Gallagher (2013) and own calculations for the elections in 2013 in AUS, CZR, GER, LUX and NOR.

^ ECOHARD is operationalised by calculating the (available) average unemployment figures between 2000 and 2012. Data from Eurostat (2014), and OECD (2014) for Switzerland.

° The values related to EURSCEP reflect the average percentage of respondents who considered their country's membership to be a 'bad thing' between 2000 and 2011, or the period for which data were available. If the question was asked in multiple surveys in a given year, the average figure for individual years was calculated first. Data from Eurobarometer, through its interactive search system (European Commission 2013b).

~ CORRUP values are based on Transparency International data between 2000 and 2013, concerning perceived public sector corruption (TI 2014). The average from the available years per country is calculated and original data are reversed, 10 meaning 'corrupt' and 0 'clean'.

Table A.3   Calculation of UNRESP values

Case	dissat04* raw	fuzzy	dissat09^ raw	fuzzy	noconfparl° raw	fuzzy	noconfparty~ raw	fuzzy	UNRESP mean fs
AUS	6.5	0.13	7.5	0.16	19.8	0.55	30.4	0.55	0.35
BEL	8.5	0.2	6.0	0.12	14.9	0.32	26.9	0.41	0.26
BUL			41.6	0.98	52.9	0.99	56.4	0.99	0.99
CRO					39.6	0.95	46.6	0.95	0.95
CYP	7.0	0.14	8.8	0.21	9.7	0.13	24.8	0.34	0.21
CZR	21.3	0.73	12.2	0.38	36.1	0.92	39.5	0.86	0.72
DEN	0.7	0.03	1.6	0.04	2.6	0.03	4.8	0.02	0.03
EST	12.0	0.37	16.2	0.57	20.6	0.57	40.1	0.87	0.60
FIN	2.9	0.06	4.0	0.07	12.8	0.23	30.4	0.55	0.23
FRA	11.8	0.36	12.6	0.4	12.2	0.21	31.1	0.58	0.39
GER	10.7	0.3	8.5	0.2	19.5	0.54	33.2	0.67	0.43
GRE	7.6	0.16	29.8	0.9	24.7	0.71	36.3	0.77	0.64
HUN	12.9	0.42	32.0	0.92	31.7	0.87	42.6	0.91	0.78
ICE					10.8	0.16	17.3	0.14	0.15
IRE	10.8	0.3	12.6	0.4	12.2	0.21	20.5	0.21	0.28
ITA	19.2	0.67	14.4	0.51	20.3	0.56	39.5	0.86	0.65
LAT	19.0	0.66	32.3	0.93	35.2	0.91	43.5	0.92	0.86
LIT			25.6	0.83	21.9	0.62	26.8	0.41	0.62
LUX	2	0.05	2.1	0.05	6.7	0.08	16.6	0.13	0.08
MAL			8.1	0.18	13.4	0.25	20.4	0.21	0.21
NET	5.2	0.1	4.0	0.07	9.6	0.13	11.9	0.07	0.09
NOR					5.4	0.06	9.5	0.05	0.06
POL	24.6	0.81	5.4	0.1	34.8	0.91	45.7	0.95	0.69
POR	14.9	0.52	20.8	0.72	23.3	0.66	41.2	0.89	0.70
ROM			35.5	0.95	31.7	0.87	41.7	0.9	0.91
SLK	20.8	0.72	9.9	0.26	12.9	0.23	24.8	0.34	0.39
SLV	14.2	0.5	15.7	0.55	8.4	0.1	13.1	0.08	0.31
SPA	1.7	0.04	8.1	0.18	12.0	0.2	31.4	0.59	0.25
SWE	3.1	0.06	5.8	0.11	6.5	0.07	14.3	0.09	0.08
SWI					4.4	0.05	15.6	0.11	0.08
UK	9.5	0.24	18.0	0.63	25.1	0.72	31.7	0.61	0.55

Notes: For each country the table shows the raw data ('raw' column) and the associated fuzzy set scores ('fuzzy' column) relating to the four survey items. The values in the final UNRESP column are used in the fsQCA and represent the mean of the (available) fuzzy set scores on the individual indicators.

* dissat04 reflects the percentage of respondents who were not at all satisfied with the way democracy works in their country. Data from European Election Study 2004 (Schmitt et al. 2009). Fuzzy set score calibration is based on the values in dissat09, as less countries were missing in the 2009 survey. Full membership (1) = 35.5 (second highest value); crossover point (0.5) = 14.2 (average value after omitting highest and lowest values); full non-membership (0) = 2.1 (second lowest value).

^ dissat09: see dissat04. Data from European Election Study 2009 (Van Egmond et al. 2013). Fuzzy set score calibration: see dissat04.

° noconfparl reflects the percentage of respondents with no confidence at all in parliament. Data from European Values Study 2008 (EVS 2011). Fuzzy set score calibration: full membership (1) = 39.6; crossover point (0.5) = 18.5; full non-membership (0) = 4.4.

~ noconfparty reflects the percentage of respondents with no confidence at all in political parties. Data from European Values Study 2008 (EVS 2011). Fuzzy set score calibration: full membership (1) = 46.6; crossover point (0.5) = 29.2; full non-membership (0) = 9.5.

Table A.4 Calculation of NATIV values

Case	notcultrich* raw	fuzzy	ancestry^ raw	fuzzy	adapt° raw	fuzzy	notallowmig˜ raw	fuzzy	NATIV mean fs
AUS	36.5	0.59	23.9	0.33	35.6	0.52	12.4	0.28	0.43
BEL	37.5	0.62	14.1	0.1	31.9	0.35	14.7	0.43	0.38
BUL	35.5	0.57	53.6	0.95	31.3	0.32	22.9	0.82	0.67
CRO	32.0	0.43	39.8	0.79			15.4	0.49	0.57
CYP	57.0	0.94	69.8	0.99	36.6	0.56	29.5	0.95	0.86
CZR	44.0	0.78	31.3	0.58	49.6	0.9	22.6	0.81	0.77
DEN	26.0	0.15	14.1	0.1	22.1	0.07	7.9	0.09	0.10
EST	28.5	0.24	34.5	0.67	40.8	0.71	23.5	0.84	0.62
FIN	21.0	0.05	21.8	0.26	45.9	0.84	9.9	0.16	0.33
FRA	25.0	0.12	15.0	0.11	37.1	0.58	9.7	0.15	0.24
GER	22.5	0.07	32.0	0.6	29.7	0.26	13.5	0.35	0.32
GRE	59.0	0.95	49.4	0.92	34.8	0.49	26.0	0.9	0.82
HUN	37.0	0.61	43.8	0.86	54.9	0.95	38.8	0.99	0.85
ICE			11.1	0.06					0.06
IRE	28.5	0.24	43.9	0.86	33.2	0.41	8.0	0.09	0.40
ITA	40.0	0.69	17.9	0.16	37.4	0.59	17.1	0.58	0.51
LAT	31.0	0.37	28.3	0.49	34.9	0.49			0.45
LIT	36.5	0.59	22.7	0.29	33.7	0.43			0.44
LUX	24.0	0.09	9.8	0.05	33.4	0.42	21.4	0.77	0.33
MAL	74.5	0.99	51.5	0.94	36.2	0.55			0.83
NET	24.0	0.09	5.5	0.03	20.1	0.05	11.5	0.23	0.10
NOR			9.2	0.05			5.5	0.05	0.05
POL	26.5	0.16	48.4	0.91	28.4	0.21	8.2	0.1	0.35
POR	30.0	0.31	33.8	0.65	12.7	0.01	30.1	0.95	0.48
ROM	24.5	0.11	48.0	0.91	25.7	0.13			0.38
SLK	40.0	0.69	26.9	0.43	41.7	0.73	14.2	0.4	0.56
SLV	42.5	0.75	32.8	0.62	42.4	0.75	13.3	0.34	0.62
SPA	28.0	0.22	18.3	0.17	32.9	0.4	15.2	0.47	0.32
SWE	12.5	0.01	15.6	0.12	23.9	0.1	2.2	0.02	0.06
SWI			11.1	0.06			6.9	0.07	0.07
UK	33.5	0.51	33.5	0.64	58.6	0.97	14.8	0.44	0.64

Notes: For each country the table shows the raw data ('raw' column) and the associated fuzzy set scores ('fuzzy' column) relating to the four survey items. The values in the final NATIV column are used in the fsQCA and represent the mean of the (available) fuzzy set scores on the individual indicators. This mean is calculated on the basis of only one or two scores for Iceland, Switzerland and Norway. These countries' low values in an additional survey item, concerning the question of whether immigrants will become a threat to society (EVS 2011), suggest that the low NATIV score of these countries is a valid indicator of the level of nativist sentiment.
* notcultrich reflects the percentage of respondents who disagreed with the statement that people from other ethnic groups enrich the cultural life of their country. Data from Eurobarometer (European Commission 2009: 46). The raw scores represent the average values from two surveys (from 2006 and 2009). Fuzzy set score calibration: full membership (1) = 59.0 (second highest value); crossover point (0.5) = 33.2 (average value after omitting highest and lowest values); full non-membership (0) = 21.0 (second lowest value).
^ ancestry reflects the percentage of respondents who found it very important to have a national ancestry. Data from European Values Study 2008 (EVS 2011). Fuzzy set score calibration: full membership (1) = 53.6; crossover point (0.5) = 28.6; full non-membership (0) = 9.2.
° adapt reflects the percentage of respondents who strongly agreed with the statement that immigrants are required to adapt to the customs of their country. Data from European Election Study 2009 (Van Egmond et al. 2013). Fuzzy set score calibration: full membership (1) = 54.9; crossover point (0.5) = 35.0; full non-membership (0) = 20.1.
˜ notallowmig reflects the percentage of respondents who preferred to allow no immigrants of a different race/ethnic group from the majority population. Data from European Social Survey Round 3, 2006 (ESS 2006), apart from data on CRO (Round 4, 2008) and CZR, GRE, ITA, LUX (Round 2, 2004). Data are weighted according to the ESS instructions. Fuzzy set score calibration: full membership (1) = 30.1; crossover point (0.5) = 15.6; full non-membership (0) = 5.5.

Table A.5 Data for the fsQCA concerning the latest election results

	Conditions								Outcome	
	LUNRESP*	LCREDIB^	LECOHARD°		LEURSCEP˜		LCORRUP†		LPOPSUC˜	
Case	*fuzzy*	*fuzzy*	raw	*fuzzy*	raw	*fuzzy*	raw	*fuzzy*	raw	*fuzzy*
AUS	*0.42*	*1*	4.3	*0.06*	25.0	*0.92*	3.1	*0.4*	26.2	*0.99*
BEL	*0.28*	*0.67*	8.3	*0.53*	12.0	*0.28*	2.9	*0.35*	10.5	*0.54*
BUL	*0.99*	*0.67*	12.3	*0.86*	10.0	*0.14*	5.9	*0.91*	39.5	*1*
CRO	*0.95*	*0.67*	13.5	*0.91*	32.0	*0.98*	6.0	*0.92*	8.0	*0.35*
CYP	*0.23*	*0*	7.9	*0.48*	25.0	*0.92*	3.7	*0.55*	0	*0*
CZR	*0.72*	*1*	7.0	*0.32*	19.0	*0.75*	5.2	*0.84*	25.6	*0.99*
DEN	*0.03*	*1*	7.6	*0.43*	16.0	*0.6*	0.6	*0.05*	12.3	*0.67*
EST	*0.67*	*0*	12.5	*0.87*	9.0	*0.1*	3.6	*0.52*	0	*0*
FIN	*0.28*	*1*	7.8	*0.46*	19.0	*0.75*	0.6	*0.05*	19	*0.94*
FRA	*0.40*	*1*	10.2	*0.72*	19.0	*0.75*	2.9	*0.35*	13.6	*0.75*
GER	*0.47*	*0.67*	5.5	*0.13*	16.0	*0.6*	2.2	*0.21*	8.6	*0.4*
GRE	*0.79*	*1*	24.3	*1*	33.0	*0.98*	6.4	*0.94*	36	*1*
HUN	*0.90*	*1*	11.2	*0.8*	15.0	*0.55*	5.3	*0.85*	69.4	*1*
ICE	*0.15*	*0*	6.0	*0.18*	–	*1*	2.2	*0.21*	0	*0*
IRE	*0.27*	*0.67*	14.7	*0.95*	12.0	*0.28*	2.5	*0.26*	9.9	*0.49*
ITA	*0.64*	*1*	10.7	*0.76*	17.0	*0.65*	5.7	*0.89*	51.3	*1*
LAT	*0.92*	*0*	16.2	*0.97*	21.0	*0.82*	5.8	*0.9*	0	*0*
LIT	*0.62*	*0.67*	13.4	*0.91*	16.0	*0.6*	4.6	*0.74*	7.3	*0.31*
LUX	*0.09*	*0.67*	5.1	*0.1*	13.0	*0.38*	2.0	*0.17*	6.6	*0.27*
MAL	*0.21*	*0*	6.4	*0.23*	18.0	*0.7*	4.4	*0.7*	0	*0*
NET	*0.09*	*0.67*	5.3	*0.12*	12.0	*0.28*	1.6	*0.12*	10.1	*0.51*
NOR	*0.06*	*1*	3.2	*0.03*	–	*1*	1.4	*0.1*	16.3	*0.87*
POL	*0.65*	*1*	9.7	*0.67*	10.0	*0.14*	4.5	*0.72*	29.9	*1*
POR	*0.76*	*0*	12.9	*0.89*	26.0	*0.93*	3.9	*0.6*	0	*0*
ROM	*0.91*	*0.67*	7.0	*0.32*	11.0	*0.2*	5.6	*0.88*	15.5	*0.84*
SLK	*0.28*	*1*	14.0	*0.93*	10.0	*0.14*	5.4	*0.86*	14.1	*0.77*
SLV	*0.24*	*0.33*	8.2	*0.52*	21.0	*0.82*	4.1	*0.64*	1.8	*0.08*
SPA	*0.32*	*0*	21.7	*1*	17.0	*0.65*	3.8	*0.57*	0	*0*
SWE	*0.09*	*0.33*	8.6	*0.56*	20.0	*0.78*	0.8	*0.06*	5.7	*0.22*
SWI	*0.08*	*1*	4.0	*0.05*	–	*1*	1.2	*0.08*	27.8	*1*
UK	*0.65*	*0*	7.8	*0.46*	33.0	*0.98*	2.4	*0.24*	0	*0*

Note: see Table 3.1 and Tables A.1–A.4 for data sources and fuzzy set score calibration. The conditions PR (most electoral systems remained the same) and NATIV (no cross-time indicators) were not recalculated.

* LUNRESP: dissat04 has been omitted from the calculation (see Table A.3).

^ LCREDIB: Scores of some countries have been raised (CRO, CZR, FIN, FRA, HUN) or lowered (ICE, LAT) due to developments in the supply of populist parties (see Chapter 2).

° LECOHARD: Unemployment rates in the respective election years have been used (or the 2012 figure if the election year was 2013).

˜ LEURSCEP: Data from the latest available survey up until 2011 have been used, or, where appropriate, data from surveys in the election year of 2010.

† LCORRUP: Transparency International data from the appropriate election years have been used.

˜ LPOPSUC: The latest (aggregate) vote shares of populist parties up until 2013 have been used.

Appendix D: List of Interviewees

The Netherlands

Politicians

- Jan de Wit (SP MP), The Hague, 23 June 2008.
- Hilbrand Nawijn (former LPF immigration minister and Party for the Netherlands leader), Zoetermeer, 8 September 2008.
- Mat Herben (former Pim Fortuyn spokesperson and LPF party leader), The Hague, 10 September 2008.
- Rita Verdonk (TON Party leader and former VVD immigration minister), The Hague, 18 December 2008.

Scholars/Researchers/Journalists

- Paul Lucardie (University of Groningen), Groningen, 19 June 2008.
- René Cuperus (Wiardi Beckman Stichting), Amsterdam, 4 September 2008.

Poland

Politicians

- Maciej Giertych (LPR MEP, former presidential candidate), Brussels, 9 September 2008.
- Mateusz Piskorski (former SO MP and spokesperson), Warsaw, 21 September 2008.
- Konrad Bonisławski (All Polish Youth member), Warsaw, 22 September 2008.

Scholars/Researchers/Journalists

- Mikolaj Czesnik (Institute for Political Studies), Warsaw, 18 September 2008.
- Miroslawa Grabowska (CBOS), Warsaw, 19 September 2008.
- Ewa Nalewajko (Institute for Political Studies), Warsaw, 22 September 2008.
- Wawrzyniec Smoczyński (*Polityka* newspaper), Warsaw, 22 September 2008.

United Kingdom

Politicians

- Graham Booth (UKIP MEP), Brussels, 9 September 2008.
- Godfrey Bloom (UKIP MEP), Brussels, 9 September 2008.
- Jeffrey Titford (former UKIP leader and MEP), Brighton, 6 April 2009.
- Alan Sked (founder of Anti-Federalist League and UKIP, former party leader), London, 10 July 2009.
- Colin and Bernadette Bullen (former Anti-Federalist League and UKIP politicians), Brighton, 17 September 2009.

Scholars/Researchers/Journalists

- Simon Usherwood (University of Surrey), Guildford, 3 November 2008.

Appendix E: Expert Survey (Case Studies)

The questionnaire was tailored slightly for each of the three case studies (Netherlands, Poland and the United Kingdom). The survey was completed online via a generated Survey Monkey webpage (see, for an example of the UK case survey, http://www.surveymonkey.com/s/ ZVSTL9X). The survey questions are listed below.

This survey focuses on new political parties that try to portray themselves as political 'outsiders', whilst systematically challenging the dominant parties for being unresponsive towards the electorate.

1. Since the early 1990s, did any such parties from your country manage to enter the national parliament or the European Parliament?
   a. If 'yes', please proceed to question 2.
   b. If 'no', please proceed to question 10 at the end of this survey.
2. What is the name of these parties?
3. How do these parties define themselves, do they employ a particular ideological label (e.g. liberal, conservative, socialist)?
4. Do these parties define themselves in terms of being left or right, or not?
5. Do any of these parties claim to represent the 'will of the people' rather than a specific ideology?
   a. No
   b. Yes (please indicate which party/parties by filling in the corresponding number(s))
6. According to you, what are the most important policy issues for these parties? Are there particular issues the parties attempt to 'own' (e.g. crime, immigration, tax and spending issues)?
7. Please select a value in each of the menus. On a scale from 1 to 10, which position would you say these parties have with regard to ...
   a. Socio-economic issues (1 = left-wing, 10 = right-wing)
   b. Moral/cultural issues like euthanasia, abortion and same-sex marriage (1 = liberal, 10 = conservative)
   c. Issues related to immigration and integration of foreigners or minority groups (1 = permissive, 10 = restrictive)
   d. European integration (1 = Europhile, 10 = Eurosceptic)
8. What are the main reasons for A. the breakthrough and B. the possible demise of these new parties in your view?
9. Would you label any of the parties listed above as 'populist'? If so, please fill in the corresponding party number(s) below.

Are any of the parties listed above often called 'populist' by others (e.g. in the media, by politicians or academics)? If so, please fill in the corresponding party number(s) below.

10. Would you like to add any information to this questionnaire?

Notes

1 Introduction: Studying Populism in European Party Systems

1. European Commission President Barroso spoke these words at the annual Brussels Think Tank Forum on 22 April 2013 (European Commission 2013a).
2. See e.g. Van Spanje (2011), Mudde (2007), and Carter (2005) for a discussion on the terminology used to describe such parties; various adjectives such as 'radical right', 'extreme right', 'far right' and 'anti-immigrant' are used rather inconsistently by different authors.
3. See also the record of the conference that yielded this volume in *Government and Opposition* (Berlin et al. 1968).
4. Since populists may be inclined to criticise certain specific 'elite actors' in practice, I am hesitant to argue that populism treats the 'elite' category as a homogeneous unit.
5. The definition deviates somewhat from the one in previous publications that stemmed from this research project (Van Kessel 2011; 2013). This more recent definition captures the essence of populist parties more precisely.
6. Collier and Mahon (1993: 849) use the example 'mother': even if a woman is not the genetic mother of a child, and hence does not belong to the central subcategory, she might still be categorised as a 'nurturing mother' or a 'stepmother'.
7. In an interview with the author, Dutch politician Rita Verdonk, for instance, saw the term 'populist' as an honorary adjective: *'Populi* means the people, and I am there for the people. And there's nothing wrong with that' (The Hague, 18 December 2008).
8. Abedi's definition of anti-political establishment parties, a concept coined by Andreas Schedler (1996), overlaps considerably with well-known definitions of populism. It is questionable, however, whether all the parties identified by Abedi as APE parties (including Green Parties and Orthodox Christian Parties) truly fit the definition.
9. Radical anti-immigration parties in Germany, for instance, are especially prone to stigmatisation due to the legacy of Nazism (e.g. Decker 2008). In some Central and Eastern European countries where xenophobic sentiments are widespread, on the other hand, political mainstream parties are found that voice extremist rhetoric (targeting, for instance, Jewish people and Roma) (see Mudde 2005; Minkenberg 2013).
10. For some cases the list of questions was more tailored, if the aim was to collect specific information about populist parties in a particular country.

2 Populist Parties across Europe

1. As the second part of the QCA focuses on the last election in each country (up until 2013), I take note of changes in the credibility of populist parties in a given country, if these occurred prior to this election.
2. Full original party names are normally only given for the identified populist parties, unless these names are excessively long.
3. Since Belgium consists of two separate party systems (Flemish and Walloon), the actual strength of the parties in their respective regions is greater than national vote shares suggest.
4. Several party members nevertheless defected in November 2013, following Berlusconi's re-launch of Forza Italia. Berlusconi himself was forced to give up his seat in the Senate in the same month, after being convicted for tax fraud.

3 Paths to Populist Electoral Success and Failure: fsQCA Analysis

1. Note that only the electoral results have been recorded of parties that have entered parliament after national elections between 2000 and 2013 (see Table A.1).
2. In this analysis, the first-round vote share in French parliamentary elections is considered.
3. The fact that many, ultimately unsuccessful, minor parties and independents competed in national elections also contributed a relatively large amount of wasted votes.
4. Unfortunately, but self-evidently, the non-EU countries at the time of the 2004 and 2009 European elections were not included in the survey, and data for 2004 are also lacking for Malta and Lithuania.
5. For the case of Switzerland, OECD (2014) data are used.
6. The data used for the CORRUP condition may point in a similar direction as the data used for the UNRESP condition, as the latter gauge satisfaction with democracy and trust in political parties and parliament. The TI data, however, exclusively relate to the issue of corruption, which make them suitable in the operationalisation of this particular condition.
7. The consistency formula for necessary conditions is $\Sigma(\min(Xi, Yi))/\Sigma(Yi)$. The 'min' indicates that for each case the lower of the two values (Xi or Yi) needs to be selected. Xi is the membership score in the condition, while Yi is the membership score in the outcome. As follows, 'if all Y values are less than or equal to their corresponding X values, the formula returns a score of 1.0' (Ragin 2009: 110). The formula is devised so that it 'gives credit for near misses and penalties for causal membership scores that exceed their mark' (Ragin 2006: 296).
8. The formula for the coverage of a necessary condition is $\Sigma(\min(Xi,Yi))/\Sigma(Xi)$ and 'expresses how much smaller the outcome set Y is in relation to set X. According to this formula, if X and Y are of roughly equal size, then the coverage of X as a necessary condition is high' (Schneider and Wagemann 2012: 144). The formula essentially provides an indication of the relevance or trivialness of the necessary condition; if membership scores in X are generally much higher than the scores in Y, the observation that X is a necessary condition is not that meaningful.

9. The consistency formula for sufficient conditions is $\Sigma(\min(Xi,Yi))/\Sigma(Xi)$. As follows, 'when all of the Xi values are less than or equal to their corresponding Yi values, the consistency score is 1.00' (Ragin 2009: 108). Note that this formula is equal to the coverage formula for necessary conditions, as for this assessment cases below the diagonal line are also 'punished' (see e.g. Schneider and Wagemann 2012, Chapter 5).

10. For example, the fuzzy set membership score of Austria in the configuration PR*UNRESP*CREDIB is 0.35; this equals the country's lowest membership score in each of these three individual conditions (in this case: the score in UNRESP) (see Table 3.2).

11. The analyses for the intermediate solution only made use of logical remainders if the outcomes were consistent with the theoretical expectation that only the presence of each of the individual conditions is conducive to the electoral success of populist parties (and *vice versa* for the analysis of populist failure). It would be implausible to assume the opposite, and 'difficult counterfactuals' are thus not included to make the intermediate solution more parsimonious (see Schneider and Wagenmann 2012: 167–177). In this chapter I will, in any case, focus predominantly on the complex solutions in which no assumptions at all are made about the logical remainders.

12. The coverage of sufficient conditions decreases when cases are far removed from the diagonal line, as this indicates that the given causal configuration does not explain these cases' membership in the outcome. As follows, the formula for coverage is $\Sigma(\min(Xi, Yi))/\Sigma(Yi)$. This is equal to the consistency formula for necessary conditions, as for this assessment cases above the diagonal line are also 'punished' (see e.g. Schneider and Wagemann 2012, Chapter 5).

13. Where '~' denotes the absence of the condition or outcome, * a logical 'AND' and + a logical 'OR'.

14. The table reports various coverage measures. The solution coverage indicates how much of the outcome is covered by the entire solution term, and is determined by calculating the coverage of the joined paths of the solution, or the 'union' of all sets. The raw coverage value, on the other hand, indicates how much of the outcome is covered by a given path, irrespective of whether other paths also cover the outcome. The unique coverage figure, finally, shows how much of the outcome is covered by the given path only. To determine the unique coverage of a particular path, the coverage of the union of all sets except for this path is subtracted from the solution coverage.

15. Exceptions are the five borderline cases (France, Finland, Germany, Ireland and Luxembourg) that had CREDIB scores higher than 0.5 and POPSUC scores lower than 0.5.

16. The data used for this analysis can be found in Appendix C, Table A.5.

17. To avoid repetition, the results have been left out here.

4 Populist Parties in the Netherlands

1. All quotes from interviews, party documents and other literature in this chapter are translated from Dutch into English by the author.

2. Although not entirely surprising in view of the pejorative connotation of the term, Jan de Wit, MP for the SP, was also not very keen on applying the label 'populism' to the SP: 'we have certain points of views, we have a certain analysis, and we will not put those aside because of what "the people" may think' (Interview, The Hague, 23 June 2008).

3. Former Fortuyn spokesperson and party leader Mat Herben was much more reluctant to use the term 'populism' to describe the LPF, and he considered it to be a term of abuse used by the party's political opponents (Interview, The Hague, 10 September 2008).

4. The Hague is the political capital of the Netherlands.

5. Wilders has required constant police protection ever since 2004, as a consequence of his controversial anti-Islam statements (Lucardie and Voerman 2012: 157).

6. Several other categories could also be created on the basis of an inductive assessment of the data, including voters who cast a strategic or negative ('the party was the least bad') vote, those who followed the outcome of an online Voting Advice Application (VAA), and PVV voters with a vague or an idiosyncratic motivation.

7. Fortuyn was far from a colourless person. As Van Holsteyn and Irwin (2003: 44) sum up his lifestyle: 'Ferrari, Bentley with chauffeur, butler, two lap dogs, portraits of John F. Kennedy in his lavishly decorated Rotterdam home which he referred to as Palazzo di Pietro'.

8. Ratelband, who had become a famous TV personality, did not have any political experience. His motivational training methods included loudly exclaiming the catchword 'Tsjakka' and convincing people to walk over hot coals barefoot.

9. One prominent scandal involved MP Eric Lucassen, who, apart from being alleged to howl unwelcome remarks at neighbours, was convicted during his time in the army for engaging in an affair with a person of a lower rank. Despite this, Lucassen remained seated in parliament for the PVV until the election of 2012.

10. Another MP and one of the closer trustees of Wilders, Louis Bontes, was expelled from the party on 29 October 2013, after having openly criticised the party's executive committee, and the decisions of party leader Wilders personally.

11. On 19 March 2014, the evening of the municipal elections, Wilders asked a crowd of supporters whether they respectively desired more or less PvdA, Europe and Moroccans. After the crowd shouted 'less' all three times, Wilders assured his supporters that his party would 'take care of that'. It was the 'fewer Moroccans' question that provoked considerable public condemnation and triggered the departure of PVV politicians.

5 Populist Parties in Poland

1. The borderline character of the LPR also became apparent in the results of the expert survey. While 12 of the 14 experts regarded SO as a populist party, only seven mentioned the LPR. Seven experts also mentioned PiS – two adding that PiS had been populist since 2005.

2. PiS, for instance, promised to end the alleged scandal of 'hungry children' and aired a television ad which 'featured a child's teddy bear, whose price would rise if the heartless PO imposed its flat tax' (Millard 2006: 1023).

3. The circumstances fed into conspiracy theories imagining Russians and domestic political opponents to be responsible for the crash.

4. The League's anti-EU rhetoric was more effective in the 'second-order' European parliament election of 2004. The LPR became the second largest party behind PO, winning 15.9 per cent of the vote. SO, voicing a more ambiguous message about European integration, became the fourth largest party, with a vote share of 10.8 per cent. In this election only about one-fifth of the eligible voters showed up.

5. Millard (2009: 109) remarked that Lepper 'could sound very convincing so long as one did not listen too attentively'.

6. Millard (1999: 120) estimated that the radio station 'reached about 40 per cent of the population by 1997 with a faithful audience of some 5 million'.

7. Both Kaczyńskis were, for instance, close trustees of Lech Wałęsa – before relations soured – and Lech Kaczyński had been mayor of Warsaw and justice minister in the Solidarity Electoral Action-dominated Buzek government. Jarosław Kaczyński's former party Centre Agreement (*Porozumienie Centrum*, PC) also took part in this government.

8. An example of such measures was the establishment of a Central Anticorruption Bureau (CBA). The CBA was controversial, however, and seen by critics as a vehicle of PiS (Stanley 2010: 241–242). PiS, moreover, made no less use of patronage than previous governing parties, and appointed party supporters to positions in, for instance, the Central Bank and the Constitutional Court (Kucharczyk and Wysocka 2008: 89). These actions were justified with the argument that such institutions needed to be cleansed of *układ*-related persons.

6 Populist Parties in the United Kingdom

1. The main focus of this chapter is on politics in Great Britain, in view of the *sui generis* character of Northern Irish politics.

2. The Northern Ireland Executive has even been comprised of all major regional parties, due to a consociationalist power-sharing agreement.

3. 'Holyrood' refers to the Scottish parliament, which is located in the Holyrood area, Edinburgh.

4. In this content analysis, paragraphs in manifestos were coded as 'populist' if statements characterised by people-centrism and anti-elitism were found (Rooduijn et al. 2014: 7).

5. As former leader Titford phrased it in a personal interview, 'We have come down to the fact that it's space, not race' (Interview, Brighton, 6 April 2009). Or, in the words of MEP Bloom, 'the racist thing is lazy journalism and political opportunism' (Interview, Brussels, 9 September 2008).

6. The Northern Ireland Assembly is elected on the basis of single transferable vote. As mentioned, Northern Irish politics has a *sui generis* character whereby the religious cleavage is of prime importance. Labour and the Conservatives are not represented in the Northern Irish Assembly.

7. Electoral system reform vanished from the political agenda after the referendum on electoral system change, held on 5 May 2011, resulted in a vote against change. It is uncertain whether the introduction of the 'alternative vote' system would have significantly affected general election results (see Sanders et al. 2011).

8. Titford revealed: 'I didn't really want to be leader. I had to be a leader of bringing people back into the party, because they had been so upset by internal politics. I was the one who poured oil on troubled waters and brought them all back in' (Interview, Brighton, 6 April 2009).

9. The BBC had sacked 'Kilroy' in January 2004 after he had made controversial statements about Muslims.

7 Conclusion: Populist Parties and Their Electoral Performance

1. During the 2014 European Consortium for Political Research (ECPR) General Conference in Glasgow, for instance, the section 'Political Radicalism in Times of Crisis' included papers touching on topics such as the role of welfare chauvinism in the programmes of radical right-wing populist parties, the nationalism of radical left parties, and the commonalities between the radical left and right in terms of ideology and support.

Bibliography

Aarts, K. and J. Thomassen (2008) 'Dutch Voters and the Changing Party Space 1989–2006', *Acta Politica*, 43(2–3), 203–234.

Abedi, A. (2004) *Anti-Political Establishment Parties. A comparative analysis*, Oxon: Routledge.

Abedi, A. and T. Lundberg (2009) 'Doomed to Failure? UKIP and the Organisational Challenges Facing Right-Wing Populist Anti-Political Establishment Parties', *Parliamentary Affairs*, 62(1), 72–87.

Abts, K. and S. Rummens (2007) 'Populism versus Democracy', *Political Studies*, 55(6), 405–424.

Abts, K. and M. Swyngedouw (2012) 'The success and failure of extreme right in Flanders. The case of Vlaams Belang', Paper presented at the IPSA Conference, Madrid, 10 July 2012.

AfD (2013) *Alternative für Deutschland Wahlprogramm*, Alternative für Deutschland federal election manifesto, 2013.

Akkerman, A., C. Mudde and A. Zaslove (2014) 'How Populist Are the People? Measuring Populist Attitudes in Voters', *Comparative Political Studies*, 47(9), 1324–1353.

Akkerman, T. (2005) 'Anti-Immigration Parties and the Defence of Liberal Values: The Exceptional Case of the List Pim Fortuyn', *Journal of Political Ideologies*, 10(3), 337–354.

Akkerman, T. and S. de Lange (2012) 'Radical Right Parties in Office: Incumbency Records and the Electoral Cost of Governing', *Government and Opposition*, 47(4), 574–596.

Albertazzi, D. (2008) 'Switzerland: Yet Another Populist Paradise', in Albertazzi, D. and McDonnell, D. (eds.) *Twenty-First Century Populism. The Spectre of Western European Democracy*, Basingstoke: Palgrave Macmillan, 100–118.

Albertazzi, D. and D. McDonnell (2005) 'The Lega Nord in the Second Berlusconi Government: In a League of Its Own', *West European Politics*, 28(5), 952–972.

Albertazzi, D. and D. McDonnell (eds.) (2008a) *Twenty-First Century Populism. The Spectre of Western European Democracy*, Basingstoke: Palgrave Macmillan.

Albertazzi, D. and D. McDonnell (2008b) 'Introduction: The Spectre and the Spectre', in Albertazzi, D. and McDonnell, D. (eds.) *Twenty-First Century Populism. The Spectre of Western European Democracy*, Basingstoke: Palgrave Macmillan, 1–11.

Albertazzi, D. and D. McDonnell (2010) 'The Lega Nord Back in Government', *West European Politics*, 33(6), 1318–1340.

Albertazzi, D. and S. Mueller (2013) 'Populism and Liberal Democracy: Populists in Government in Austria, Italy, Poland and Switzerland', *Government and Opposition*, 48(3), 343–371.

Andeweg, R. (2001) 'Lijphart versus Lijphart: The Cons of Consensus Democracy in Homogeneous Societies', *Acta Politica*, 36(2), 117–128.

Andeweg, R. and G. Irwin (2009) *Governance and Politics of the Netherlands*, 3rd edition, Houndmills: Palgrave Macmillan.

Andreescu, G. (2005) 'Romania', in Mudde, C. (ed.) *Racist Extremism in Central and Eastern Europe*, London: Routledge, 184–209.

Antić, M. (2012) 'The Parliamentary Elections in Croatia, December 2011', *Electoral Studies*, 31(3), 636–639.

Arditi, B. (2005) 'Populism as an Internal Periphery of Democratic Politics', in Panizza, F. (ed.) *Populism and the Mirror of Democracy*, London: Verso, 72–98.

Arter, D. (2007) 'The End of the Social Democratic Hegemony? The March 2007 Finnish General Election', *West European Politics*, 30(5), 1148–1157.

Arter, D. (2010) 'The Breakthrough of Another West European Populist Radical Right Party? The Case of the True Finns', *Government and Opposition*, 45(4), 484–504.

Arzheimer, K. (2009) 'Contextual Factors and the Extreme Right Vote in Western Europe, 1980–2002', *American Journal of Political Science*, 53(2), 259–275.

Arzheimer, K. and E. Carter (2006) 'Political Opportunity Structures and Right-Wing Extremist Party Success', *European Journal of Political Research*, 45(3), 419–443.

Auers, D. (2010) 'Europe and the 2010 Parliamentary Election in Latvia', EPERN Election Briefing Paper, no. 60.

Auers, D. (2013) 'Latvia', in Berglund, S., Ekman, J., Deegan-Krause, K. and Knutsen, T. (eds.) *The Handbook Of Political Change In Eastern Europe*, 3rd edition, Cheltenham: Edward Elgar, 85–123.

Backes, U. and C. Mudde (2000) 'Germany: Extremism without Successful Parties', *Parliamentary Affairs*, 53(3), 457–468.

Baker, D., A. Gamble, N. Randall and D. Seawright (2008) 'Euroscepticism in the British Party System: "A Source of Fascination, Perplexity, and Sometimes Frustration" ', in Szczerbiak, A. and Taggart, P. (eds.) *Opposing Europe? The Comparative Party Politics of Euroscepticism. Volume 1 Case Studies and Country Surveys*, Oxford: Oxford University Press, 83–116.

Balcere, I. (2012) 'Baltic Countries', in Havlík, V. et al. (eds.) *Populist Political Parties in East-Central Europe*, Brno: Masarykova Univerzita, 39–71.

Bale, T. (2003) 'Cinderella and Her Ugly Sisters: The Mainstream and Extreme Right in Europe's Bipolarising Party Systems', *West European Politics*, 26(3), 67–90.

Bale, T. (2006) 'Between a Soft and a Hard Place? The Conservative Party, Valence Politics and the Need for a New "Eurorealism" ', *Parliamentary Affairs*, 59(3), 385–400.

Bale, T. (2010) 'Europe and the UK General Election of 6 May 2010', EPERN Election Briefing Paper, no. 53.

Bale, T., D. Hough and S. van Kessel (2012) 'In or out of Proportion? Labour and Social Democratic Parties' Responses to the Radical Right', in Rydgren, J. (ed.) *Class Politics and the Radical Right*, Oxon: Routledge, 91–106.

Bale, T, S. van Kessel and P. Taggart (2011) 'Thrown around with Abandon? Popular Understandings of Populism as Conveyed by the Print Media: a UK Case Study', *Acta Politica*, 46(2), 111–131.

Balent, M. (2013) 'The French National Front from Jean-Marie to Marine Le Pen: Between Change and Continuity', in Grabow, K. and Hartleb, F. (eds.) *Exposing the Demagogues. Right-Wing and National Populist Parties in Europe*, Brussels: CES-KAS, 161–186.

Barr, R. (2009) 'Populists, Outsiders and Anti-Establishment Politics', *Party Politics*, 15(1), 29–48.

Bartlett, J., C. Froio, M. Littler and D. McDonnell (2013) *New Political Actors in Europe: Beppe Grillo and the M5S*, London: Demos.

Batory, A. (2008) *The Politics of EU Accession. Ideology, Party Strategy and the European Question in Hungary*, Manchester: Manchester University Press.

Batory, A. (2010) 'Europe and the Hungarian Parliamentary Elections of April 2010', EPERN Election Briefing Paper, no. 51.

BBC (2013) 'Local Elections: Nigel Farage Hails Results as a "Game Changer"', 3 May 2013, in http://www.bbc.co.uk/news/uk-politics-22382098, accessed 1 February 2014.

Bélanger, É. and K. Aarts (2006) 'Explaining the Rise of the LPF: Issues, Discontent, and the 2002 Dutch Election', *Acta Politica*, 41(1), 4–20.

Bellucci, P., D. Garzia and M. Lewis-Beck (2013) 'Issues and Leaders as Vote Determinants: The Case of Italy', *Party Politics*, Published online, doi: 10.1177/1354068812472583.

Berlin, I. et al. (1968) 'To Define Populism', *Government and Opposition*, 3(2), 137–179.

Bernáth, G., G. Miklósi and C. Mudde (2005) 'Hungary', in Mudde, C. (ed.) *Racist Extremism in Central and Eastern Europe*, London: Routledge, 80–100.

Betz, H.-G. (1994) *Radical Right-Wing Populism in Western Europe*, New York: St. Martin's Press.

Betz, H.-G. and S. Immerfall (eds.) (1998) *The New Politics of the Right. Neo-Populist Parties and Movements in Established Democracies*, New York: St. Martin's Press.

Betz, H.-G. (2002) 'Conditions Favouring the Success and Failure of Radical Right-Wing Populist Parties in Contemporary Democracies', in Mény, Y. and Surel, Y. (eds.) *Democracies and the Populist Challenge*, Basingstoke: Palgrave, 197–213.

BNP (2005) *Rebuilding British Democracy*, British National Party general election manifesto, 2005.

BNP (2010a) *Democracy, Freedom, Culture and Identity*, British National Party general election manifesto, 2010.

BNP (2010b) 'A message from BNP Leader Nick Griffin MEP', British National Party website, in http://www.bnp.org.uk/introduction, accessed 20 July 2010.

Bolin, N. (2007) 'New Party Entrance – Analyzing the Impact of Political Institutions', Umeå Working Papers in Political Science, no. 2.

Bolleyer, N. (2013) *New Parties in Old Party Systems. Persistence and Decline in Seventeen Democracies*, Oxford: Oxford University Press.

Bordignon, F. and L. Ceccarini (2013) 'Five Stars and a Cricket. Beppe Grillo Shakes Italian Politics', *South European Society and Politics*, 18(4), 427–449.

Bornschier, S. (2010) *Cleavage Politics and the Populist Right. The New Cultural Conflict in Western Europe*, Philadelphia: Temple University Press.

Bornschier, S. (2012) 'Why a right-wing populist party emerged in France but not in Germany: Cleavages and actors in the formation of a new cultural divide', *European Political Science Review*, 4(1), 121–145.

Bos, L. and W. van der Brug (2010), 'Public images of leaders of anti-immigration parties: Perceptions of legitimacy and effectiveness', *Party Politics*, 16(6), 777–799.

Bovens, M. and A. Wille (2011) 'Politiek vertrouwen in Nederland: tijdelijke dip of definitieve daling?', in Andeweg, R. and Thomassen, J. (eds.) *Democratie Doorgelicht, het functioneren van de Nederlandse democratie*, Leiden: Leiden University Press, 21–43.

Budge, I. and D. Farlie (1983) *Explaining and Predicting Elections: Issue Effects and Party Strategies in Twenty-Three Democracies*, London: Allen & Unwin.

Bustikova, L. and H. Kitschelt (2009) 'The Radical Right in Post-Communist Europe. Comparative Perspectives on Legacies and Party Competition', *Communist and Post-Communist Studies*, 42(4), 459–483.

Canovan, M. (1981) *Populism*, New York and London: Harcourt Brace Jovanovich.

Canovan, M. (1982) 'Two Strategies for the Study of Populism', *Political Studies*, 30(4), 544–552.

Canovan, M. (1999) 'Trust the People! Populism and the Two Faces of Democracy', *Political Studies*, 47(1), 2–16.

Carter, E. (2005) *The Extreme Right in Western Europe. Success or Failure?*, Manchester: Manchester University Press.

Casal Bértoa, F. (2013) 'Post-Communist Politics: On the Divergence (and/or Convergence) of East and West', *Government and Opposition*, 48(3), 398–433.

Castle, M. and R. Taras (2002) *Democracy in Poland*, 2nd edition, Oxford: Westview Press.

CBOS (2001a) 'Polish Public Opinion July–August 2001', Centrum Badania Opinii Społecznej, Warsaw, August 2001.

CBOS (2001b) 'Polish Public Opinion October 2001', Centrum Badania Opinii Społecznej, Warsaw, October 2001.

CBOS (2001c) 'Poglądy elektoratów partii politycznych', Centrum Badania Opinii Społecznej, Research Report 136, Warsaw, October 2001.

CBOS (2003a) 'Polish Public Opinion May 2003', Centrum Badania Opinii Społecznej, Warsaw, May 2003.

CBOS (2003b) 'Polish Public Opinion June 2003', Centrum Badania Opinii Społecznej, Warsaw, June 2003.

CBOS (2005) 'Polish Public Opinion September 2005', Centrum Badania Opinii Społecznej, Warsaw, September 2005.

CBOS (2006a) 'Polish Public Opinion August 2006', Centrum Badania Opinii Społecznej, Warsaw, August 2006.

CBOS (2006b) 'Polish Public Opinion October 2006', Centrum Badania Opinii Społecznej, Warsaw, October 2006.

CBS, SKON, M. Brinkman, H. van der Kolk, C. Aarts and M. Rosema (2007) *Dutch Parliamentary Election Study 2006*, The Hague: DANS.

Cholova, B. (2012) 'Bulgaria', in Havlík, V. et al. (eds.) *Populist Political Parties in East-Central Europe*, Brno: Masarykova Univerzita, 73–96.

Clarke, H., D. Sanders, M. Steward and P. Whiteley (2010) *British Election Study 2010*, Colchester: University of Essex.

Collier, D. and J. Mahon (1993) 'Conceptual "Stretching" Revisited: Adapting Categories in Comparative Analysis', *American Political Science Review*, 87(4), 845–855.

Conservative Party (2010) *Invitation to Join the Government of Britain*, Conservative Party general election manifesto, 2010.

Copsey, N. (1996) 'Contemporary Fascism in the Local Arena: The British National Party and "Rights for Whites" ', in M. Cronin (ed.) *The Failure of British Fascism. The Far Right and the Fight for Political Recognition*, Houndmills: Macmillan.

Copsey, N. (2007) 'Changing Course or Changing Clothes? Reflections on the Ideological Evolution of the British National Party 1999–2006', *Patterns of Prejudice*, 41(1), 61–82.

Copsey, N. (2008) *Contemporary British Fascism. The British National Party and the Quest for Legitimacy*, 2nd edition, Houndmills: Palgrave Macmillan.

Crewe, I., B. Sarlvik and J. Alt (1977) 'Partisan Dealignment in Britain 1964–1974', *British Journal of Political Science*, 7(2), 129–190.

Cronin, M. (ed.) (1996) *The Failure of British Fascism. The Far Right and the Fight for Political Recognition*, Houndmills: Macmillan.

Crowther, W. and O. Suciu (2013) 'Romania', in Berglund, S., Ekman, J., Deegan-Krause, K. and Knutsen, T. (eds.) *The Handbook of Political Change in Eastern Europe*, 3rd edition, Cheltenham: Edward Elgar, 369–406.

Čular, G. (2004) 'Organisational Development of Parties and Internal Party Democracy in Croatia', *Politička misao*, XLI(5), 28–51.

Cutts, D., R. Ford and M. Goodwin (2011) 'Anti-Immigrant, Politically Disaffected or Still Racist after All? Examining the Attitudinal Drivers of Extreme Right Support in Britain in the 2009 European Elections', *European Journal of Political Research*, 50(3), 418–440.

Cutts, D. and M. Goodwin (2014) 'Getting out the Right-Wing Extremist Vote: Extreme Right Party Support and Campaign Effects at a Recent British General Election', *European Political Science Review*, 6(1), 93–114.

Dalton, R., I. McAllister and M. Wattenberg (2000) 'The Consequences of Partisan Dealignment', in Dalton, R. and Wattenberg, M. (eds.) *Parties without Partisans. Political Change in Advanced Industrial Democracies*, Oxford: Oxford University Press, 37–63.

Daniel, M. (2005) *Cranks and Gadflies: The Story of UKIP*, London: Timewell Press.

Davoliute, V. (2012) 'Mob Justice in Lithuania: Who Can Stand up to the Madding Crowd?', Open Democracy, 11 May 2012, in http://www.opendemocracy.net/od-russia/violeta-davoliute/mob-justice-in-lithuania-who-can-stand-up-to-madding-crowd, accessed 20 December 2013.

Decker, F. (2008) 'Germany: Right-Wing Populist Failures and Left-wing Successes', in Albertazzi, D. and McDonnell, D. (eds.) *Twenty-First Century Populism. The Spectre of Western European Democracy*, Basingstoke: Palgrave Macmillan, 119–134.

Deegan-Krause, K. and T. Haughton (2009) 'Toward a More Useful Conceptualization of Populism: Types and Degrees of Populist Appeals in the Case of Slovakia', *Politics & Policy*, 37(4), 821–841.

Deegan-Krause, K. (2012) 'Populism, Democracy, and Nationalism in Slovakia', in Mudde, C. and Rovira Kaltwasser, C. (eds.) *Populism in Europe and the Americas. Threat or Corrective for Democracy?*, Cambridge: Cambridge University Press, 182–204.

De Lange, S. and T. Akkerman (2012) 'Populist Parties in Belgium: A Case of Hegemonic Liberal Democracy?', in Mudde, C. and Rovira Kaltwasser, C. (eds.) *Populism in Europe and the Americas. Threat or Corrective for Democracy?*, Cambridge: Cambridge University Press, 27–45.

De Lange, S. and D. Art (2011) 'Fortuyn versus Wilders: An Agency-Based Approach to Radical Right Party Building', *West European Politics*, 34 (6), 1229–1249.

De Lange, S. and S. Guerra (2009) 'The League of Polish Families between East and West, Past and Present', *Communist and Post-Communist Studies*, 42(4), 527–549.

De Lange, S. and M. Rooduijn (2011) 'Een populistische *Zeitgeist* in Nederland? Een inhoudsanalyse van de verkiezingsprogramma's van populistische en gevestigde politieke partijen', in Andeweg, R. and Thomassen, J. (eds.) *Democratie Doorgelicht, het functioneren van de Nederlandse democratie,* Leiden: Leiden University Press, 319–334.

De Meur, G., B. Rihoux and S. Yamasaki (2009) 'Addressing the Critiques of QCA', in Rihoux, B. and Ragin, C. (eds.) *Configurational Comparative Methods. Qualitative Comparative Analysis (QCA) and Related Techniques,* Thousand Oaks: Sage, 147–165.

De Vries, C. and E. Edwards (2009) 'Taking Europe to its Extremes: Extremist Parties and Public Euroscepticism', *Party Politics,* 15(1), 5–28.

Dinas, E. (2008) 'The Greek General Election of 2007: You Cannot Lose If Your Opponent Cannot Win', *West European Politics,* 31(3), 600–607.

Di Tella, T. (1997) 'Populism into the Twenty-first Century', *Government and Opposition,* 32(2), 187–200.

Dumont, P. and P. Poirier (2005) 'Luxembourg', *European Journal of Political Research,* 44(7–8), 1102–1118.

Dumont, P., R. Kies and P. Poirier (2011) 'Luxembourg', *European Journal of Political Research,* 50(7–8), 1058–1064.

Dumont, P., R. Kies and P. Poirier (2012) 'Luxembourg', *European Journal of Political Research Political Data Yearbook,* 51(1), 201–209.

Dunleavy, P. (2005) 'Facing Up to Multi-Party Politics: How Partisan Dealignment and PR Voting Have Fundamentally Changed Britain's Party Systems', *Parliamentary Affairs,* 58(3), 503–532.

Durham, M. (1996) 'The Conservative Party, the British Extreme Right and the Problem of Political Space, 1967–83', in M. Cronin (ed.) *The Failure of British Fascism. The Far Right and the Fight for Political Recognition,* Houndmills: Macmillan.

Duverger, M. (1959) *Political Parties,* 2nd edition, London: Methuen.

Duvold, K. and M. Jurkynas (2013) 'Lithuania', in Berglund, S., Ekman, J., Deegan-Krause. K. and Knutsen, T. (eds.) *The Handbook of Political Change in Eastern Europe,* 3rd edition, Cheltenham: Edward Elgar, 125–166.

Eatwell, R. (1996) 'The Esoteric Ideology of the National Front in the 1980s', in Cronin, M. (ed.) *The Failure of British Fascism. The Far Right and the Fight for Political Recognition,* Houndmills: Macmillan.

Eatwell, R. (2000) 'The Extreme Right and British Exceptionalism. The Primacy of Politics', in Hainsworth, P. (ed.) *The Politics of the Extreme Right. From the Margins to the Mainstream,* London: Pinter, 172–192.

Eatwell, R. (2003) 'Ten Theories of the Extreme Right', in Merkl, P. and Weinberg, L. (eds.) *Right-Wing Extremism in the Twenty-first Century,* London: Frank Cass, 47–73.

Eatwell, R. (2004) 'The Extreme Right in Britain. The Long Road to "Modernization"', in Eatwell, R. and Mudde, C. (eds.) *Western Democracies and the New Extreme Right Challenge,* London: Routledge.

Eatwell, R. (2010) 'Responses to the Extreme Right in Britain', in Eatwell, R. and Goodwin, M. (eds.) *The New Extremism in 21st Century Britain,* Oxon: Routledge, 211–230.

Eatwell, R. and M. Goodwin (eds.) (2010) *The New Extremism in 21st Century Britain,* Oxon: Routledge.

Economist (2013) 'Take Me to Your Leader', 18 May 2013, in www.economist.com/node/21578096, accessed 30 January 2014.

Economist (2014) 'UKIP gets serious', 18 January 2014, in www.economist.com/node/21594261, accessed 1 Feburary 2014.

Ellemers, J. (2004) 'Het fenomeen Fortuyn. De revolte verklaard', in Voerman, G. (ed.) *Jaarboek DNPP 2002*, Groningen: Rijksuniversiteit Groningen, 252–266.

ESS (2006) *European Social Survey Round 3 Data*, Data file edition 3.4. Norwegian Social Science Data Services, Norway – Data Archive and distributor of ESS data.

European Commission (2009) 'Table of Results. Standard Eurobarometer 71', in http://ec.europa.eu/public_opinion/archives/eb/eb71/eb713_anx_future.pdf, accessed 13 January 2014.

European Commission (2012) 'Tables of Results', Standard Eurobarometer 78, Autumn 2012, in http://ec.europa.eu/public_opinion/archives/eb/eb78/eb78_anx_bd_fr.pdf, accessed 7 July 2014.

European Commission (2013a) 'Speech: More Integration Would Boost European Cooperation', 22 April 2013, in http://ec.europa.eu/debate-future-europe/ongoing-debate/articles/barroso_federalism_20130422_en.htm, accessed 4 December 2013.

European Commission (2013b) 'Eurobarometer Interactive Search System', in http://ec.europa.eu/public_opinion/cf/index_en.cfm, accessed 22 December 2013.

Eurostat (2014) 'Unemployment Rate by Sex and Age Groups – Annual Average, %', in http://appsso.eurostat.ec.europa.eu/nui/show.do?dataset=une_rt_a&lang=en, accessed 13 January 2014.

EVS (2011) *European Values Study 2008: Integrated Dataset (EVS 2008)*, GESIS Data Archive, Cologne. ZA4800 Data file Version 3.0.0, doi:10.4232/1.11004.

Eyerman, R. (1981) 'False Consciousness and Ideology in Marxist Theory', *Acta Sociologica*, 24(1–2), 43–56.

Fallend, F. (2012) 'Populism in Government: The Case of Austria', in Mudde, C. and Rovira Kaltwasser, C. (eds.) *Populism in Europe and the Americas. Threat or Corrective for Democracy?*, Cambridge: Cambridge University Press, 113–135.

Fella, S. (2008) 'Britain: Imperial Legacies, Institutional Constraints and New Political Opportunities', in Albertazzi, D. and McDonnell, D. (eds.) *Twenty-First Century Populism. The Spectre of Western European Democracy*, Basingstoke: Palgrave Macmillan.

Fitzgibbon, J. and S. Guerra (2010) 'Not Just Europeanization, Not Necessarily Populism: Potential Factors Underlying the Mobilization of Populism in Ireland and Poland', *Perspectives on European Politics and Society*, 11(3), 273–291.

Ford, R. (2010) 'Who Might Vote for the BNP? Survey Evidence on the Electoral Potential of the Extreme Right in Britain', in Eatwell, R. and Goodwin, M. (eds.) *The New Extremism in 21st Century Britain*, Oxon: Routledge, 145–168.

Ford, R. and M. Goodwin (2010) 'Angry White Men: Individual and Contextual Predictors of Support for the British National Party', *Political Studies*, 58(1), 1–25.

Ford, R., M. Goodwin, and D. Cutts (2012) 'Strategic Eurosceptics and Polite Xenophobes: Support for the United Kingdom Independence Party (UKIP) in the 2009 European Parliament Elections', *European Journal of Political Research*, 51(2), 204–234.

Ford, R. and M. Goodwin (2014) *Revolt on the Right. Explaining Support for the Radical Right in Britain*, Oxon: Routledge.

Fortuyn, P. (2002) *De Puinhopen van acht jaar paars*. *Een genadeloze analyse van de collectieve sector en aanbevelingen voor een krachtig herstelprogramma*, Uithoorn-Rotterdam: Karakter Uitgevers-Speakers Academy.

Freeden, M. (1998) 'Is Nationalism a Distinct Ideology?', *Political Studies*, 46(4), 748–765.

Fry, G. (1998) 'Parliament and "morality": Thatcher, Powell and Populism', *Contemporary British History*, 12(1), 139–147.

Gallagher, M. (1991) 'Proportionality, disproportionality and electoral systems', *Electoral Studies*, 10(1), 33–51.

Gallagher, M. (2013) Electoral Systems Website, in http://www.tcd.ie/Political_Science/staff/michael_gallagher/ElSystems/index.php, accessed 20 December 2013.

Gardner, P. (2006) *Hard Pounding: The Story of the UK Independence Party*, Totnes: June Press.

Garzia, D. (2013) 'The 2013 Italian Parliamentary Election: Changing Things So Everything Stays the Same', *West European Politics*, 36(5), 1095–1105.

Gemenis, K. and E. Dinas (2010) 'Confrontation Still? Examining Parties' Policy Positions in Greece', *Comparative European Politics*, 8(2), 179–201.

Gherghina, S. and S. Soare (2013) 'From TV to Parliament. Populism and Communication in the Romanian 2012 Elections', Paper prepared for the XXVII Congress of the Italian Society of Political Science, University of Florence, 12–14 September 2013.

Ghodsee, K. (2008) 'Left Wing, Right Wing, Everything. Xenophobia, Neo-totalitarianism, and Populist Politics in Bulgaria', *Problems of Post-Communism*, 55(3), 26–39.

Gifford, C. (2006) 'The Rise of Post-Imperial Populism: The Case of Right-Wing Euroscepticism in Britain', *European Journal of Political Research*, 45(5), 851–869.

Givens, T. (2005) *Voting Radical Right in Western Europe*, Cambridge: Cambridge University Press.

Goertz, G. (2006) *Social Science Concepts. A User's Guide*, Princeton: Princeton University Press.

Golder, M. (2003) 'Explaining Variation in the Success of Extreme Right Parties in Western Europe', *Comparative Political Studies*, 36(4), 432–466.

Goodwin, M. (2008) 'Backlash in the 'Hood: Determinants of Support for the British National Party (BNP) at the Local Level', *Journal of Contemporary European Studies*, 16(3), 347–361.

Goodwin, M. (2010) 'In Search of the Winning Formula. Nick Griffin and the 'Modernization' of the British National Party', in Eatwell, R. and Goodwin, M. (eds.) *The New Extremism in 21st Century Britain*, Oxon: Routledge, 169–190.

Goodwin, M. (2011) *New British Fascism. The Rise of the British National Party*, Oxon: Routledge.

Griffin, R. (1993) *The Nature of Fascism*, Oxon: Routledge.

Guardian (2010) 'Lord Pearson Stands Down as UKIP Leader because he is "Not Much Good" ', 17 August 2010, in http://www.guardian.co.uk/politics/2010/aug/17/lord-pearson-stands-down-as-ukip-leader, accessed 9 May 2011.

Guardian (2011) 'BNP Faces Meltdown at Local Polls after Defections and Infighting', 22 April 2011, in http://www.theguardian.com/politics/2011/apr/22/bnp-faces-local-election-meltdown, accessed 30 January 2014.

Hagelund, A. (2005) 'The Progress Party and the Problem of Culture: Immigration Politics and Right Wing Populism in Norway' in Rydgren, J. (ed.) *Movements of Exclusion: Radical Right-Wing Populism in the Western World*, New York: Nova Science Publishers, 147–164.

Hainsworth, P. and P. Mitchell (2000) 'France: The Front National from Crossroads to Crossroads', *Parliamentary Affairs*, 53(3), 443–456.

Hakhverdian, A. and C. Koop (2007) 'Consensus Democracy and Support for Populist Parties in Western Europe', *Acta Politica*, 42(4), 401–420.

Halasz, K. (2009) 'The Rise of the Radical Right in Europe and the Case of Hungary: "Gypsy Crime" Defines National Identity?', *Development*, 52(4), 490–494.

Hanley, S. and A. Sikk (2014) 'Economy, corruption or floating voters? Explaining the breakthroughs of anti-establishment reform parties in eastern Europe', *Party Politics*, Online First, doi: 10.1177/1354068814550438.

Hardarson, O. and G. Kristinsson (2010) 'Iceland', *European Journal of Political Research*, 49(7–8), 1009–1016.

Harmel, R. and J. Robertson (1985) 'Formation and Success of New Parties. A Cross-National Analysis', *International Political Science Review*, 6(4), 501–523.

Hauss, C. and D. Rayside (1978) 'The Development of New Parties in Western Democracies since 1945', in Maisel, L. and Cooper, J. (eds.) *Political Parties: Development and Decay*, London: Sage, 32–58.

Havlík, V. (2012) 'The Czech Republic', in Havlík, V. et al. (eds.) *Populist Political Parties in East-Central Europe*, Brno: Masarykova Univerzita, 97–134.

Havlík, V. et al. (eds.) (2012) *Populist Political Parties in East-Central Europe*, Brno: Masarykova Univerzita.

Hawkins, K. (2009) 'Is Chavez Populist? Measuring Populist Discourse in Comparative Perspective', *Comparative Political Studies*, 42(8), 1040–1067.

Hayes, P. (1973) *Fascism*, London: Allen and Unwin.

Hayton, R. (2010) 'Towards the Mainstream? UKIP and the 2009 Elections to the European Parliament', *Politics*, 30(1), 26–35.

HBS (2013) 'Political Earthquake in the Czech Republic: Rejection of Established Parties', Heinrich Böll Stiftung, 28 October 2013, in http://www.boell.de/en/2013/10/31/political-earthquake-czech-republic-rejection-established-parties, accessed 8 December 2013.

Heinisch, R. (2003) 'Success in Opposition – Failure in Government: Explaining the Performance of Right-Wing Populist Parties in Public Office', *West European Politics*, 26(3), 91–130.

Heinisch, R. (2008) 'Austria: The Structure and Agency of Austrian Populism', in Albertazzi, D. and McDonnell, D. (eds.) *Twenty-First Century Populism. The Spectre of Western European Democracy*, Basingstoke: Palgrave Macmillan, 67–83.

Heinisch, R. (2013) 'Austrian Right-wing Populism: A Surprising Comeback under a New Leader', in Grabow, K. and Hartleb, F. (eds.) *Exposing the Demagogues. Right-wing and National Populist Parties in Europe*, Brussels: CES-KAS, 47–80.

Henjak, A. (2007) 'The Croatian Parliamentary Elections of November 2007', EPERN Election Briefing Paper, no. 40.

Henjak, A., N. Zakošek and G. Čular (2013) 'Croatia', in Berglund, S., Ekman, J., Deegan-Krause, K. and Knutsen, T. (eds.) *The Handbook of Political Change in Eastern Europe*, 3rd edition, Cheltenham: Edward Elgar, 443–480.

Herben, M. (2005) *Vrij Denken: over religie, politiek en vrijmetselarij*, The Hague: Synthese.

Hloušek, V. and P. Kaniok (2010) 'The Absence of Europe in the Czech Parliamentary Election, May 28–29 2010', EPERN Election Briefing Paper, no. 56.

Hloušek, V. and P. Kaniok (2014) 'Europe and the 2013 Czech Parliamentary Election, October 25–26 2013', EPERN Election Briefing Paper, no. 74.

Hooghe, L., G. Marks and C. Wilson (2002) 'Does Left/Right Structure Party Positions on European Integration?', *Comparative Political Studies*, 35(8), 965–989.

Hornát, J. (2013) 'A Czech Election with Consequences', Open Democracy, 14 October 2013, in http://www.opendemocracy.net/can-europe-make-it/jan-horn%C3%A1t/czech-election-with-consequences, accessed 08 December 2014.

Hough, D. (2010) 'From Pariah to Prospective Partner? The German Left Party's Winding Path towards Government', in Olsen, J., Koss, M. and Hough, D. (eds.) *Left Parties in National Governments*, London: Palgrave Mcmillan, 138–154.

Hough, D. and M. Koß (2009) 'Populism Personified or Reinvigorated Reformers? The German Left Party in 2009 and Beyond', *German Politics and Society*, 27(2), 76–91.

Huberty, M. (2009) 'The National Legislative and European Parliament Elections in Luxembourg, 7 June 2009', EPERN European Parliament Elections briefing no. 40.

Hug, S. (2001) *Altering Party Systems. Strategic Behavior and the Emergence of New Political Parties in Western Democracies*, Ann Arbor: University of Michigan Press.

ICM (2006) 'State of the Nation 2006', ICM Research and Joseph Rowntree Reform Trust Report, 30 October 2006, in http://www.jrrt.org.uk/sites/jrrt.org.uk/files/documents/SoN%202006%20summary%20of%20findings.pdf, accessed 30 January 2014.

Ignazi, P. (1992) 'The Silent Counter-Revolution. Hypotheses on the Emergence of Extreme Right-Wing Parties in Europe', *European Journal of Political Research* 22(1), 3–34.

Ignazi, P. (1996) 'The Crisis of Parties and the Rise of New Political Parties', *Party Politics*, 2(4), 549–566.

Ikstens, J. (2012) 'Latvia', *European Journal of Political Research Political Data Yearbook*, 51(1), 175–186.

Inglehart, R. (1977) *The Silent Revolution: Changing Values and Political Styles among Western Publics*, Princeton: Princeton University Press.

Inglehart, R. (1997) *Modernization and Postmodernization: Cultural, Economic, and Political Change in 43 Societies*, Princeton: Princeton University Press.

Ionescu, G. and E. Gellner (eds.) (1969) *Populism, its Meanings and National Characteristics*, London: Weidenfeld and Nicolson.

Ipsos MORI (2010) 'Importance of Key Issues to Voting', 24 March 2010, in http://www.ipsos-mori.com/researchpublications/researcharchive/poll.aspx?oItemId=54&view=wide, accessed 29 January 2014.

Ipsos MORI (2011) 'Satisfaction with the System of Governing Britain 1973–2010', 30 March 2011, in http://www.ipsos-mori.com/researchpublications/researcharchive/poll.aspx?oItemId=2442&view=wide, accessed 1 February 2014.

Ipsos MORI (2012a) 'The Most Important Issues Facing Britain Today', 1 October 2012, in http://www.ipsos-mori.com/researchpublications/researcharchive/poll.aspx?oItemId=56&view=wide, accessed 29 January 2014.

Ipsos MORI (2012b) 'European Union Membership – Trends', 30 November 2012, in http://www.ipsos-mori.com/researchpublications/researcharchive/poll.aspx?oItemId=2435&view=wide, accessed 30 January 2014.

Ivanov, C. and M. Ilieva (2005) 'Bulgaria', in Mudde, C. (ed.) (2005) *Racist Extremism in Central and Eastern Europe*, London: Routledge, 1–29.

Ivarsflaten, E. (2008) 'What Unites the Populist Right in Western Europe? Reexamining Grievance Mobilization Models in Seven Successful Cases', *Comparative Political Studies*, 41(1), 3–23.

Jackman, R. and K. Volpert (1996) 'Conditions Favouring Parties of the Extreme Right in Western Europe', *British Journal of Political Science*, 26(4), 501–521.

Jagers, J. and S. Walgrave (2007) 'Populism as Political Communication Style: An Empirical Study of Political Parties' Discourse in Belgium', *European Journal of Political Research*, 46(3), 319–345.

Jasiewicz, K. (2003) 'Pocketbook or Rosary? Economic and Identity Voting in 2000–2001 Elections in Poland', *Studies in Public Policy*, no. 379, Glasgow: Centre for the Study of Public Policy.

Jasiewicz, K. (2008) 'The New Populism in Poland', *Problems of Post-Communism*, 55(3), 7–25.

John, P. and H. Margetts (2009) 'The Latent Support for the Extreme Right in British Politics', *West European Politics*, 32(3), 496–513.

Jupskås, A. (2013) 'The Progress Party: A Fairly Integrated Part of the Norwegian Party System?', in Grabow, K. and Hartleb, F. (eds.) *Exposing the Demagogues. Right-wing and National Populist Parties in Europe*, Brussels: CES-KAS, 205–236.

Karasimeonov, G. and M. Lyubenov (2013) 'Bulgaria', in Berglund, S., Ekman, J., Deegan-Krause, K. and Knutsen, T. (eds.) *The Handbook Of Political Change In Eastern Europe*, 3rd edition, Cheltenham: Edward Elgar, 407–442.

Katz, R. and P. Mair (1995) 'Changing Models of Party Organization and Party Democracy. The Emergence of the Cartel Party', *Party Politics*, 1(1), 5–28.

Kazin, M. (1998) *The Populist Persuasion: American History*, Ithaca: Cornell University Press, 2nd edition.

Kitschelt, H. (1988) 'Left-Libertarian Parties: Explaining Innovation in Competitive Party Systems', *World Politics*, 40(2), 194–234.

Kitschelt, H. and A. McGann (1995) *The Radical Right in Western Europe: A Comparative Analysis*, Ann Arbor: University of Michigan Press.

Klein, A. (2013) 'The End of Solidarity? On the Development of Right-wing Populist Parties in Denmark and Sweden', in Grabow, K. and Hartleb, F. (eds.) *Exposing the Demagogues. Right-wing and National Populist Parties in Europe*, Brussels: CES-KAS, 105–131.

Kleinnijenhuis, J., D. Oegema, J. de Ridder, A. van Hoof and R. Vliegenthart (2003) *De puinhopen in het nieuws: de rol van de media bij de Tweede Kamer verkiezingen van 2002*, Alphen aan den Rijn: Kluwer.

Knigge, P. (1998) 'The Ecological Correlates of Right-Wing Extremism in Western Europe', *European Journal of Political Research*, 34(2), 249–279.

Knudsen, A. (2005) 'The Danish General Election of February 2005', EPERN Election Briefing Paper, no. 19.

Koopmans, R. and J. Muis (2009) 'The Rise of Right-Wing Populist Pim Fortuyn in the Netherlands: A Discursive Opportunity Approach', *European Journal of Political Research*, 48(5), 642–664.

Krašovec, A. (2012) 'Slovenia', in Havlík, V. et al. (eds.) *Populist Political Parties in East-Central Europe*, Brno: Masarykova Univerzita, 259–284.

Kriesi, H. et al. (2006) 'Globalization and the Transformation of the National Political Space: Six European Countries Compared', *European Journal of Political Research*, 45(6), 921–956.

Kriesi, H. et al. (2008) *West European Politics in the Age of Globalization*, Cambridge: Cambridge University Press.

Krouwel, A. (2012) *Party Transformations in European Democracies*, Albany: SUNY Press.

Krouwel, A. and P. Lucardie (2008) 'Waiting in the Wings: New Parties in the Netherlands', *Acta Politica*, 43(2–3), 278–307.

Krupavicius, A. (2004) 'Lithuania', *European Journal of Political Research*, 43(7–8), 1059–1069.

Kucharczyk, J. and O. Wysocka (2008) 'Poland', in Mesežnikov, G., Gyárfášová, O. and Smilov, D. (eds.) *Populist Politics and Liberal Democracy in Central and Eastern Europe*, Bratislava: Institute for Public Affairs.

Laclau, E. (2005) 'Populism: What's in a Name?', in Panizza, F. (ed.) *Populism and the Mirror of Democracy*, London: Verso, 32–49.

Lagerspetz, M. and H. Vogt (2013) 'Estonia', in Berglund, S., Ekman, J., Deegan-Krause, K. and Knutsen, T. (eds.) *The Handbook of Political Change in Eastern Europe*, 3rd edition, Cheltenham: Edward Elgar, 51–84.

Lang, K. (2005) 'Populism in Central and Eastern Europe – A Threat to Democracy or Just Political Folklore?', *Slovak Foreign Policy Affairs*, I, 6–17.

Lewis, D. (1987) *Illusions of Grandeur. Mosley, Fascism and British Society, 1931–81*, Manchester: Manchester University Press.

Liberal Democrats (2010) *Change That Works for You. Building a Fairer Britain*, Liberal Democrats Party general election manifesto, 2010.

Lieberman, E. (2005) 'Nested Analysis as a Mixed-Method Strategy for Comparative Research', *American Political Science Review*, 99(3), 435–452.

Lijphart, A. (1975) *The Politics of Accommodation: Pluralism and Democracy in the Netherlands*, 2nd edition, Berkeley: University of California Press.

Little, C. (2011) 'The General Election of 2011 in the Republic of Ireland: All Changed Utterly?', *West European Politics*, 34(6), 1304–1313.

LN (2002) *Leefbaar Nederland komt er nu aan!*, Leefbaar Nederland parliamentary election manifesto 2002, in http://www.parlement.com/9291000/d/vtk2002_vp_ln.pdf, accessed 15 January 2014.

LPF (2002) *Lijst Pim Fortuyn. Zakelijk met een hart.* Lijst Pim Fortuyn parliamentary election manifesto 2002, in http://www.parlement.com/9291000/d/vtk2002_vp_lpf.pdf, accessed 15 January 2014.

Lubbers, M., M. Gijsberts and P. Scheepers (2002) 'Extreme Right-Wing Voting in Western Europe', *European Journal of Political Research*, 41(3), 345–378.

Lucardie, P. (1998) 'The Netherlands: The Extremist Center Parties', in Betz, H.-G. and Immerfall, S. (eds.) *The New Politics of the Right. Neo-Populist Parties and Movements in Established Democracies*, New York: St. Martin's Press, 111–124.

Lucardie, P. (2000) 'Prophets, Purifiers and Prolocutors. Towards a Theory on the Emergence of New Parties', *Party Politics*, 6(2), 175–185.

Lucardie, P. (2008) 'The Netherlands: Populism versus Pillarization', in Albertazzi, D. and McDonnell, D. (eds.) *Twenty-First Century Populism. The Spectre of Western European Democracy*, Basingstoke: Palgrave Macmillan, 151–165.

Lucardie, P. and G. Voerman (2012) *Populisten in de Polder*, Amsterdam: Boom.

Luther, K. (2011) 'Of Goals and Own Goals: A Case Study of Right-Wing Populist Party Strategy for and during Incumbency', *Party Politics*, 17(4), 453–470.

Lynch, P. (2007) 'Party System Change in Britain: Multi-Party Politics in a Multi-Level Polity', *British Politics*, 2(3), 323–346.

Lynch, P. and R. Whitaker (2013) 'Rivalry on the Right: The Conservatives, the UK Independence Party (UKIP) and the EU Issue', *British Politics*, 8(3), 285–312.

Mair, P. (2002) 'Populist Democracy vs. Party Democracy', in Mény, Y. and Surel, Y. (eds.) *Democracies and the Populist Challenge*, Basingstoke: Palgrave, 81–98.

Mair, P. (2006) 'Ruling the Void: The Hollowing of Western Democracy', *New Left Review*, 42, 25–51.

Mair, P. (2008) 'Electoral Volatility and the Dutch Party System: A Comparative Perspective', *Acta Politica*, 43(2–3), 235–253.

Mair, P. and C. Mudde (1998) 'The Party Family and its Study', *Annual Review of Political Science*, 1, 211–229.

Marantzidis, N. (2008) 'The Communist Party of Greece after the Collapse of Communism (1989–2006): From Proletarian Internationalism to Ethno-Populism', in Backes, U. and Moreau, P. (eds.) *Communist and Post-Communist Parties in Europe*, Göttingen: Vandenhoeck & Ruprecht, 245–258.

March, L. (2011) *Radical Left Parties in Europe*, Oxon: Routledge.

March, L. and C. Mudde (2005) 'What's Left of the Radical Left? The European Radical Left after 1989: Decline *and* Mutation', *Comparative European Politics*, 3(1), 23–49.

March, L. and C. Rommerskirchen (2012) 'Out of Left Field? Explaining the Variable Electoral Success of European Radical Left Parties', *Party Politics*, Published online, doi: 10.1177/1354068812462929.

Markowski, R. (2006) 'The Polish Elections of 2005: Pure Chaos or a Restructuring of the Party System?', *West European Politics*, 29(4), 814–832.

Markowski, R. (2008) 'The 2007 Polish Parliamentary Election: Some Structuring, Still a Lot of Chaos', *West European Politics*, 31(5), 1055–1068.

Marthaler, S. (2007) 'The French Legislative Elections of 10 and 17 June 2007', EPERN Election Briefing Paper, no. 34.

Mazzoleni, G. (2008) 'Populism and the Media', in Albertazzi, D. and McDonnell, D. (eds.) *Twenty-First Century Populism. The Spectre of Western European Democracy*, Basingstoke: Palgrave MacMillan, 49–64.

Mazzoleni, G., J. Steward and B. Horsfield (eds.) (2003) *The Media and Neo-Populism: A Contemporary Comparative Analysis*, Westport: Praeger.

Mazzoleni, O. (2013) 'Between Opposition and Government: The Swiss People's Party', in Grabow, K. and Hartleb, F. (eds.) *Exposing the Demagogues. Right-Wing and National Populist Parties in Europe*, Brussels: CES-KAS, 237–259.

McDonnell, D. (2006) 'A Weekend in Padania: Regionalist Populism and the Lega Nord', *Politics*, 26(2), 126–132.

McDonnell, D. (2008) 'The Republic of Ireland: The Dog That Hasn't Barked in the Night?', in Albertazzi, D. and McDonnell, D. (eds.) *Twenty-First Century Populism. The Spectre of Western European Democracy*, Basingstoke: Palgrave Macmillan, 198–216.

McDonnell, D. (2013) 'Silvio Berlusconi's Personal Parties: From Forza Italia to the Popolo Della Libertà', *Political Studies*, 61(S1), 217–233.

McManus-Czubinska, C. et al. (2004) *Polish National Election Study, 2001* [computer file], Colchester, Essex: UK Data Archive [distributor], November 2004. SN: 5036.

Meguid, B. (2008) *Party Competition between Unequals: Strategies and Electoral Fortunes in Western Europe*, Cambridge: Cambridge University Press.

Mény, Y. and Y. Surel (2002) 'The Constitutive Ambiguity of Populism', in: Mény, Y. and Surel, Y. (eds.) *Democracies and the Populist Challenge*, Basingstoke: Palgrave, 1–21.

Messina, A. (2007) *The Logics and Politics of Post-WWII Migration to Western Europe*, Cambridge: Cambridge University Press.

Millard, F. (1999) *Polish Politics and Society*, London: Routledge.

Millard, F. (2003) 'Elections in Poland 2001: Electoral Manipulation and Party Upheaval', *Communist and Post-Communist Studies*, 36(1), 69–86.

Millard, F. (2006) 'Poland's Politics and the Travails of Transition after 2001: The 2005 Elections', *Europe-Asia Studies*, 58(7), 1007–1031.

Millard, F. (2009) *Democratic Elections in Poland, 1991–2007*, Oxon: Routledge.

Minkenberg, M. (2002) 'The Radical Right in Post-Socialist Central and Eastern Europe: Comparative Observations and Interpretations', *East European Politics and Society* 16(2), 335–362.

Minkenberg, M. (2013) 'From Pariah to Policy-Maker? The Radical Right in Europe, West and East: Between Margin and Mainstream', *Journal of Contemporary European Studies*, 21(1), 5–24.

Moffitt, B. and S. Tormey (2013) 'Rethinking Populism: Politics, Mediatisation and Political Style', *Political Studies*, 62(2), 381–397. Mudde, C. (2002a) 'In the Name of the Peasantry, the Proletariat, and the People: Populisms in Eastern Europe', in: Mény, Y. and Surel, Y. (eds.) *Democracies and the Populist Challenge*, Basingstoke: Palgrave, 214–232.

Mudde, C. (2002b) 'The Pink Populist: Pim Fortuyn for Beginners', e-Extreme 2, in http://www.tufts.edu/~dart01/extremismanddemocracy/newsletter/News3_2. htm, accessed 19 July 2011.

Mudde, C. (2004) 'The Populist Zeitgeist'. *Government and Opposition*, 39(4), 542–563.

Mudde, C. (ed.) (2005) *Racist Extremism in Central and Eastern Europe*, London: Routledge.

Mudde, C. (2007) *Populist Radical Right Parties in Europe*, Cambridge: Cambridge University Press.

Mudde, C. (2010) 'The Populist Radical Right: A Pathological Normalcy', *West European Politics*, 33(6), 1167–1186.

Mudde, C. and C. Rovira Kaltwasser (eds.) (2012) *Populism in Europe and the Americas. Threat or Corrective for Democracy?*, Cambridge: Cambridge University Press.

Mudde, C. and C. Rovira Kaltwasser (2013) 'Exclusionary vs. Inclusionary Populism: Comparing Contemporary Europe and Latin America', *Government and Opposition*, 48(2), 147–174.

Mudde, C. and J. van Holsteyn (2000) 'The Netherlands: Explaining the Limited Success of the Extreme Right', in Hainsworth, P. (ed.) *The Politics of the Extreme Right. From the Margins to the Mainstream*, London: Pinter, 144–171.

Müller, W. (2002) 'Evil or the "Engine of Democracy"? Populism and Party Competition in Austria', in Mény, Y. and Surel, Y. (eds.) *Democracies and the Populist Challenge*, Basingstoke: Palgrave, 155–175.

Müller-Rommel, F. (1998) 'Explaining the Electoral Success of Green Parties: A Cross-National Analysis', *Environmental Politics*, 7(4), 145–154.

Nordsieck, W. (2013) *Parties and Elections in Europe*, in http://www.parties-and-elections.eu/index.html, accessed 16 December 2013.

Norris, P. (2005) *Radical Right. Voters and Parties in the Electoral Market*, Cambridge: Cambridge University Press.

Novinite (2009) 'EU Conservatives Stand Firm behind Bulgaria's Order, Law and Justice Party', 05 April 2009, in http://www.novinite.com/view_news.php?id=102523, accessed 16 December 2010.

OECD (2014) 'Harmonised unemployment rates', via http://www.oecd.org/statistics/, accessed 13 January 2014.

Oesch, D. (2008) 'Explaining Workers' Support for Right-Wing Populist Parties in Western Europe: Evidence from Austria, Belgium, France, Norway and Switzerland', *International Political Science Review*, 29(3), 349–373.

Oosterwaal, A. and R. Torenvlied (2010) 'Politics Divided from Society? Three Explanations for Trends in Societal and Political Polarisation in the Netherlands', *West European Politics*, 33(2), 258–279.

Panizza, F. (2005) 'Introduction: Populism and the Mirror of Democracy', in Panizza, F. (ed.) *Populism and the Mirror of Democracy*, London: Verso, 1–31.

Pankowski, R. (2010) *The Populist Radical Right in Poland*, Oxon: Routledge.

Pappas, T. (2014a) 'Populist Democracies: Post-Authoritarian Greece and Post-Communist Hungary', *Government and Opposition*, 49(1), 1–23.

Pappas, T. (2014b) *Populism and Crisis Politics in Greece*, Basingstoke: Palgrave Macmillan.

Pasquino, G. (2007) 'The Five Faces of Silvio Berlusconi: The Knight of Anti-Politics', *Modern Italy*, 12(1), 39–54.

Pasquino, G. (2008) 'Populism and Democracy', in Albertazzi, D. and McDonnell, D. (eds.) *Twenty-First Century Populism. The Spectre of Western European Democracy*, Basingstoke: Palgrave Macmillan, 15–29.

Pattie, C. and R. Johnston (2012), 'The Electoral Impact of the UK 2009 MPs' Expenses Scandal', *Political Studies*, 60(4), 730–750.

Pauwels, T. (2010) 'Explaining the Success of Neoliberal Populist Parties: The Case of Lijst Dedecker in Belgium', *Political Studies*, 58(5), 1009–1029.

Pauwels, T. (2011a) 'Measuring populism: A quantitative text analysis of Party Literature in Belgium', *Journal of Elections, Public Opinion and Parties*, 21(1), 97–119.

Pauwels, T. (2011b) 'Explaining the Strange Decline of the Populist Radical Right Vlaams Belang in Belgium: The Impact of Permanent Opposition', *Acta Politica*, 46(1), 60–82.

Pauwels, T. (2013) 'Belgium: Decline of National Populism?', in Grabow, K. and Hartleb, F. (eds.) *Exposing the Demagogues. Right-Wing and National Populist Parties in Europe*, Brussels: CES-KAS, 81–104.

Pauwels, T. (2014) *Populism in Western Europe. Comparing Belgium, Germany and The Netherlands*, Oxon: Routledge.

Payne, S. (1980) *Fascism. Comparison and Definition*, Wisconsin: University of Wisconsin Press.

Pellikaan, H., T. van der Meer and S. de Lange (2007) 'Fortuyn's Legacy: Party System Change in the Netherlands', *Comparative European Politics*, 5(3), 282–302.

Pennings, P. and H. Keman (2003) 'The Dutch Parliamentary Elections in 2002 and 2003: The Rise and Decline of the Fortuyn Movement', *Acta Politica*, 38(1), 51–68.

Petrocik, J. (1996) 'Issue Ownership in Presidential Elections, with a 1980 Case Study', *American Journal of Political Science*, 40(3), 825–850.

Pirro, A. (2014a) 'Populist Radical Right Parties in Central and Eastern Europe: The Different Context and Issues of the Prophets of the Patria', *Government and Opposition*, 49(4), 600–629.

Pirro, A. (2014b) 'Digging into the breeding ground: insights into the electoral performance of populist radical right parties in Central and Eastern Europe', *East European Politics*, 30(2), 246–270.

Piskorski, M. (2004) 'Self Defence of the Republic of Poland – Who We Are and What We Stand for', 18 November 2004, in http://www.samoobrona.org. pl/pages/20.english/index.php?document=presentation.html, accessed 25 February 2010.

Plaid Cymru (2010) *Think Different. Think Plaid*, Plaid Cymru Manifesto, General Election 2010.

Pop-Eleches, G. (2008) 'A Party for all Seasons: Electoral Adaptation of Romanian Communist Successor Parties', *Communist and Post-Communist Studies*, 41(4), 465–479.

Pop-Eleches, G. (2010) 'Throwing out the Bums: Protest Voting and Unorthodox Parties after Communism', *World Politics*, 62(2), 221–260.

Prins, B. (2002) 'The Nerve to Break Taboos: New Realism in the Dutch Discourse on Multiculturalism', *Journal of International Migration and Integration*, 3(3–4), 363–380.

PVV (2006) *Verkiezingspamflet*. Partij voor de Vrijheid parliamentary election manifesto, 2006.

PVV (2010) *Partij voor de Vrijheid: De agenda van hoop en optimisme. Een tijd om te kiezen*. Partij voor de Vrijheid parliamentary election manifesto, 2010.

PVV (2012) *Hún Brussel, óns Nederland*, Partij voor de Vrijheid parliamentary election manifesto, 2012.

Rae, D. (1971) *The Political Consequences of Electoral Laws*, revised edition, New Haven: Yale University Press.

Ragin, C. (1987) *The Comparative Method: Moving beyond Qualitative and Quantitative Strategies*, Berkeley and Los Angeles: University of California Press.

Ragin, C. (2000) *Fuzzy-Set Social Science*, Chicago: University of Chicago Press.

Ragin, C. (2006) 'Set Relations in Social Research: Evaluating Their Consistency and Coverage', *Political Analysis*, 14(3), 291–310.

Ragin, C. (2008) *Redesigning Social Inquiry. Fuzzy Sets and Beyond*, Chicago: University of Chicago Press.

Ragin, C. (2009) 'Qualitative Comparative Analysis using Fuzzy Sets (fsQCA)', in Rihoux, B. and Ragin, C. (eds.) *Configurational Comparative Methods. Qualitative Comparative Analysis (QCA) and Related Techniques*, Thousand Oaks: Sage.

Ragin, C. and S. Davey (2012) *fs/QCA Version 2.5* [Computer program], Irvine, CA: University of California.

Rajacic, A. (2007) 'Populist Construction of the Past and Future: Emotional Campaigning in Hungary between 2002 and 2006', *East European Politics & Societies*, 21(4), 639–660.

Ramonaitė, A. and V. Ratkevičiūtė (2013) 'The Lithuanian Case: National Populism without Xenophobia', in Grabow, K. and Hartleb, F. (eds.) *Exposing the Demagogues*. *Right-Wing and National Populist Parties in Europe*, Brussels: CES-KAS, 263–291.

Raniolo, F. (2006) 'Forza Italia: A Leader with a Party', *South European Society and Politics*, 11(3), 439–455.

Raunio, T. (2007) 'Europe and the Finnish Parliamentary Elections of March 2007', EPERN Election Briefing Paper, no. 32.

Raunio, T. (2013) 'The Finns: Filling a Gap in the Party System', in Grabow, K. and Hartleb, F. (eds.) *Exposing the Demagogues*. *Right-Wing and National Populist Parties in Europe*, Brussels: CES-KAS, 133–160.

Reif, K. and Schmitt, H. (1980) 'Nine Second Order National Elections: A Conceptual Framework for the Analysis of European Election Results', *European Journal of Political Research*, 8(1), 3–44.

Respect (2005) *Peace, Justice, Equality*, Respect Party general election manifesto, 2005.

Reykjavik Grapevine (2009) 'The Citizen Movement', 03 April 2009, in http://www.grapevine.is/Home/ReadArticle/Citizen-Movement-Borgarahreyfingin-Iceland-Elections-2009, accessed 22 September 2010.

Rhodes, J. (2009) 'The Banal National Party: The Routine Nature of Legitimacy', *Patterns of Prejudice*, 43(2), 142–160.

Rihoux, B. and C. Ragin (eds.) (2009) *Configurational Comparative Methods. Qualitative Comparative Analysis (QCA) and Related Techniques*, Thousand Oaks: Sage.

Roberts, K. (2006) 'Populism, Political Conflict, and Grass-Root Organisation in Latin America', *Comparative Politics*, 38(2), 127–148.

Rooduijn, M. (2014a) 'The Nucleus of Populism: In Search of the Lowest Common Denominator', *Government and Opposition*, 49(4), 573–599.

Rooduijn, M. (2014b) 'Van protest- naar pluchepartij? Een analyse van de ontwikkeling van de SP', Stuk Rood Vlees, 23 June 2014, in http://stukroodvlees.nl/populisme/van-protest-naar-pluchepartij-een-analyse-van-de-ontwikkeling-van-de-sp/, accessed 30 June 2014.

Rooduijn, M., S. de Lange and W. van der Brug (2014) 'A Populist Zeitgeist? Programmatic Contagion by Populist Parties in Western Europe', *Party Politics*, 20(4), 563–575.

Rose, R. (1995) 'Mobilizing Demobilized Voters in Post-Communist Societies', *Party Politics*, 1(4), 549–563.

Rovira Kaltwasser, C. (2014) 'The Responses of Populism to Dahl's Democratic Dilemmas', *Political Studies*, 62(3), 470–487.

Rupnik, J. (2007) 'Is East-Central Europe Backsliding? From Democracy Fatigue to Populist Backlash', *Journal of Democracy*, 18(4), 17–25.

Ruzza, C. and S. Fella (2009) *Re-inventing the Italian Right. Territorial Politics, Populism and 'Post-Fascism'*, Oxon: Routledge.

Rydgren, J. (2004) 'Explaining the Emergence of Radical Right-Wing Populist Parties: The Case of Denmark', *West European Politics*, 27(3), 474–502.

Rydgren, J. (2005) 'Is Extreme Right-Wing Populism Contagious? Explaining the Emergence of a New Party Family', *European Journal of Political Research*, 44(3), 413–437.

Rydgren, J. (2008a) 'France: The *Front National*, Ethnonationalism and Populism', in Albertazzi, D. and McDonnell, D. (eds.) *Twenty-First Century Populism. The Spectre of Western European Democracy*, Basingstoke: Palgrave Macmillan, 166–180.

Rydgren, J. (2008b) 'Sweden: The Scandinavian Exception', in Albertazzi, D. and McDonnell, D. (eds.) *Twenty-First Century Populism. The Spectre of Western European Democracy*, Basingstoke: Palgrave Macmillan, 135–150.

Sanders, D., H. Clarke, M. Steward and P. Whiteley (2011) 'Simulating the Effects of the Alternative Vote in the 2010 UK General Election', *Parliamentary Affairs*, 64(1), 5–23.

Sanford, G. (1999) *The Conquest of History*, Amsterdam: Harwood Academic Press.

Sartori, G. (1970) 'Concept Misformation in Comparative Politics', *American Political Science Review*, 64(4), 1033–1053.

Sartori, G. (1984) 'Guidelines for Concept Analysis', in Sartori, G. (ed.) *Social Science Concepts*, Beverly Hills: Sage, 15–85.

Sartori, G. (1991) 'Comparing and Miscomparing', *Journal of Theoretical Politics*, 3(3), 243–257.

Schedler, A. (1996) 'Anti-Political-Establishment Parties', *Party Politics*, 2(3), 291–312.

Schmitt, H. et al. (2009) *European Election Study 2004*, 2nd edition. GESIS Data Archive, Cologne. ZA4566 Data file Version 2.0.0, doi:10.4232/1.10086.

Schneider, C. and C. Wagemann (2006) 'Reducing Complexity in Qualitative Comparative Analysis (QCA): Remote and Proximate Factors and the Consolidation of Democracy', *European Journal of Political Research*, 45(5), 751–786.

Schneider, C. and C. Wagemann (2012) *Set-Theoretic Methods: A User's Guide for Qualitative Comparative Analysis and Fuzzy Sets in Social Science*, Cambridge: Cambridge University Press.

Schumacher, G. and M. Rooduijn (2013) 'Sympathy for the "devil"? Voting for populists in the 2006 and 2010 Dutch general elections', *Electoral Studies*, 32(1), 124–133.

Shils, E. (1956) *The Torment of Secrecy: The Background and Consequences of American Security Policies*, London: Heinemann.

Sikk, A. (2009) 'Parties and Populism', Centre for European Politics, Security and Integration, University College London, Working paper 2009–02.

Sikk, A. (2012) 'Newness as a Winning Formula for New Political Parties', *Party Politics*, 18(4), 465–486.

Skinner, M. (2013) 'Different Varieties of Euroscepticism? Conceptualizing and Explaining Euroscepticism in Western European Non-Member States', *Journal of Common Market Studies*, 51(1), 122–139.

SKON, CBS, H. van der Kolk, C. Aarts and J. Tillie (2012) *Dutch Parliamentary Election Study 2010*, The Hague: DANS.

SKON, CBS, H. van der Kolk, J. Tillie, P. Van Erkel, M. van der Velden and A. Damstra (2013) *Dutch Parliamentary Election Study 2012*, The Hague: DANS.

Smith, J. (2010) 'Does Crime Pay? Issue Ownership, Political Opportunity, and the Populist Right in Western Europe', *Comparative Political Studies*, 43(11), 1471–1498.

Smrčková, M. (2012) 'Romania', in Havlík, V. et al. (eds.) *Populist Political Parties in East-Central Europe*, Brno: Masarykova Univerzita, 199–226.

SNP (2010) *Elect a Local Champion*, Scottish National Party general election manifesto, 2010.

SP (2010) *Een beter Nederland, voor minder geld. Verkiezingsprogramma SP 2011–2015*, Socialistische Partij parliamentary election manifesto, 2010.

Spáč, P. (2012) 'Slovakia', in Havlík, V. et al. (eds.) *Populist Political Parties in East-Central Europe*, Brno: Masarykova Univerzita, 227–258.

Spies, D. (2013) 'Explaining Working-Class Support for Extreme Right Parties: A Party Competition Approach', *Acta Politica*, 48(3), 296–325.

Spies, D. and S. Franzmann (2011) 'A Two-Dimensional Approach on the Political Opportunity Structure of Extreme Right Parties in Western Europe', *West European Politics*, 34(5), 1044–1069.

SSP (2005) *Make Capitalism History*, Scottish Socialist Party general election manifesto, 2005.

Stanley, B. (2008) 'The Thin Ideology of Populism', *Journal of Political Ideologies*, 13(1), 95–110.

Stanley, B. (2010) *Populism in the Polish Party System: Party Appeals and Voter Mobilization*, Doctoral Dissertation, Colchester: University of Essex.

Stanley, B. (2013) 'Poland', in Berglund, S., Ekman, J., Deegan-Krause, K. and Knutsen, T. (eds.) *The Handbook of Political Change in Eastern Europe*, 3rd edition, Cheltenham: Edward Elgar, 167–215.

Stavrakakis, Y. and G. Katsambekis (2014) 'Left-Wing Populism in the European Periphery: The Case of SYRIZA', *Journal of Political Ideologies*, 19(2), 119–142.

Steward, A. (1969) 'The Social Roots', in Ionescu, G. and Gellner, E. (eds.) *Populism, its Meanings and National Characteristics*, London: Weidenfeld and Nicolson, 180–196.

Sum, P. (2010) 'The Radical Right in Romania: Political Party Evolution and the Distancing of Romania from Europe', *Communist and Post-Communist Studies*, 43(1), 19–29.

Swank, D. and H.-G. Betz (2003) 'Globalization, the Welfare State and Right-Wing Populism in Western Europe', *Socio-Economic Review*, 1(2), 215–245.

Swyngedouw, M. (1998) 'The Extreme Right in Belgium: Of a Non-existent Front National and an Omnipresent Vlaams Blok', in Betz, H.-G. and Immerfall, S. (eds.) *The New Politics of the Right. Neo-Populist Parties and Movements in Established Democracies*, New York: St. Martin's Press, 59–75.

Szczerbiak, A. (2002a) 'Poland's Unexpected Political Earthquake: The September 2001 Parliamentary Election', *Journal of Communist Studies and Transition Politics*, 18(3), 41–76.

Szczerbiak, A. (2002b) 'Dealing with the Communist Past or the Politics of the Present? Lustration in Post-Communist Poland', *Europe-Asia Studies*, 54(4), 553–572.

Szczerbiak, A. (2004) 'The Polish Centre-Right's (Last?) Best Hope: The Rise and Fall of Solidarity Electoral Action', *Journal of Communist Studies and Transition Politics*, 20(3), 55–79.

Szczerbiak, A. (2007) ' "Social Poland" Defeats "Liberal Poland"? The September–October 2005 Polish Parliamentary and Presidential Elections', *Journal of Communist Studies and Transition Politics*, 23(2), 203–232.

Szczerbiak, A. (2008) 'The Birth of a Bipolar Party System or a Referendum on a Polarizing Government? The October 2007 Polish Parliamentary Election', *Journal of Communist Studies and Transition Politics*, 24(3), 415–443.

Szczerbiak, A. (2013) 'Poland (Mainly) Chooses Stability and Continuity: The October 2011 Polish Parliamentary Election', *Perspectives on European Politics and Society*, 14(4), 480–504.

Szczerbiak, A. and M. Bil (2009) 'When in Doubt, (Re-)Turn to Domestic Politics? The (Non-)Impact of the EU on Party Politics in Poland', *Journal of Communist Studies and Transition Politics*, 25(4), 447–467.

Taagepera, R. (2006) 'Meteoric Trajectory: The Res Publica Party in Estonia', *Democratization*, 13(1), 78–94.

Taggart, P. (1996) *The New Populism and the New Politics. New Protest Parties in Sweden in a Comparative Perspective*, London: Macmillan.

Taggart, P. (2000) *Populism*, Buckingham and Philadelphia: Open University Press.

Taggart, P. (2002) 'Populism and the Pathology of Representative Politics', in Mény, Y. and Surel, Y. (eds.) *Democracies and the Populist Challenge*, Basingstoke: Palgrave, 62–80.

Taggart, P. (2004) 'Populism and Representative Politics in Contemporary Europe', *Journal of Political Ideologies*, 9(3), 269–288.

Tarchi, M. (2008) 'Italy: A Country of Many Populisms', in Albertazzi, D. and McDonnell, D. (eds.) *Twenty-First Century Populism. The Spectre of Western European Democracy*, Basingstoke: Palgrave Macmillan, 84–99.

Tavits, M. (2006) 'Party System Change: Testing a Model of New Party Entry', *Party Politics*, 12(1), 99–119.

Team Stronach (2013) *Grundsatzprogramm. Juli 2013*, Team Stronach Party Consitution, in http://www.teamstronach.at/de/programm/fuer-ein-starkes-europa?file=files/team-stronach/content/downloads/grundsatzprogramm/Grundsatzprogramm.pdf, accessed 6 December 2013.

Tetteh, E. (2009) 'Electoral Performance of the British National Party in the UK', House of Commons Standard Note, SN/SG/5064, 15 May 2009.

Thomassen, J. (2000) 'Politieke veranderingen en het functioneren van de parlementaire democratie in Nederland', in Thomassen, J., Aarts, K. and van der Kolk, H. (eds.) *Politieke veranderingen in Nederland 1971–1998. Kiezers en de smalle marges van de politiek*, The Hague: SDU, 203–218.

TI (2014) 'Corruption Perception Index', via http://www.transparency.org/, accessed 13 January 2014.

Tóka, G. and S. Popa (2013) 'Hungary', in Berglund, S., Ekman, J., Deegan-Krause, K. and Knutsen, T. (eds.) *The Handbook of Political Change in Eastern Europe*, 3rd edition, Cheltenham: Edward Elgar, 291–338.

Tworzecki, H. (2012) 'The Polish Parliamentary Elections of October 2011', *Electoral Studies*, 31(3), 617–621. Učeň, P. (2007) 'Parties, Populism, and Anti-Establishment Politics in East Central Europe', *SAIS Review*, 27(1), 49–62.

Učeň, P., O. Gyárfášová and V. Krivý (2005) 'Centrist Populism in Slovakia from the Perspective of Voters and Supporter', *Slovak Foreign Policy Affairs*, I, 28–46.

UKIP (1994) *U.K. Independence Party Interim Manifesto*, UK Independence Party manifesto, November 1994.

UKIP (2005) *We Want our Country Back*, UK Independence Party general election manifesto, 2005.

UKIP (2010) *Empowering the People*, UK Independence Party general election manifesto, 2010.

Usherwood, S. (2008) 'The Dilemmas of a Single-Issue Party – The UK Independence Party', *Representation*, 44(3), 255–264.

Van Assche, M. (2003) 'The Belgian Federal Elections of 18 May 2003', EPERN Election Briefing Paper, no. 13.

Van Biezen, I., P. Mair and T. Poguntke (2012) 'Going, Going, ... Gone? The decline of party membership in contemporary Europe', *European Journal of Political Research*, 51(1), 24–56.

Van Biezen, I. and H. Wallace (2013) 'Old and New Oppositions in Contemporary Europe', *Government and Opposition*, 48(3), 289–313.

Van der Brug, W. (2003) 'How the LPF Fuelled Discontent: Empirical Tests of Explanations of LPF Support', *Acta Politica*, 38(1), 89–106.

Van der Brug, W., C. de Vries and J. van Spanje (2011) 'Nieuwe strijdpunten, nieuwe scheidslijnen? Politieke vertegenwoordiging in Nederland', in Andeweg, R. and Thomassen, J. (eds.) *Democratie Doorgelicht, het functioneren van de Nederlandse democratie*, Leiden: Leiden University Press, 283–300.

Van der Brug, W., M. Fennema and J. Tillie (2000) 'Anti-Immigrant Parties in Europe: Ideological or Protest Vote?' *European Journal of Political Research*, 37(1), 77–102.

Van der Brug, W., M. Fennema and J. Tillie (2005) 'Why Some Anti-Immigrant Parties Fail and Others Succeed: A Two-Step Model of Aggregate Electoral Support', *Comparative Political Studies*, 38, 537–573.

Van der Brug, W. and A. Mughan (2007) 'Charisma, Leader Effects and Support for Right-Wing Populist Parties', *Party Politics*, 13(1), 29–51.

Van der Brug, W. and J. van Spanje (2009) 'Immigration, Europe and the 'New' Cultural Dimension', *European Journal of Political Research*, 48(3), 309–334.

Van der Meer, T., R. Lubbe, E. van Elsas, M. Elff and W. van der Brug (2012) 'Bounded Volatility in the Dutch Electoral Battlefield: A Panel Study on the Structure of Changing Vote Intentions in the Netherlands during 2006–2010', *Acta Politica*, 47(4), 333–355.

Van der Pas, D., C. De Vries and W. van der Brug (2013) 'A Leader without a Party: Exploring the Relationship between Geert Wilders' Leadership Performance in the Media and his Electoral Success', *Party Politics*, 19(3), 458–476.

Van der Steen, P. (1995) 'De doorbraak van de "gewone mensen"-partij. De SP en de Tweede-Kamerverkiezingen van 1994', in Voerman, G. (ed.) *Jaarboek DNPP 1994*, Groningen: DNPP, 172–189.

Van Egmond, M. et al. (2013) *European Parliament Election Study 2009*, Voter Study. GESIS Data Archive, Cologne. ZA5055 Data file Version 1.1.0, doi:10.4232/1.11760.

Van Heerden S., S. de Lange, W. Van der Brug and M. Fennema (2013) 'The Immigration and Integration Debate in the Netherlands: Discursive and Programmatic Reactions to the Rise of Anti-Immigration Parties', *Journal of Ethnic and Migration Studies*, 40(1), 119–136.

Van Holsteyn, J. and G. Irwin (2003) 'Never a Dull Moment: Pim Fortuyn and the Dutch Parliamentary Election of 2002', *West European Politics*, 26(2), 41–66.

Van Holsteyn, J., G. Irwin and J. den Ridder (2003) 'In the Eye of the Beholder: The Perception of the List Pim Fortuyn and the Parliamentary Elections of 2002', *Acta Politica*, 38(1), 69–87.

Van Kersbergen, K. and A. Krouwel (2008) 'A Double-Edged Sword! The Dutch Centre-Right and the "Foreigners Issue" ', *Journal of European Public Policy*, 15(3), 398–414.

Van Kessel, S. (2010) 'The Dutch General Election of June 2010', EPERN Election Briefing Paper, no. 54.

Van Kessel, S. (2011) 'Explaining the Electoral Performance of Populist Parties: the Netherlands as a Case Study', *Perspectives on European Politics and Society*, 12(1), 68–88.

Van Kessel, S. (2013) 'A Matter of Supply and Demand: The Electoral Performance of Populist Parties in Three European Countries', *Government and Opposition*, 48(2), 175–199.

Van Kessel, S. (2014) 'The Populist Cat-Dog. Applying the Concept of Populism to Contemporary European Party Systems', *Journal of Political Ideologies*, 19(1), 99–118.

Van Kessel, S. and S. Hollander (2012) 'Europe and the Dutch Parliamentary Election, September 2012', EPERN Election Briefing Paper, no. 71.

Van Kessel, S. and A. Krouwel (2011) 'Van vergankelijke radicale dissidenten tot kwelgeesten van de gevestigde orde. Nieuwe politieke partijen in Nederland en en de toekomst van de representative democratie', in Andeweg, R. and Thomassen, J. (eds.) *Democratie Doorgelicht, het functioneren van de Nederlandse democratie*, Leiden: Leiden University Press, 301–317.

Van Spanje, J. (2011) 'The Wrong and the Right: A Comparative Analysis of "Anti-Immigration" and "Far Right" Parties', *Government and Opposition*, 46(3), 293–320.

Verney, S. (2004) 'The End of Socialist Hegemony: Europe and the Greek Parliamentary Election of 7th March 2004', Sussex European Institute, working paper no. 80/European Parties Elections and Referendums Network, working paper no.15.

Veugelers, J. and A. Magnan (2005) 'Conditions of Far-Right Strength in Contemporary Western Europe', *European Journal of Political Research*, 44(6), 749–918.

Voerman, G. and P. Lucardie (2007) 'De Sociaal-Democratisering van de SP', in Becker, F. and Cuperus, R. (eds.) *Verloren Slag. De PvdA en de verkiezingen van november 2006*, Amsterdam: Mets and Schilt/Wiardi Beckman Stichting, 139–164.

Vossen, K. (2010) 'Populism in the Netherlands after Fortuyn: Rita Verdonk and Geert Wilders Compared', *Perspectives on European Politics and Society*, 11(1), 22–38.

Vossen, K. (2011) 'Classifying Wilders: The Ideological Development of Geert Wilders and His Party for Freedom', *Politics*, 31(3), 179–189.

Ware, A. (2002) 'The United States: Populism as Politics Strategy', in Mény, Y. and Surel, Y. (eds.) *Democracies and the Populist Challenge*, Basingstoke: Palgrave, 101–119.

Webb, P. (2000) *The Modern British Party System*, London: Sage.

Webb, P. (2005) 'The Continuing Advance of the Minor Parties', *Parliamentary Affairs*, 58(4), 575–775.

Webb, P. (2008) 'The Attitudinal Assimilation of Europe by the Conservative Parliamentary Party', *British Politics*, 3(4), 427–444.

Werts, H., P. Scheepers and M. Lubbers (2012) 'Euro-Scepticism and Radical Right-Wing Voting in Europe, 2002–2008: Social Cleavages, Socio-Political Attitudes and Contextual Characteristics Determining Voting for the Radical Right', *European Union Politics*, 14(2), 183–205.

Weyland, K. (2001) 'Clarifying a Contested Concept – Populism in the Study of Latin American Politics', *Comparative Politics*, 34(1), 1–22.

Whitaker, R. and P. Lynch (2011) 'Explaining Support for the UK Independence Party at the 2009 European Parliament Elections', *Journal of Elections, Public Opinion and Parties*, 21(3), 359–379.

Widfeldt, A. (2000) 'Scandinavia: Mixed Success for the Populist Right', *Parliamentary Affairs*, 53(3), 486–500.

Widfeldt, A. (2008) 'Party Change as a Necessity – the Case of the Sweden Democrats', *Representation*, 44(3), 265–276.

Wilders, G. (2005) *Groep Wilders. Onafhankelijkheidsverklaring*, Party Document, Groep Wilders, The Hague.

Wiles, P. (1969) 'A Syndrome, not a Doctrine', in Ionescu, G. and Gellner, E. (eds.) *Populism, its Meanings and National Characteristics*, London: Weidenfeld and Nicolson, 166–179.

Willey, J. (1998) 'Institutional Arrangements and the Success of New Parties in Old Democracies', *Political Studies*, 46(3), 651–668.

Worsley, P. (1969) 'The Concept of Populism', in Ionescu, G. and Gellner, E. (eds.) *Populism, its Meanings and National Characteristics*, London: Weidenfeld and Nicolson, 212–250.

Wysocka, O. (2010) *Populism. The Polish Case*, Doctoral Dissertation, June 2010, Florence: European University Institute.

YouGov (2005) 'Current Political Issues', YouGov/Daily Telegraph Survey, 29 March 2005, in http://today.yougov.co.uk/sites/today.yougov.co.uk/files/YG-Archives-pol-dTel-CurrentPolIssues-050329.pdf, accessed 27 July 2010.

YouGov (2009a) 'Megapoll Euro Elections', YouGov/Channel 4 News Survey Results, 4 June 2009, in http://www.yougov.co.uk/extranets/ygarchives/content/pdf/Megapoll_EuroElections.pdf, accessed 8 May 2011.

YouGov (2009b) 'Voting intention, BNP and Question Time', YouGov/Daily Telegraph Survey, 26 October 2009, in http://today.yougov.co.uk/sites/today.yougov.co.uk/files/YG-Archives-pol-dTel-vi-091026.pdf, accessed 9 May 2011.

YouGov (2010a) 'Immigration', YouGov/The Sun Survey, 22 March 2010, in http://today.yougov.co.uk/sites/today.yougov.co.uk/files/YG-Archives-Pol-SunImmigration-100322.pdf, accessed 26 July 2010.

YouGov (2010b) 'Islam', YouGov/Apex Communications Survey, 07 June 2010, in http://today.yougov.co.uk/sites/today.yougov.co.uk/files/YG-Archives-Pol-ApexCommunicationsExploringIslamFoundation2-100520.pdf, accessed 26 July 2010.

YouGov (2010c) 'Voting intention, issues, leader characteristics', YouGov/The Sun Survey, 03 May 2010, in http://today.yougov.co.uk/sites/today.yougov.co.uk/files/YG-Archives-Pol-Suntrackers-100503.pdf, accessed 27 July 2010.

YouGov (2010d) 'Issues facing Britain + behaviour of Brown', YouGov/The Sun Survey, 23 February 2010, in http://today.yougov.co.uk/sites/today.yougov.co.uk/files/YG-Archives-Pol-Suntopical-100223.pdf, accessed 28 July 2010.

Zajc, D. (2013) 'Slovenia', in Berglund, S., Ekman, J., Deegan-Krause, K. and Knutsen, T. (eds.) *The Handbook of Political Change in Eastern Europe*, 3rd edition, Cheltenham: Edward Elgar, 339–368.

Zaslove, A. (2008) 'Here to Stay: Populism as a New Party Type?', *European Review*, 16(3), 319–336.

Zaslove, A. (2009) 'The Populist Radical Right: Ideology, Party Families, and Core Principles', *Political Studies Review*, 7(3), 309–318.

Zaslove, A. (2012) 'The Populist Radical Right in Government: The Structure and Agency of Success and Failure', *Comparative European Politics*, 10(4), 421–448.

Index

Aarts, Kees, 109, 110
Abedi, Amir, 18, 198
abortion, 105, 126, 130
Abts, Koen, 9
agency of political actors, 3, 4, 20–1,
    73, 93, 118, 141, 167, 174–5,
    181–2
    see also credibility of populist
    parties; responsiveness of
    established parties
agriculture, 125
Åkesson, Jimmie, 68
Albertazzi, Daniele, 6
All For Latvia (VL), 56–7, 72
Alliance for the Future of Austria
    (BZÖ), 35, 71
Alliance of the New Citizen (ANO,
    Slovakia), 65
Alternative Democratic Reform Party
    (ADR, Luxembourg), 59, 72
Alternative for Germany (AfD), 47
Andeweg, Rudy, 108
ANO 2011 (Czech Republic), 41, 71
anti-capitalism, 25, 40, 47, 48, 125–6,
    175
anti-establishment
    discourse/rhetoric, 11, 22, 26, 28,
        70–1, 118, 140–2, 170–1, 177–9,
        181, 183
    sentiments, 4, 23, 70, 141–2, 167,
        170–1, 183
    see also individual political parties
Anti-Federalist League (AFL, UK), 150
anti-political establishment (APE)
    parties, 19, 25, 198
anti-Semitism, 38, 40, 63, 65, 105,
    162, 198
    see also culture and ethnicity
Arditi, Benjamin, 10, 11
Arter, David, 44
Arzheimer, Kai, 25
Association of Workers of Slovakia
    (ZRS), 64

asylum seekers, 156–8
    see also immigration
Attack Party (Bulgaria), 38, 40, 71
austerity, 48–50, 54, 106, 132–3
Austria, 29, 34–6, 70–1, 77, 84, 170
Austrian Freedom Party (FPÖ), 29,
    34–6, 70, 71, 77, 170
AWS, *see* Solidarity Electoral Action
    (AWS, Poland)

Babiš, Andrej, 41–2
Baker, David, 159
Balcerowicz, Leszek, 123, 132
Bale, Tim, 21
Balent, Magali, 46
bank(er)s, 13, 40, 48, 51, 54, 58
Barr, Robert, 12
Barroso, José Manuel, 1, 198
Băsescu, Traian, 63
Becali, George, 64
Bélanger, Éric, 110
Belgium, 16, 36–8, 69, 71, 84, 170,
    174, 199
Berlusconi, Silvio, 53–5, 199
Betz, Hans-Georg, 7, 9, 18
Blair, Tony, 146–7
Blocher, Christoph, 68–9
Bloom, Godfrey, 150–1, 202
BNP, *see* British National Party (BNP)
Bolkestein, Frits, 109
Bomhoff, Eduard, 114
Bontes, Louis, 201
Booth, Graham, 160, 164
Borissov, Boyko, 39
Bossi, Umberto, 55–6
Bovens, Mark, 108
Brinkman, Hero, 117
British National Party (BNP), 144, 147,
    172, 176–8
    credibility, 161–3, 166–7
    electorate, 153, 161
    profile and electoral results, 148–50
Brown, Gordon, 157

Bulgaria, 38–40, 51, 64, 71, 77, 79, 84, 86, 92, 97, 170, 174
Buzek, Jerzy, 123, 133, 134

Cameron, David, 146, 157, 160, 165
Canovan, Margaret, 6, 9, 26
Carter, Elisabeth, 18, 21, 25, 37, 45, 198
Catholicism, 62, 126, 134, 138, 140, 171
see also religion
CBOS (Public Opinion Research Centre, Poland), 133–5
CDA, *see* Christian Democratic Appeal (CDA, Netherlands)
Central and Eastern Europe
communism, legacy of, 3, 16–17, 25
corruption, 16, 26–7, 70, 170, 183
populism in, 4, 17, 33, 70–1, 98, 170, 179–80, 183
transition losers, 16, 121, 133, 136, 140
trust and satisfaction, political, 4, 16–17, 26–7, 70, 170–1, 183
volatility and party system instability, 16–17, 70, 182
see also individual countries
Centre Agreement (PC, Poland), 202
Centre Democrats (CD, Netherlands), 100, 113
Centre Party (CP, Netherlands), 100, 113
charisma, *see* leadership
Christian Democratic Appeal (CDA, Netherlands), 101, 103–4, 106, 109
Christianity, 38
see also Catholicism; religion
Citizens for European Development of Bulgaria (GERB), 39–40, 71, 77
Citizens' Movement (BF, Iceland), 51–2, 72
Civic List (DL, Slovenia), 67
Civic Platform (PO, Poland), 123–4, 127–30, 135–6, 140, 142, 202
cleavages, 8, 18, 107, 202
clientelism, 42, 53, 48, 63, 66, 134
see also corruption
Coalition of the Radical Left (SYRIZA, Greece), 48–9, 72

communism, 3, 15–16
see also Central and Eastern Europe
Communist Party of Slovakia (KSS), 64–5
concept formation, 13–14
conservatism, 2
Netherlands, 100, 103, 105
in party ideologies, 43, 49–50, 52–3, 55–9, 62, 65, 68
Poland, 121–2, 126–7, 129, 134, 138–9, 140–2, 171
United Kingdom, 148, 157–8, 165
see also culture and ethnicity
Conservative Party (UK), 144–8, 150, 152–4, 156–61, 164–7, 172, 176
convergence, ideological, 20, 109
Copsey, Nigel, 149
corruption, 6, 12–13, 16, 23, 26–7, 30, 70, 92–3, 97–8, 170–2, 174–5, 183
Netherlands, 102, 106, 119
in party programmes, 35–6, 38–43, 48–9, 53–9, 61–4, 66–7
Poland, 62, 121, 123, 127–8, 134–6, 139, 141–2
QCA operationalisation, 82–4
United Kingdom, 150, 167
see also Central and Eastern Europe
credibility of populist parties, 3, 21–3, 32, 33–4, 176–9, 181–2
Netherlands, 112–17
Poland, 136–40
QCA operationalisation, 22–3, 80
QCA results, 85–6, 88–90, 96–7
United Kingdom, 161–6
see also individual parties
crime, *see* law and order
crisis, 6, 16, 136
economic/Eurozone, 1, 26, 31, 44, 48–50, 51, 54–5, 63, 81–2, 92–3, 96–7, 101, 106, 119–20, 173, 181, 203
Croatia, 40–1, 71, 79, 82, 84
Croatian Labourists – Labour Party (HL-SR), 40–1, 71
Croatian Party of Rights – dr. Ante Starčević (HSP-AS), 40–1, 71
cronyism, 26, 35, 127, 141, 175
see also corruption
Csurka, István, 50

culture and ethnicity, 24, 73, 97, 112, 175
  minorities, 9, 12, 24, 49, 56, 65, 100, 103, 109, 172, 179
  multiculturalism, 2, 24, 92, 103, 109–10, 112, 141, 146, 151, 157, 172, 179
  norms and values, 105, 179
  protection of culture, 2, 24, 57, 103, 112, 118
  QCA operationalisation, 80–1
  racism, 22, 36, 63, 148–9, 151, 161–2
  xenophobia, 1–2, 9, 12, 35–7, 42, 50–1, 64, 68, 116–17, 144, 148, 161, 172, 182, 198
  see also immigration; *individual parties*, Islam; Roma
Cyprus, 34, 84
Czech Republic, 41–2, 71, 84

Danish People's Party (DF), 42–3, 60, 70, 71, 78
Dawn of Direct Democracy (Úsvit, Czech Republic), 41–2, 71
De Jong, Winny, 115
De Lange, Sarah, 101
De Wit, Jan, 201
dealignment, partisan, 17–18
  see also party systems; voting behaviour
Dedecker, Jean-Marie, 37–8, 71
Deegan-Krause, Kevin, 65
democracy
  consensus, 108
  direct, 12–13, 41–2, 47, 58
  liberal, 9–10, 169, 182
  majoritarian, 147, 167
  populism and, 9–10, 182
Democratic Left Alliance (SLD, Poland), 122–4, 126, 130–5
Democratic Political Turning Point (DPK, Netherlands), 117
Denmark, 42–3, 60, 61, 70, 71, 78, 83, 84, 90, 97, 170, 174
deregulation, 106, 175
Dewinter, Filip, 37
Diaconescu, Dan, 63–4, 72
Dijkstal, Hans, 109

Direction (Smer, Slovakia), 65, 72, 77
discrimination, 103
  see also culture and ethnicity
dissatisfaction, *see* trust and satisfaction, political
drugs, 103, 130
Duncan Smith, Ian, 160
Durham, Martin, 157
Duverger, Maurice, 155

Eastern Europe, *see* Central and Eastern Europe
Eatwell, Roger, 163
economy
  hardship, 23, 25–6, 81, 92–3, 96–7, 119, 141, 175
  populist party performance and, 25–6
  unemployment, 25–6, 67, 81, 92, 98, 109–10, 125, 129, 133, 135–6, 139, 159
  see also crisis
Eerdmans, Joost, 115
elderly and pensions, 59, 105, 111, 149, 159
electoral system, effect of, 19–20, 29, 89, 97, 155, 174, 178
  Netherlands, 107–8
  Poland, 122, 130–1
  QCA operationalisation, 78–9
  UK (SMP system), 31, 144, 153–6, 166–7, 178
elites, *see* anti-establishment; responsiveness of established parties
England, *see* United Kingdom (UK)
Estonia, 43–4, 56, 84, 93
Europe of Freedom and Democracy (EFD), 164
European Conservatives and Reformists (ECR), 160
European integration, 26–7, 73, 97, 175, 179, 181
  Netherlands, 106, 111–12, 118–19
  Poland, 126, 133, 138, 141, 202
  QCA operationalisation, 82
  United Kingdom, 144, 150–1, 158–61, 164–6
  see also Euroscepticism

European Parliament elections, 106,
117, 140, 144, 150, 152, 155,
160–1, 163, 165–6, 175
European People's Party (EPP), 64, 160
European Union, *see* crisis; European
integration; European Parliament
elections; European Union
membership; Euroscepticism
European Union membership, 82,
104, 112, 126, 133, 141, 150, 158,
160
see also European integration;
Euroscepticism
Euroscepticism, 26, 30, 82, 92, 96–7,
173, 176
Netherlands, 106, 112
in party programmes, 35, 41–2,
44–5, 47–8, 50, 52, 59, 65–8
Poland, 126, 133, 138, 141, 202
United Kingdom, 150–2, 158–61,
165–6
see also European integration
extreme right/extremism, 1–2, 5, 15,
21–2, 28, 113, 115, 145, 148, 152,
162, 169, 172, 177, 182, 198
explanations for performance,
17–28
see also individual political parties

Farage, Nigel, 153, 165, 167, 176
farmers, 100, 125, 133
Farmers Party (Boerenpartij,
Netherlands), 100
fascism, 15, 55, 67, 145, 148–9, 162,
176
federalism and devolution, 19, 53,
146, 154, 159
see also minority nationalism/
regionalism
Fella, Stefano, 164
Fianna Fáil (Ireland), 53
Fico, Robert, 65
FIDESZ-Hungarian Civic Alliance,
50–1, 70, 72, 77, 89
Finland, 44, 71, 83, 84, 89
Five Star Movement (M5S, Italy),
54–5, 72, 96
Flemish Interest (VB, Belgium), 16,
36–8, 71, 170

For Fatherland and Freedom/LNNK
(TB/LNNK, Latvia), 57
Ford, Robert, 161
Fortuyn, Pim, 59–60, 100–5, 108–10,
112–15, 118–19, 176, 201
see also List Pim Fortuyn (LPF)
Forza Italia, 54–5, 72, 77, 89, 199
FPÖ, 29, 34–6, 70, 71, 77, 170
France, 37, 45–6, 71, 78–9, 84, 89, 97,
131, 148, 170, 178, 199
Freeden, Michael, 7
Freedom Party (PVV, Netherlands), 60,
72, 172, 176–7, 179, 201
credibility, 60, 115–20
electorate, 110–12
profile and electoral results, 104–7
Freedom Union (UW, Poland), 123–4
free-market economy, 16, 103, 105–6,
125–6, 132, 141, 146, 152, 175
see also anti-capitalism; liberalism
Front National (France), 45–6, 71, 89,
148, 170, 178
fsQCA, *see* Qualitative Comparative
Analysis (QCA)

Gellner, Ernest, 5–6
Geneva Citizens' Movement (MCG,
Switzerland), 68, 72
German People's Union (DVU), 46
Germany, 46–7, 48–9, 71, 79, 84, 89,
170, 198
Ghodsee, Kristen, 39
Giertych, Maciej, 126, 128
Giertych, Roman, 128, 138–9
Gifford, Chris, 158
globalisation, 18, 26, 45, 67, 152, 181
winners and losers, 18, 26
Go Italy (FI, Italy), 54–5, 72, 77, 89,
199
Golden Dawn (Greece), 49
Goldsmith, James, 152
Goodwin, Matthew, 158, 161
Greater Romania Party (PRM), 63–4,
72
Greece, 44, 48–50, 72, 76, 79, 82, 84,
89, 92, 96, 97, 106, 117, 173
Greek Communist Party (KKE), 48–9
green parties, 18, 27, 104, 147, 155,
198

Green Party (UK), 147, 155
Griffin, Nick, 148–50, 162–3
Grillo, Beppe, 54–5, 96
Gysi, Gregor, 47

Hagen, Carl I., 61
Hague, William, 160
Haider, Jörg, 35–6
healthcare, 103, 106, 129, 132, 159
Heinisch, Richard, 36
Heinsbroek, Herman, 114
Herben, Mat, 103, 115, 201
Hernandez, Marcial, 117
Holmes, Michael, 163
Holocaust, 162
homosexuality, 103, 105, 126, 130, 157
Hough, Daniel, 47
Howard, Michael, 160
Hungary, 50–1, 63, 64, 66, 70, 72, 77, 79, 84, 89, 92, 96, 97, 173

Iceland, 3, 51–2, 72, 82, 84
Ignazi, Piero, 18
immigration
    anti-, 2, 12, 24, 26, 35–7, 42–5, 48–9, 52–3, 59, 61, 66–8, 172
    attitudes towards, 24, 26, 80–1, 141
    Netherlands, 92, 100, 103, 106, 109–10, 111–12, 113, 118–19, 175, 177
    United Kingdom, 144–5, 148, 150–2, 156–62, 164–7, 176
    see also culture and ethnicity
Independent Greeks (ANEL), 49, 72
Inglehart, Ronald, 18
Ionescu, Ghiţa, 5–6
Ireland, Republic of, 44, 52–3, 72, 78, 79, 84, 89
irredentism, 48, 50, 63, 66
Irwin, Galen, 114, 201
Islam, 24, 45, 53, 60, 68, 102, 103–5, 115, 118, 148, 152, 157, 166, 172, 176, 201
    cultural influence/Islamisation, 68, 103, 105, 118, 148, 166, 172
    Muslims, 67, 100, 103, 116, 157, 203
    see also culture and ethnicity
issues

ownership, 21–2, 98, 110, 119, 136, 138, 142, 144, 158, 161, 166–7, 176–9, 182
    salience, 4, 18, 21–4, 26–7, 32, 70, 97–8, 119–20, 140–1, 166–7, 170–1, 173–4, 177–9, 182–3
Italy, 16, 53–6, 69, 72, 78–9, 84, 89, 92, 96–7, 173

Jaerling, Aly, 59
Jagers, Jan, 7
Janmaat, Hans, 100, 113, 116
Jelinčič, Zmago, 66–7
Jensen, Siv, 61
Jews, *see* anti-Semitism
Jobbik, *see* Movement for a Better Hungary (Jobbik)
John, Peter, 156
John, Radek, 42
judiciary, 54
Justice and Life Party (MIÉP, Hungary), 50–1

Kaczyński, Jarosław, 62, 123, 128–9, 138–9, 140, 202
Kaczyński, Lech, 62, 123, 128–9, 138, 140, 202
Kammenos, Panos, 49
Karatzaferis, Georgios, 48–9
Kilroy-Silk, Robert, 163–4, 203
Kitschelt, Herbert, 27
Kjærsgaard, Pia, 42–3
Knapman, Roger, 163–4
Komorowski, Bronisław, 129
Koopmans, Ruud, 114
Kortenoeven, Wim, 117
Koß, Michael, 47
Kotlinowski, Marek, 137
Kriesi, Hanspeter, 18
Kucharczyk, Jacek, 127
Kwaśniewski, Aleksander, 123

Labour Party (DP, Lithuania), 58, 72, 77
Labour Party (PvdA, Netherlands), 101, 104, 107, 113–14, 201
Labour Party (UK), 145–8, 150, 152–4, 156–9, 163, 165, 167, 172, 202
Labour Union (UP, Poland), 123–4

Laclau, Ernesto, 10
Lafontaine, Oskar, 47
Lange, Anders, 60–1
Latin America, 5, 7, 10, 12, 15
Latvia, 56–7, 72, 84, 93
Law and Justice (PiS, Poland), 62, 70,
    72, 77, 121, 171–2, 177, 201–2
  credibility, 62, 138–43
  electorate, 138–40
  profile and electoral results, 123–4,
    127–30, 136
law and order, 53, 58, 103, 111, 123,
    128, 152, 159
  capital punishment, 152
  crime, 39, 41, 62, 138, 148
  police, 102, 136, 201
Law, Order and Justice (RZS,
    Romania), 38, 40, 71
Le Pen, Jean-Marie, 45–6
Le Pen, Marine, 45–6
leadership, 21–3, 177
  charismatic, 6, 14, 112–13
  populism and, 6–7, 13–15
  see also credibility of populist
    parties; individual parties; party
    organisation
League of Polish Families (LPR), 62,
    121–3, 140–3, 171, 177, 201–2
  credibility, 137–9
  electorate, 134
  profile and electoral results, 124–6,
    128–9, 134–5
League of Ticinesians (LdTi,
    Switzerland), 68, 72
Left, The (Die Linke, Germany), 46–7,
    48, 71, 170
Lega Nord (Italy), 16, 53–5, 70, 72,
    78, 170
Lepper, Andrzej, 61–2, 125,
    128–30, 133, 136–7, 140–2,
    177, 202
Lesar, Dragutin, 40–1
Liberal Democratic Party (LDP,
    Lithuania), 57
Liberal Democrats (UK), 145, 147–8,
    151, 154–5, 158, 160, 165–6, 178
Liberal Party (FF, Iceland), 52
Liberal Party (VVD, Netherlands), 101,
    103–4, 106–7, 109, 114, 116

liberalism, 13, 50, 59, 61, 103, 115,
    118, 125, 127–8, 136, 140, 178
  economic/neo-, 7, 26, 37, 48, 56,
    123, 130, 136, 175
  social, 18, 51, 67, 103, 125, 130,
    132, 156–7, 165
  see also anti-capitalism, democracy,
    free-market economy
Linke, see Left, The (Die Linke,
    Germany)
List Dedecker (LDD, Belgium), 37–8,
    71
List Pim Fortuyn (LPF, Netherlands),
    59–60, 71–2, 108, 118, 172, 176–8
  credibility, 60, 114–15, 118
  electorate, 109–10
  profile and electoral results, 101–4
Lithuania, 57–9, 72, 77, 79, 84, 89, 92
Liveable Netherlands (LN), 59–60, 72
  credibility, 60, 114–15
  electorate, 114
  profile and electoral results, 101–2,
    104
LN, see Liveable Netherlands (LN)
LPF, see List Pim Fortuyn (LPF,
    Netherlands)
LPR, see League of Polish Families (LPR)
Lucassen, Eric, 201
Luxembourg, 59, 72, 82, 84, 89

M5S, see Five Star Movement (M5S,
    Italy)
McCarthy, Joseph, 5
McDonnell, Duncan, 6, 52, 55
Mahon, James, 198
Major, John, 157
Malta, 34, 79, 84
March, Luke, 3, 16, 25, 47
Marcinkiewicz, Kazimierz, 128
Margetts, Helen, 156
Marijnissen, Jan, 113
Markowski, Radoslav, 127
Mečiar, Vladimír, 65
media, 13, 19, 22, 54
  attention/skills, 36, 44, 46, 47, 49,
    55, 57, 61, 67, 69
  Netherlands, 100, 114–16, 118
  Poland, 135, 136–9
  United Kingdom, 164–5

Mégret, Bruno, 45
Meguid, Bonny, 21
Mény, Yves, 9, 70
Merkel, Angela, 48
Millard, Frances, 127–8, 132, 135, 137, 202
Miller, Leszek, 123, 126, 135, 137
minorities, *see* culture and ethnicity
minority governments, 43, 60, 70, 106, 117, 123, 128, 177
minority nationalism/regionalism, 15–16, 53, 68, 145–6, 153, 155, 167, 172
see also federalism and devolution
Moffitt, Benjamin, 8
Mote, Ashley, 164
Movement for a Better Hungary (Jobbik), 50–1, 72
Movement for a Democratic Slovakia (HZDS), 65, 72
Mudde, Cas, 3, 6–8, 10, 12, 14, 16, 21, 24, 45, 63, 102, 198
Muis, Jasper, 114
Müller-Rommel, Ferdinand, 27
multiculturalism, *see* culture and ethnicity
Muslims, *see* Islam

National Alliance (AN, Italy), 55
National Alliance (NA, Latvia), 57
National Democratic Party of Germany (NPD), 46
National Front (FN, Belgium), 37–8, 71
National Front (FN, France), 45–6, 71, 89, 148, 170, 178
National Front (NF, UK), 148, 157, 162
National Movement Simeon the Second (NDSV, Bulgaria), 39–40, 71
National Revival Party (TPP, Lithuania), 57
nationalism, 2, 16, 203
Netherlands, 100, 105
in party ideology, 35–6, 38, 42, 44–5, 50, 52, 58, 62–3
patriotism, 105, 125, 127, 149, 172
Poland, 125–6, 127, 134, 142
United Kingdom, 145–6, 152, 153, 167

see also culture and ethnicity; minority nationalism/ regionalism; nativism; protectionism
nativism, 24, 30, 77, 80–1, 92–3, 96–7, 110, 173–4, 177
in party ideology, 40–1, 57, 61
see also culture and ethnicity, nationalism
Nawijn, Hilbrand, 102–3, 115
Nazism, 46, 49, 148, 162, 198
neo-liberalism, *see* liberalism
Netherlands, 31, 59–60, 76, 84, 92, 175–9
credibility of populist parties, 60, 112–17
economy, 101, 106, 109–12, 119–20
electoral system, 79, 107–8
European integration, 106, 111–12, 118–20
homosexuality, 103, 105
immigration and multiculturalism, 100, 103, 106, 109–13, 118–19
Islam and Muslims, 100, 102–5, 115–16, 118
issue salience and ownership, 109–12, 119–20
liberalism, 103, 115, 118
partisan (de)alignment, 107–8
populism/populist parties, 59–60, 71–2, 100–6
Purple Coalition, 101–3
responsiveness of established parties, 108–12, 118–19
trust and satisfaction, political, 97, 108, 110, 118–19
women, emancipation of, 103, 105
see also individual parties
New Democracy (ND, Greece), 48
New Era (JL, Latvia), 56
New Flemish Alliance (N-VA, Belgium), 37–8, 69
New Generation Party-Christian Democrats (PNG-CD, Romania), 64
New Union (NS, Lithuania), 57
NF, *see* National Front (NF, UK)
niche parties, 17, 21, 179
Northern Ireland, *see* United Kingdom (UK)

Northern League (LN, Italy), 16, 53–5, 70, 72, 78, 170
Norway, 3, 60–1, 72, 81–2, 84, 90, 97, 174

Okamura, Tomio, 41–2
oligarchy, 48, 56–8, 127
One NL (EénNL), 115
Orbán, Viktor, 50
Order and Justice Party (TT, Lithuania), 57–8, 72
Ordinary People and Independent Personalities (OĽaNO, Slovakia), 66, 72

Paksas, Rolandas, 57–8
Palikot, Janusz, 130
Palikot Movement (RP, Poland), 124, 130
pan-European research, 3, 30, 76, 183
Panhellenic Socialist Movement (PASOK, Greece), 48–9
Panizza, Francisco, 10
Pappas, Takis, 48
party families, 7–8, 15, 181
Party for the Netherlands (PVN), 115
Party of Civic Understanding (SOP, Slovakia), 64
Party of Democratic Socialism/The Left, *see* Left, The (Die Linke, Germany)
party organisation, 16, 21–3, 98, 178
   populism and, 6–7, 14–15, 21–3, 28
   see also credibility of populist parties; *individual parties*; leadership
party systems, 1–3, 16–17, 180, 183
   (in)stability and volatility, 16–17, 30, 70, 107–8, 122–4, 131, 153–4, 170
   partisan (de)alignment, 17–18, 107–8, 131, 141, 182
   see also individual countries
Party X (Partia X, Poland), 124
Pasquino, Gianfranco, 10
Pastors, Marco, 115
Pauwels, Teun, 37
Pearson of Rannoch, Malcolm, 151, 164–5

Pellikaan, Huib, 109
People of Freedom (PdL, Italy), 55, 72, 89
People's Party (PP-DD, Romania), 63–4, 72
Pirate Party (Iceland), 52
PiS, *see* Law and Justice (PiS, Poland)
Piskorski, Mateusz, 125, 138–9
Plaid Cymru (PC, Wales), 145–6, 153, 154, 167
pluralism, 12, 24
PO, *see* Civic Platform (PO, Poland)
Poland, 31, 61–2, 77–8, 84, 92, 175–9
   Catholicism, 62, 125–6, 134, 138, 140
   CBA (Central Anticorruption Bureau), 202
   communist successors, 124, 132, 137, 140–1
   corruption/clientelism/cronyism, 62, 121, 134–6, 139, 140–2
   credibility of populist parties, 62, 136–43
   decommunisation and lustration, 127–8, 132
   economy, 81, 132–4, 136, 139–41
   electoral system, 130–1
   EU and foreign policy, 126, 132–3, 138, 141, 202
   issue salience and ownership, 127, 133–6, 138–9, 141–3
   liberal and solidaristic, 122, 127, 136, 138, 141, 177–8
   partisan (de)alignment, 131, 135, 141
   populism/populist parties, 61–2, 71–2, 123–30, 140–2
   privatisation, 125, 132–4
   Radio Maryja, 138, 141
   responsiveness of established parties, 131–6, 141–2
   Round-Table Negotiations, 122, 126
   Rywin affair, 135
   Smolensk plane crash, 129, 202
   Solidarity and post-Solidarity, 122–4, 131–2, 137, 140–1
   transition losers, 121, 125, 133, 136, 140

trust and satisfaction, political, 97,
121, 131, 133–6, 141–3
układ, 127, 202
see also individual parties
Poland is the Most Important (PJN), 140
polarisation, 48, 50, 141
Polish Peasant Party (PSL), 122–4,
129–30, 134–5
Polish United Worker's Party (PZPR),
122
Politics can be Different (LMP,
Hungary), 51
Popular Orthodox Rally (LAOS,
Greece), 48–9, 72
popular sovereignty/will, 2, 5, 9,
11–13, 16, 39, 43, 62, 70, 126,
147, 171
populism
compared with other ideologies,
15–16
definitions, 5–9, 11, 13
democracy and, 9–10, 182
heartland, 6–7, 12, 15, 125–6, 166
ideology (thin), 2, 6–7, 11, 14, 23,
70, 172, 181
manifestation, 1–2, 5–12, 15–17, 31,
69–73, 140–2, 147, 170–2, 179–81
measurement, 8, 180
see also populist parties
populist parties
classification, 4, 8–9, 11, 13, 15–17,
33, 69–71, 170–2, 179–81, 183
definition, 13
electoral appeal, 21–3, 33–4, 176–9,
181–2
explanatory model for performance,
17–28
governing, 22, 35–6, 39–40, 41–3,
49, 53–5, 58, 60, 62, 64–6, 69, 70,
117, 119–20, 139, 177–8, 181
left-wing/social, 7, 12, 16, 24–6, 40,
47, 61, 100–1, 125, 127, 146–7,
170, 181
organisation, 6–7, 14–15, 21–3, 28
right-wing, 2, 5, 7, 16–17, 24–6,
169–70, 172, 181, 198
themes (four), 23–8, 30, 73, 80–3,
97–8, 119, 141, 166–7, 172–5,
179, 181

voter motivations, 23, 175, 178–9,
182–3
*see also individual countries and
parties*; credibility of populist
parties; populism
(populist) radical right, 2, 5, 7, 16–17,
24–6, 169–70, 172, 181, 198
explanations for performance,
17–28
*see also individual countries and
parties*; populism
Portugal, 34, 82, 84, 96, 174
Positive Slovenia (PS), 67
post-communist Europe, *see* Central
and Eastern Europe
Powell, Enoch, 145
Progress Party (FrP, Norway), 60–1, 72
protectionism, economic, 26, 49, 65,
125–6, 152
protest voting, 23, 111, 119, 137, 182
see also anti-establishment; populist
parties
Proud of the Netherlands (TON),
116–17
PSL, *see* Polish Peasant Party (PSL)
Public Affairs (VV, Czech Republic),
41–2, 71, 78
PvdA, *see* Labour Party (PvdA,
Netherlands)
PVV, *see* Freedom Party (PVV,
Netherlands)

Qualitative Comparative Analysis
(QCA), 3, 29–31, 74–98, 173–4

racism, *see* culture and ethnicity
radical left, 16, 24–6, 181, 203
see also anti-capitalism;
communism; populism;
socialism/social democracy
Ratelband, Emile, 115, 201
Raunio, Tapio, 44
Referendum Party (UK), 152
referendums, 12, 160, 203
regionalism, *see* minority nationalism/
regionalism
religion, 14, 107, 133–4, 138, 142,
202
see also Catholicism; Islam

Republicans (Republikaner, Germany), 46
Res Publica (RP, Estonia), 43, 56
Respect (UK), 146–8, 155
responsiveness of established parties, 4, 10, 20–1, 27, 97, 175–6, 182
    Netherlands, 108–12, 118–19
    Poland, 131–6, 141–2
    QCA operationalisation, 79–80
    United Kingdom, 156–61, 166–7
Roma, 24, 38, 40, 42, 50, 51, 63, 66, 198
    see also culture and ethnicity
Romania, 63–4, 72, 79, 83, 84, 97, 106, 170, 174
Rommerskirchen, Charlotte, 25
Rooduijn, Matthijs, 16, 101, 147, 180
Rovira Kaltwasser, Cristóbal, 10, 12
Rummens, Stefan, 9
Russia, 5, 129, 202
Rutte, Mark, 116
Rydgren, Jens, 42
Rydzyk, Tadeusz, 138

Sartori, Giovanni, 180
Scandinavia, 42
Schneider, Carsten, 75, 83
Scotland, *see* United Kingdom (UK)
Scottish National Party (SNP), 145–6, 153, 154, 167
Scottish Socialist Party (SSP), 146
Self Defence (SO, Poland), 61–2, 71–2, 78, 172, 177–8
    credibility, 62, 136–43
    electorate, 133, 142
    profile and electoral results, 124–5, 128–9
Shils, Edward, 5
Siderov, Volen, 38
Simeon II, 39
Sinclaire, Nikki, 164
Sinke, Ed, 116
Sinn Fein (SF, Ireland), 52–3, 72
Sked, Alan, 150–1, 163
SLD, *see* Democratic Left Alliance (SLD, Poland)
Slovak National Party (SNS), 65–6, 72, 78

Slovakia, 64–6, 72, 77, 81, 84, 92, 170, 173
Slovenia, 66–7, 72, 82, 84, 174
Slovenian National Party (SNS), 66–7, 72
SO, *see* Self Defence (SO, Poland)
socialism/social democracy, 100–1, 125, 126, 127, 145
Socialist Party (SP, Netherlands), 60, 69, 100–1, 104, 113, 118, 171, 201
Soini, Timo, 44
Solidarity Electoral Action (AWS, Poland), 123–4, 131–2, 134, 138, 141, 202
Solidarity (Solidarność, Poland), 122
sovereignty, national, 26, 47, 52, 106, 126, 150, 166
SP, *see* Socialist Party (SP, Netherlands)
Spain, 34, 81, 82, 84, 96
Stanley, Ben, 7, 11, 128, 139
Steward, Angus, 6
Strache, Heinz-Christian, 35–6
Stronach, Frank, 35–6
Stuger, Olaf, 115
Surel, Yves, 9, 70
Sweden, 67–8, 72, 84
Sweden Democrats (SD), 67–8, 72
Swiss Democrats (SD), 68, 72
Swiss People's Party (SVP), 29, 68–9, 70, 72, 170
Switzerland, 3, 29, 68–9, 70, 72, 81, 82, 84, 90, 97, 170, 174
SYRIZA, *see* Coalition of the Radical Left (SYRIZA, Greece)
Szczerbiak, Aleks, 137, 140

Taggart, Paul, 6, 7, 9, 12
Tarchi, Marco, 55
Team Stronach (TS, Austria), 35, 71
terrorism, 53, 148
Thatcher, Margaret, 61, 145, 157, 159
Thomassen, Jacques, 109
Titford, Jeffrey, 163, 202, 203
Tomašić, Ruža, 41
TON, *see* Proud of the Netherlands (TON)
Tormey, Simon, 8
True Finns (PS), 44, 71

trust and satisfaction, political, 16, 18, 20, 25, 27, 32, 43, 49, 51, 53, 56, 58, 66, 79–80, 90, 92, 97, 98, 174, 175, 178, 179, 183
Netherlands, 97, 108, 110, 118–19
Poland, 97, 121, 131, 133–6, 141–3
United Kingdom, 149, 160, 161, 165, 167
see also anti-establishment
Tsipras, Alexis, 48–9
Tuđman, Franjo, 40
Tudor, Vadim, 63–4
Tusk, Donald, 123, 128, 129
Tymiński, Stanisław, 124
Tyndall, John, 148

Učeň, Peter, 43
UK Independence Party (UKIP), 144–5, 172, 176, 178
credibility, 163–8
electorate, 153, 160–1
profile and electoral results, 150–3
unemployment, *see* economy
United Kingdom (UK), 31, 34, 82, 84, 175–9electoral system, 144, 153–5
European integration, 158–61
immigration and ethnicity, 148–50, 151–2, 156–8
Islam and Muslims, 148, 151–2, 157, 166, 203
issue ownership and salience, 144, 156–9, 166–7
Northern Ireland, 52, 146, 202
partisan (de)alignment, 153–4
populism/populist parties, 145–8, 166, 172
regionalism and devolution, 145–6, 154–5
Scotland and Wales, 145–6, 153, 154, 167, 172, 202
trust and satisfaction, political, 149, 160, 161, 165, 167
see also individual parties
United States, 5, 67
Usherwood, Simon, 164
Uspaskich, Victor, 58

Van Bemmel, Jhim, 117
Van de Linde, Kay, 115, 116
Van der Brug, Wouter, 26, 110
Van Holsteyn, Joop, 114, 201
Van Spanje, Joost, 26, 110, 198
Verdonk, Rita, 116, 117, 198
Veritas (UK), 164
Vlaams Belang, *see* Flemish Interest (Belgium)
volatility, electoral, *see* party systems
VVD, *see* Liberal Party (VVD, Netherlands)

Wagemann, Claudius, 75, 83
Wales, *see* United Kingdom (UK)
Wałęsa, Lech, 122, 202
Walgrave, Stefaan, 7
Way of Courage (DK, Lithuania), 58
Webb, Paul, 160
welfare
chauvinism, 26, 35, 42, 45, 65–7, 112, 181, 203
protectionism, 100, 105, 111, 118, 177
state, 25–6, 105, 132, 151, 152
Western Europe, 2–3, 5, 8, 17, 18, 24, 70, 170, 180–1, 182–3
Weyland, Kurt, 7
Widfeldt, Anders, 61, 68
Wilders, Geert, 60, 100, 104–6, 108, 110–12, 115–20, 152, 176–7, 179, 201
Wiles, Peter, 5
Wille, Anchrit, 108
Wise, Tom, 164
women, emancipation of, 103, 105
Worsley, Peter, 6
Wysocka, Olga, 127

xenophobia, *see* culture and ethnicity

Yanev, Yane, 40

Zatlers Reform Party (ZRP, Latvia), 56
Zatlers, Valdis, 56
Zimmer, Gabi, 47

CPI Antony Rowe
Chippenham, UK
2017-02-07 21:25